WITNESSES TO FREEDOM

A DAY BY DAY ACCOUNT OF THE WAR OF INDEPENDENCE IN CORK 1919-1921

This book is sold subject to the condition that it shall not, by way of trade or otherwise, be lent, resold, hired out or otherwise circulated without the author's prior consent in any form of binding or cover other than that in which it is published and without a similar condition including this condition being imposed on the subsequent purchaser.

© Diarmuid Grainger, 2019

List of Abbreviations

IO	Intelligence Officer
IRA	Irish Republican Army
QM	Quartermaster
RIC	Royal Irish Constabulary
HQ	Headquarters
ASU	Active Service Unit
BMH	Bureau of Military History
WS	Witness Statement
YMCA	Young Men's Christian Association
DI	District Inspector RIC
OC	Officer Commanding

Dedicated to my wife Jean in gratitiude for all her help with this book.

Table of Contents

List of Abbreviations iii

Foreword vii

January 1919 1

February 1919 4

March 1919 6

April 1919 8

May 1919 11

June 1919 13

July 1919 15

August 1919 17

September 1919 19

October 1919 24

November 1919 26

December 1919 29

January 1920 31

February 1920 37

March 1920 43

April 1920 50

May 1920 55

June 1920 62

July 1920 75

August 1920 90

September 1920 109

October 1920 121

November 1920 141

December 1920 164

January 1921 184

February 1921 207

March 1921.. 241

April 1921.. 269

May 1921 284

June 1921 315

July 1921 337

Appendix 1 350

Appendix 2 367

Appendix 3 373

Bibliography 393

Foreword

The Irish Government created the Bureau of Military History in the late 1940s. Entrusted to the Department of Defence, the remit of the Bureau was to record and gather the recollections of those who had played a part in the formative years of the revolutionary period leading up to the foundation of the State.

Almost 1,800 witnesses throughout the country recorded on paper their memories, impressions and experiences of the 1913-1921 period, from the formation of the Irish Volunteers to the Truce on 11 July 1921. A few witnesses went on to give their account of the Civil War, although usually not in any detail. Some 350 witnesses, representing roughly one fifth of all those interviewed nationwide by the Bureau, came from Cork city and county. Of the 36,000 pages of witness statements given to the Bureau of Military History, 6,500 pertain to Cork city and county. By far the majority of these were members of the Irish Volunteers, generally known as the Irish Republican Army by 1919; others who contributed included members of Cumann na mBan, ex-RIC men, and members of the Dáil courts.

This study restricts the scope of its research to Cork city and county, and it is a day by day account of the War of Independence in that county alone.

Early January 1919 saw the county of Cork, hitherto consisting of one brigade, now divided up into three. Each of these brigades consisted of a number of battalions, and these were further divided up into companies, the smallest fighting unit of the IRA. A typical company might consist of eighty or one hundred volunteers, though in some areas the figure was much lower.

The opening shots of the Irish War of Independence are usually placed at Soloheadbeg, Co Tipperary, when two RIC men were shot dead by members of the IRA's South Tipperary Brigade on 21 January 1919 – coincidentally the day of the first sitting of Dáil Éireann. The war got off to a slow start in Cork, with just two members of the Crown forces – an army private and an RIC constable – being killed in 1919; that year saw the deaths of two volunteers. The first three months of 1920 were quiet, and it was not until the shooting of Lord Mayor of Cork Tomás Mac Curtain in March that the city and county gained the reputation it has held since, that of being to the forefront in the fight for Irish independence.

As the war progressed into the summer of 1920, and with British casualties and 'old' RIC resignations becoming a frequent occurrence, the government in London unleashed two forces which have entered the folk consciousness of Ireland – the Black and Tans and the Auxiliaries, both special semi-military police forces.

The IRA, as well as the civilian population, soon felt the heavy hand of the newly augmented RIC and the autumn of 1920 saw the republican army organise training camps to form flying columns, often under the instruction of ex-RIC and ex-British Army personnel, the most famous of whom was Tom Barry, although he was regarded with suspicion at first when he offered his services to the republican cause.

A lack of firearms and ammunition was the chief hurdle to be overcome by the volunteers, but this was soon rectified by an ever-growing number of raids on police and British military. The IRA system of communication – the use of semaphore, horn blowing, lighting of fires on hilltops, and in at least one case the planting of an extra telephone into the house of a resident magistrate – gave the republicans the advantage in battle as well as assisting them in avoiding contact with the enemy. The effectiveness of the IRA was greatly enhanced by Cumann na mBan in their willingness to provide safe houses and transfer information. Many volunteers had sisters in that organisation.

And yet the crown forces seemed to have a great deal of foreknowledge of the IRA's intentions, as the reader will see from the number of planned ambushes in which there was no appearance from the enemy.

The IRA victories of 1920, where the spring time saw the destruction of a great many RIC barracks throughout the county, and where the Sinn Féin courts system filled the vacuum of the British code of justice, culminated in the enormous publicity value to the republican cause of Terence Mac Swiney's death by hunger strike in October and the victory of Barry's flying column at Kilmichael the following month.

The first weeks of 1921 appeared to show the British authorities gaining the upper hand; the almost complete annihilation of the East Cork flying column in Clonmult, together with the series of executions of republicans caught in arms, must have caused the British to believe that the IRA were a beaten force.

The IRA victory at Crossbarry, however, along with other smaller engagements, slowly tipped the balance in their favour. An accelerant in this development was the systematic shooting of spies and informers by the IRA, the great majority of them in the First Cork Brigade area, under its O.C. Sean O'Hegarty.

The last few weeks of the war saw no major confrontations, the crown forces being content not to venture out of barracks in motorised patrols, while the IRA kept up its efforts to seek out and kill spies and informers.

Certain patterns emerge in reading these pages: the chronic lack of arms and ammunition in certain battalions of the IRA; the amount of ambushes where the IRA were 'given away', pointing to informers in the ranks or in the wider community; the willingness of the crown forces, armed or unarmed, to leave their barracks to go for a walk in the evening, putting themselves in mortal danger of attack; a dearth of knowledge within the IRA of the manufacture and handling of explosives, causing many an ambush to fail; unfamiliarity of republicans in handling weapons, leading to the element of surprise being lost due to accidental gunfire at an ambush site; and the phenomenon of IRA men in captivity being shot dead by crown forces as a matter of policy.

The Bureau of Military History is a wonderful resource, created in the same mould as the Irish Folklore Commission of a previous decade. It was conceived by far- sighted people, and it will serve as a repository of national history, local history, and genealogical information to millions of Irish people throughout the world.

WITNESSES TO' FREEDOM

A DAY BY DAY ACCOUNT OF THE WAR OF INDEPENDENCE IN CORK 1919-1921

January 1919

1 January 1919

Lisheen Company paraded in Ballydehob on New Year's Day 1919; their purpose was to form a Sinn Féin club in the locality.

(A subsequent meeting in the same village was addressed in Irish by Seán Lehane. Arrested and charged with making a seditious speech, the Crown prosecutor Jasper Wolfe declared, 'This young man came to Ballydehob to revive the embers of a dying revolution and spoke in the Hottentot language'. Lehane was sent to prison for three months.)

WILLIAM CROWLEY BMH WS 1502, 4; SEÁN O'DRISCOLL BMH WS 1518, 10

6 January 1919

Up to this date, all volunteers in Cork county made up one brigade. The new Second Cork Brigade met in Fermoy, Tomás Mac Curtain presiding. Liam Lynch was unanimously elected brigade OC.

GEORGE POWER BMH WS 451, 2

Thomas Roche, training officer with Newmarket Battalion, related that his battalion was now known as the Sixth and attached to the Second Cork Brigade, a decision taken at a convention at Dromahane.

THOMAS ROCHE BMH WS 1222, 5

9 January 1919

Charles Browne, OC Macroom Battalion, gives an account of an attack on British military. The soldiers, having arrived at Macroom railway station in the evening, were on their way to their quarters in Mount Massey House when they were overcome by the local IRA and relieved of their arms. The following IRA personnel took part: Charles Browne, Tim Crowley, S O'Connor, Jack Kelleher of Codrum, Paddy Buckley, Daniel Mullane, Pat Manning, William Kelleher, Tom Donovan, Denis Kelleher and Denis O'Connell.

CHARLES BROWNE BMH WS 873, 10

January 1919 (no date available)

Owen Harold, later captain of Mallow Company and vice-commandant of Mallow Battalion, was arrested and jailed for illegal military drilling. After a month in prison he was released, only to be re-arrested, this time for possession of illegal documents, for which he received a two-year sentence. Having staged a hunger strike with other prisoners, he spent six months in solitary confinement before being released.

OWEN HAROLD BMH WS 991, 5

Edward Horgan, first lieutenant H Company, First Cork Brigade, along with several comrades raided the house of a British Army captain at the Lough, Cork. Following a struggle, they came away with a rifle, but their masks had slipped off and they were identified and arrested subsequently.

EDWARD HORGAN BMH WS 1644, 3

February 1919

7 February 1919

Duhallow Fox Hounds were prevented from hunting at Seeds' fox-covert by Freemount Company, Newmarket Battalion. The hunt included several British officers who had taken part in courts martial against the Volunteers.

DENIS MULLANE BMH WS 789, 10

February 1919 (no date available)

A British military post was established at Inchegeela; this led to the constant raiding of the Ballingeary Company area. In one such raid, at the Guagán Barra Hotel, Sergeant Maunsell of the RIC, seeing Tomás Mac Curtain and three others in one of the rooms, spoke briefly to him in Irish; he then told the military that he had already searched the room, and as a result the volunteers were not discovered.

CORNELIUS CRONIN BMH WS 1726, 3

Cobh Company of the Irish Volunteers held up a party of British military tasked with guarding the Admiralty reservoir at the eastern end of the town. One British soldier was wounded, and all enemy weaponry and ammunition was captured. Later that day a party of British military, along with District Inspector Murphy of Cobh RIC, called to the workplace of Commdt Michael Leahy at Midleton. Leahy, out on bail from Belfast Jail, was not arrested.

MICHAEL LEAHY BMH WS 1421, 9; MICHAEL J BURKE BMH WS 1424, 5; JOHN P O'CONNELL BMH WS 1444, 3

March 1919

17 March 1919

Liam O'Dwyer, OC Castletownbere Battalion, relates that several member of Eyeries Company lay in ambush for a patrol of RIC at Drohadeenagath near Eyeries village, but no action took place.

LIAM O'DWYER BMH WS 1527, 7

March 1919 (no date available)

William Desmond, lieutenant and later captain of Newcestown Company, says that £30 was raised for the Volunteer arms fund at a dance at Murragh.

WILLIAM DESMOND BMH WS 832, 6

The third council meeting of the Third Cork Brigade was held at Mike Donoghue's house Fearlehanes. The Crown forces, having got prior knowledge of the meeting, held the approach roads. Kilmeen Company got outside the cordon and diverted the Republican officers to an alternative location, which was John O'Donoghue's house, Ballinvard.

PATRICK O'BRIEN BMH WS 812, 5

Eleven men of D Company, Second Battalion, First Cork Brigade attended Ballinrea point-to-point race meeting four miles south of Cork city with a view to disarming a patrol of RIC men. The planned attack had to be called off when it became evident that the police took a different route.

JEROME COUGHLAN BMH WS 1568, 3

Fifteen volunteers from Kilbrittain Company stole cattle by force of arms from Kilbrittain Castle. They also sabotaged of a cargo of timber at Burrin Pier, renering it unsellable.

JAMES O'MAHONY/DENIS CROWLEY/JOHN FITZGERALD BMH WS 560, 3

April 1919

8 April 1919

Four members of the RIC, led by Sergeant O'Connell, were fired on by volunteers from Inches Company, Castletownbere Battalion. Constables Cummins, Quinlan and Ronan were present, the latter being seriously wounded.

JAMES MC CARTHY BMH WS 1567, 8

9 April 1919

Following the attack of 8 April, martial law was enforced in the Castletownbere area for the second time and Eyeries fair was banned.

JAMES MC CARTHY BMH WS 1567, 8

20 April 1919

Seven members of Araglin Company, Fermoy Battalion, Second Cork Brigade – Con Leddy (OC), Michael Fitzgerald, Seán Mahony, Tom Brennan, Owen Mc Carthy, Maurice Hyland and Tom Donovan – entered Araglin RIC barracks while Constable O'Malley was out fetching water. They siezed arms and ammunition as well as books and records belonging to the barracks.

CON LEDDY BMH WS 756, 5

John Kelleher, lieutenant Midleton Company, Fourth Battalion, First Cork Brigade, along with Volunteer Jerry Ahern (who died at Clonmult), flew the Irish tricolour at Midleton town hall in commemoration of the third anniversary of the 1916 Rising

–the informant calls this "the first open gesture of defiance to British authority by us". Having heard of the police's determination to remove it, Captain Diarmuid Hurley and a dozen volunteers entered the building and barricaded the stairway, but the RIC did not engage.

JOHN KELLEHER BMH WS 1456, 3

28 April 1919

An explosion occurred at an IRA bomb factory in Grattan Street, Cork, as a result of which Lieutenant Mícheál Tobin died of his injuries on 20 May. Captain Murphy, QM O'Connell, Volunteers Varian, Downey and Madden, along with Miss C Moore of Cumann na mBan, were injured.[1]

SEÁN O'CONNELL BMH WS 1706, 3; LEO BUCKLEY BMH WS 1714, 1; MATTHEW O'CALLAGHAN BMH WS 561, 1

---

[1] Keane, B. *Cork's Revolutionary Dead*, Mercier Press (Cork) p108

April 1919 (no date available)

Lieutenant John Barrett of Shanbally Company raided a pavilion in the naval training grounds at Ringaskiddy, the intention being to obtain arms and ammunition. No arms being secured, the pavilion was burned down.

JOHN BARRETT BMH WS 1538, 2

Some time in April 1919 UCC Company Irish Volunteers captured British military bicycles which had been stored in Marsh's auction rooms in the South Mall, Cork. Marsh, the owner, was shot and injured when he tried to prevent the seizure.

MICHAEL J CROWLEY BMH WS 1603, 3; ROBERT AHERN BMH WS 1676, 3

QM Seán O'Connell of G Company, First Battalion, First Cork Brigade, and others raided the home of British Army Captain Clarke at Farran, during which incident Clarke was injured in the hand and several guns were captured.

SEÁN O'CONNELL BMH WS 1706, 4

May 1919

14 May 1919

Following the rescue of Seán Hogan from Knocklong railway station in Co Limerick on 13 May 1919, two volunteers who were wounded in this engagement, Jim Scanlon and Ned O'Brien, were driven to Dr Molan's of Conna, where they recuperated for a month. James Coss, Fermoy Battalion intelligence officer, acted as their driver while in Co Cork. The wounded men also stayed in the Mitchelstown area.

JAMES COSS 1056, 5; JOSEPH KEARNEY BMH WS 704, 1; THOMAS DELARUE BMH WS 1224, 13; PETER KEARNEY BMH WS 444, 1; MICHAEL O'SULLIVAN BMH WS 1186, 11

24 May 1919

Seán Moylan, commandant Newmarket Battalion, Second Cork Brigade, escaped from Cork Mental Hospital on this date. Feigning mental illness, he had been transferred there from Cork Jail.

MATTHEW MURPHY BMH WS 1375, 7

25 May 1919

An aeríocht (an athletic and cultural gathering held outdoors) was organised for Raenagoshell in the Cullen district, the venue only being revealed at the last moment in order to baffle the Crown forces.

MATTHEW MURPHY BMH WS 1375, 7

May 1919 (no date available)

The RIC barracks at Kenneigh, which had been abandoned by its garrison, was destroyed.

JACK HENNESSY BMH WS 1234, 1

IRA intelligence agent Miss Annie Barrett, a telephonist at Mallow post office, intercepted messages regarding a proposed raid on a house in Mitchelstown. As a result of this information, Volunteers Jim Scanlon and Ned O'Brien, who had rescued Seán Hogan from Knocklong railway station, were moved to a safer location.

ANNIE BARRETT BMH WS 1133, 3

June 1919

11 June 1919

Volunteer J Danagher of Broadford, Co Limerick, was brought to the house of PD Casey of Newmarket; he had been badly injured and burned in the destruction of Drumcollogher barracks. He died the next day, his remains being buried temporarily at Rockchapel.

CHRISTOPHER JW O'KEEFFE BMH WS 761, 19

16 June 1919

A party of volunteers from Kilbrittain attacked and disarmed a British Army and RIC patrol at Rathclarin without a shot being fired. Volunteer Michael O'Neill (who died at Ballygroman in April of 1922) had his head split open by a blow from a rifle butt. He spent several weeks recovering at a house in Ahiohill.

JAMES O'MAHONY/ DENIS CROWLEY/ JOHN FITZGERALD BMH WS 560, 4

29 June 1919

A council meeting of the Third Cork Brigade was held at McCarthy's of Dunmanway. Michael McCarthy, one of the three Irish fatalities at Kilmichael on 28 November 1920, was appointed brigade adjutant.

PATRICK O'BRIEN BMH WS 812, 5

June 1919 (no date available)

Liam Lynch, OC Second Cork Brigade, and Second Lieutenant Leo Callaghan were stopped and questioned while driving from Newmarket to Kanturk. They were not recognised.

LEO CALLAGHAN BMH WS 978, 2

An aeríocht (an outdoor cultural event) was organised for Newmarket sometime in June 1919. Having been banned by the British military and by the RIC, it was held successfully at Bawnmore.

JOHN WINTERS BMH WS 948, 2

July 1919

4 July 1919

A group of about thirty volunteers from Midleton Company, under the command of Captain Diarmuid Hurley, lay in wait at Ballyquirke aerodrome, nine miles from the town, for a detachment of volunteers to arrive from Cork. The city men having taken a wrong turn, the attack was called off.

MICHAEL LEAHY BMH WS 1421, 10; JOHN KELLEHER BMH WS 1456, 4

July 1919 (no date available)

Volunteers Christy O'Connell, Michael Foley and Peter Harrington of Eyeries Company were released from prison on this date. The three volunteers had prevented the arrest of Volunteer Con Dwyer in August 1918, when Volunteer O'Connell, though unarmed, attacked an armed RIC party. They were later arrested by a strong police force.

JAMES MC CARTHY BMH WS 1567, 9

August 1919

9 August 1919

A training camp for officers of the Third Cork Brigade was held in Glandore, up to one hundred men taking part. Dick McKee, OC Dublin Brigade, was in charge, with Leo Henderson giving lectures in use of arms, map-reading, compass work and tactics. A large force of British military surrounded the camp on the fifth day, and they arrested several volunteers.

SEÁN COTTER BMH WS 1493, 4; TED O'SULLIVAN BMH WS 1478, 7

15 August 1919

Peggy Bowen-Colthust, whose brother murdered Francis Sheehy-Skeffington and several others during the Easter Rising in Dublin, had established a cheese factory in Dripsey, in direct opposition to the local creamery. Some farmers 'with an imperialist outlook' ignored the boycott placed on the family. On 15 August they were held up by the Volunteers, their milk poured down the drain, and given a warning not to continue. The cheese factory closed.

MAURICE BREW BMH WS 1695, 10; JOHN MANNING BMH WS 1720, 10

16 August 1919

Michael Collins, director of intelligence GHQ, presided at a meeting in Caheragh of the Third Cork Brigade council. Several changes were made in brigade and battalion staff.

TED O'SULLIVAN BMH WS 1478, 9

August 1919 (no date available)

The many raids by police following the Rathclarin ambush (see 16 June) having proved fruitless, the RIC sergeant at Kilbrittain was transferred to divisional headquarters in Bandon and demoted in rank; the sergeant, sympathetic to the volunteer cause, provided the Volunteers valuable information right up to the Truce. He was replaced in Kilbrittain RIC barracks by 'a most hostile man'.

JAMES O'MAHONY/ DENIS CROWLEY/ JOHN FITZGERALD BMH WS 560, 6

A cycle patrol of RIC and British military passed by Daly's Rocks, Foxe's Bridge, on the Blarney road from Donoughmore. A party of IRA men from Courtbrack Company lay in wait for their return, but the Crown forces chose a different route.

THOMAS J GOLDEN BMH WS 1680, 13

A Sinn Féin organiser, J Madden, was introduced to speak at a meeting outside mass in Shanagarry, whereupon Sergeant Donaldson and Constable Hughes moved in to arrest him. The policemen were held by the Volunteers until Madden finished his speech and left the scene.

EDMOND O'BRIEN BMH WS 623, 1

September 1919

4 September 1919

Volunteer Leo Callaghan of Mallow Company was ordered by his OC, Jack Cunningham, to have a car ready for the following Sunday. Although Callaghan was not told it at the time, this car was to be used in what became known as the Wesleyan raid at Fermoy on 7 September 1919.

LEO CALLAGHAN BMH WS 978, 2

5 September 1919

The final meeting to finalise plans for the Wesleyan raid at Fermoy took place in the Sinn Féin Hall on this date.

JOHN FANNING BMH WS 990, 8

7 September 1919

A party of armed soldiers of the Shropshire Regiment were observed attending service every Sunday at Fermoy. On 7 September volunteers from Fermoy, Mallow, Araglin and Ballynoe were in waiting near the church. At the sound of a whistle from Liam Lynch, OC Second Cork Brigade, the volunteers moved in, seizing sixteen rifles. These were hidden at Kilbarry woods some miles distant in the Kilmagner direction. Private Jones was shot dead in this incident, and Lynch received a minor shoulder wound. [2]

---

[2] Keane p109

JOHN FANNING BMH WS 990, 8; JOHN J HOGAN BMH WS 1030, 5; OWEN HAROLD BMH WS 991, 5; CON LEDDY BMH WS 756, 8; LAURENCE CONDON BMH WS 859, 5; LEO CALLAGHAN BMH WS 978, 2; PATRICK AHERN BMH WS 1003, 9; JOHN J HOGAN BMH WS 1030, 4; SEÁN HENNESSY BMH WS 1090, 9

Following an attack on Crown forces near Ballyvourney, reprisals were anticipated in Macroom; most of the local company was deployed throughout the town.

DANIEL MC SWEENEY BMH WS 1651, 5

Members of Riverstown Company took part in a bowling match at Glanmire. The local sergeant of the RIC followed them and endeavoured to take names, bowling on a public road being regarded as an illegal activity. He was manhandled and thrown into a ditch.

JOSEPH CASHMAN BMH WS 1466, 1

A large detachment of British military from Buttevant and Ballyvonaire camps surrounded Mallow and searched all vehicles and people entering and leaving. Nothing was found.

JOHN BOLSTER/ RICHARD WILLIS BMH WS 808, 15

8 September 1919

John Fanning, OC Fermoy Company, and five fellow volunteers were arrested and held by the RIC on suspicion of partaking in the Wesleyan raid the previous day.

JOHN FANNING BMH WS 990, 11

9 September 1919

While being driven under armed escort to Cork prison, the British Army vehicle carrying those arrested in Fermoy the previous day collided with a cyclist, killing him instantly. The dead man was Volunteer Bryan Crowley of Glanmire. [3]

JOHN FANNING BMH WS 990, 12.

10 September 1919

Three days after the Wesleyan raid in Fermoy, members of the local IRA company held a parade in Rice's field, Pa Gallagher in charge. Volunteers were ordered 'to keep their ears open and their mouths shut'.

PATRICK AHERN BMH WS 1003, 14

13 September 1919

Instructions from the First Cork Brigade headquarters that no action should be taken against the RIC without its prior authority were discussed at a meeting of Donoughmore Battalion council.

MAURICE BREW BMH WS 1695, 11

16 September 1919

Volunteers Peter O'Callaghan and John J Hogan, suspected of taking part in the Wesleyan raid at Fermoy on 7 September, were arrested at their respective homes.

JOHN J HOGAN BMH WS 1030, 8

---

[3] Keane p110

28 September

Despite instructions from brigade headquarters (see 13 September), five volunteers from Donoughmore Company held up two RIC men after mass at Berrings, during which incident Constable McSweeney was seriously wounded, and Volunteer Ben Hickey wounded slightly. Two revolvers were captured by the IRA. Extensive raiding by Crown forces took place subsequently.

MAURICE BREW BMH WS 1695, 11

September 1919 (no date available)

A meeting of Kilbrittain Sinn Féin club was ordered to disperse by two RIC men. When this order was ignored, the policemen left, to return later with rifles to arrest some of the volunteers, who escaped under fire.

JAMES O'MAHONY/ DENIS CROWLEY/ JOHN FITZGERALD BMH WS 560, 5

Two British soldiers at the Beach in Cobh were overpowered and disarmed by volunteers from Cobh Company.

MICHAEL BURKE BMH WS 1424, 6

Volunteers Denis Manning, John O'Neill, John Fitzgerald and P O'Sullivan were sentenced to four months' prison for illegal assembly at Kilbrittain.

JAMES O'MAHONY/ DENIS CROWLEY/ JOHN FITZGERALD BMH WS 560, 6

October 1919

14 October 1919

Seán Murphy, OC Aultagh Company and QM Dunmanway Battalion, was released from Mountjoy Jail. He had been arrested at an IRA training camp at Glandore with three others and charged with unlawful assembly and being in possession of seditious documents.

SEÁN MURPHY BMH WS 1445, 4

25 October 1919

Cornelius Connolly, later OC Fourth (Skibbereen) Battalion, Third Cork Brigade and a member of the brigade flying column, escaped from Manchester prison along with Austin Stack, Piaras Beasley, Paddy McCarthy of Charleville, DP Walsh of Fethard and Seán Doran of Co Down.

CORNELIUS CONNOLLY BMH WS 602, 1; DENNY MULLANE BMH WS 789, 30

October 1919 (no date available)

A soldier of the Manchester Regiment based at Mount Massey got detached from his patrol in Castle Street in Macroom; he was relieved of his rifle by unarmed volunteers of the local A Company.

CHARLES BROWNE BMH WS 873, 11

A train from Cork to Cobh was stopped at Carrigaloe, and six members of Cobh Company IRA sought out three British soldiers known to be on board. Their weaponry and equipment were captured.

MICHAEL LEAHY BMH WS 1421, 11

Daniel Canty, OC Newcestown Company, and others entered several houses in the Newcestown area, where they seized some shotguns and ammunition.

DANIEL CANTY BMH WS 1619, 5

Newmarket Battalion QM Patrick McCarthy escaped from Strangeways prison, Manchester.

THOMAS ROCHE BMH WS 1222, 2

'General training towards war started' following a reorganisation of the Third Cork Brigade at Caheragh, according to Patrick O'Brien of Girlough, Adjutant Third (Dunmanway) Battalion.

PATRICK O'BRIEN BMH WS 812, 7

November 1919

4 November 1919

Michael Murphy, commandant Second Battalion, First Cork Brigade, and nine men of C Company scaled the outer wall of Passage West docks and broke into the wheelhouse of a trawler, taking three rifles and some ammunition.

MICHAEL MURPHY BMH WS 1547, 11

11 November 1919

A second raid on Ballyquirke aerodrome was planned on this date, the first raid, on 4 July 1919, having been cancelled. A British soldier carrying mails from the aerodrome to Killeagh was taken prisoner, and his comrades became suspicious when he failed to return. The searchlights of the aerodrome were turned on and the IRA withdrew.

MICHAEL KEARNEY BMH WS 148, 3

12 November 1919

Dr Sanderford, an ex-British officer, was fowling in the Donoughmore area when he was accosted and disarmed of a shotgun and a .38 revolver by four members of Donoughmore Company.

JOHN MANNING BMH WS 1720, 12

17 November 1919

Some local volunteers, ten in all, boarded a British Navy boat, the ML121, at Bantry pier. They captured six Ross-Canadian rifles and three revolvers.

SEÁN COTTER BMH WS 1493, 6

18 November 1919

Murray's gun shop in Patrick's Street in Cork was raided by men of the First Battalion, FirstCork Brigade. Upwards of fifty shotguns and other equipment were taken and hidden at a farm near White's Cross.

SEÁN O'CONNELL BMH WS 1706, 6

20 November 1919

Officials of the Munster and Leinster and the National Bank were waylaid and robbed of £18,000 on their way to Knocknagree fair. The robbers, who were operating for their own gain, were eventually apprehended by members of the Seventh Battalion, Second Cork Brigade, and forced to leave the country. A little more than half of the money was eventually recovered.

CON MEANY BMH WS 787, 8

22 November 1919

An IRA convention was held in Dromahane, in the Mallow Battalion area. Denny Mullane, captain Freemount Company, spoke out about an oath of allegiance being taken by the Volunteers. 'I was guided by the failure of secret oath-bound societies in past history. A good man was not in need of the oath, and it was useless to a slacker.'

DENNY MULLANE BMH WS 789, 10

November 1919 (no date available)

Morton's gun shop in Oliver Plunkett Street was raided by members of D Company, Second Battalion, First Cork Brigade, and a small amount of armaments taken, according to Robert C Ahern, intelligence officer of the First Cork Brigade.

ROBERT C AHERN BMH WS 1676, 4

Twenty volunteers from Mallow Company raided the town hall and seized musical instruments of the local fife and drum band, which had intended playing at a British Legion gathering on 11 November.

JOHN C MURPHY BMH WS 1217, 2

Volunteer Peter Donovan of C Company, Second Battalion, First Cork Brigade, held up an RIC man at gunpoint at Union Quay in Cork, taking a mailbag from him. The letters yielded valuable information regarding agents who were passing on information to the Crown forces.

MICHAEL MURPHY BMH WS 1547, 12

Sinn Féin courts sat at Cullinane's (old house) in D (Aherla) Company, Third Battalion, First Cork Brigade area, Seán Buckley as chairman. A man called Thompson and the Herons, senior and junior, who were suspected of being spies, were expelled from the country.

TIM HERLIHY/ DAN KEANE/ TIM O'KEEFFE/ JIM AHERN/ DICK COTTER/ PAT CRONIN/ JEREMIAH CARROLL/ DAN FORDE BMH WS 810, 10

December 1919

6 December 1919

Nine men from Courtbrack Company were in position for an attack on Rathduff (Grenagh) RIC barracks. By some misunderstanding 'men from another Company failed to turn out', and the attack was cancelled.

THOMAS J GOLDEN BMH WS 1680, 13

14 December 1919

Constable Edward Bolger became the first RIC fatality in the War of Independence in Cork when he was shot dead by two members of the local IRA company on his way to Kilbrittain RIC barracks. Constable Bolger was a native of Co Kilkenny. [4]

MARY WALSH BMH WS 556, 4; MICHAEL J CROWLEY BMH WS 1603, 4; JAMES O'MAHONY/ DENIS CROWLEY/ JOHN FITZGERALD BMH WS 560, 6

---

[4] Keane, p110; Abbott, p47; Kingston, D, *Beleagured: a History of the RIC in West Cork during the War of Independence*, Inspire (Cork), 2013, p70.

December 1919 (no date available)

Volunteer Dan Hegarty of Mallow Battalion was arrested.

JOHN J HOGAN BMH WS 1030, 10

Tomás Mac Curtain, OC First Cork Brigade, travelled to GHQ in Dublin, where Michael Collins, director of intelligence, included him in a plan to kill Lord French.

MICHAEL J LEAHY BMH WS 1421, 13

Captain James O'Sullivan, OC Bantry Company, led a raid on Roycroft's Stores, Main Street, Bantry, in which gunpowder and cartridges were taken.

JAMES O'SULLIVAN BMH WS 1455, 5

Ted O'Sullivan, vice-OC Third Cork Brigade, received written instructions from Michael Collins to deploy guncotton captured from Bere Island. It was eventually moved to Kealkill and was used in the attacks against Mount Pleasant and Timoleague RIC barracks in February of 1920.

TED O'SULLIVAN BMH WS 1478, 10

January 1920

1 January 1920

John J Hogan, adjutant of Ballynoe Company, incarcerated in Cork Jail and isolated from the other prisoners, went on hunger strike on this date. He was involved in the raid on the Shropshire Light Infantry at Fermoy on 7 September 1919, and had been jailed, having been identified by Private Preece of that regiment. The Lord Mayor of Cork, Tomás Mac Curtain, intervened and the strike was called off after six days.

JOHN J HOGAN BMH WS 1030, 9

3 January 1920

Inchegeela RIC barracks was attacked on this date. Having failed to gain entry, the local IRA attacking party settled down to an exchange of fire with the seven members of constabulary within, eventually withdrawing due to lack of ammunition. Constable Tobin, who was outside the barracks when the attack began, was wounded. Approximately thirty men guarded the approaches to the village, while twenty took part in the attack, two with rifles, the rest with shotguns.

MICHAEL O'SULLIVAN BMH WS 793, 4

The RIC barracks at Kilmurry was attacked by a force of about sixty men under the command of Dan Corkery, OC Macroom Battalion. The local company, Kilmurry, were engaged in scouting and road-blocking duties. The attack on the barracks went on for two hours, when the attacking party withdrew.

Although there was intense enemy activity in the neighbourhood following this incident, no arrest was made.

WILLIAM POWELL BMH WS 1699, 5; CORNELIUS KELLEHER BMH WS 1654, 4; DAN CORKERY BMH WS 1719, 9

Carrigadrohid RIC barracks was attacked and burned down.

DANIEL HARRINGTON BMH WS 1532, 4

The RIC barracks at Carrigtwohill, with a complement of one sergeant and nine constables, was attacked by members of Cobh and Midleton companies under Commandant Michael Leahy. At 10 pm that night, telephone and telegraph wires were cut, and roads blocked. The forty or so attackers fired for an hour on the barracks, finally blowing a hole in the side wall with gelignite; the policemen surrendered. No one was injured in this attack, and the captured arms and ammunition were removed by Commandant Joseph Ahern and Volunteer Tadhg Manley.

PATRICK J WHELAN BMH WS 1449, 11

4 January 1920

Joseph Ahern, captain of Midleton Company and commandant Fourth Battalion, First Cork Brigade, having partaken in the IRA attack on Carrigtwohill RIC barracks the previous evening, was questioned at his home by a police patrol. 'They went off saying they would see me again.'

JOSEPH AHERN BMH WS 1367, 8

7 January 1920

Cousins Joseph and Jeremiah Ahern, two Desmond brothers and M Hallinan were arrested and paraded before Carrigtwohill RIC. These volunteers, as well as a number from Cobh, were released immediately. Carrigtwohill RIC barracks had been attacked four days previously.

JOSEPH AHERN BMH WS 1367, 8

13 January 1920

First Lieutenant Edward Horgan of H Company, First Battalion, First Cork Brigade, was arrested along with three other comrades on a charge of raiding for arms, went on hunger strike. After eleven days, in a weakened condition and suffering from tonsillitis, he was moved to the Mercy Hospital. Despite being under armed guard day and night, he managed to don the uniform of a nurse and escape, making his way to the shop of the Misses Wallace in St Augustine Street and from there to freedom.

EDWARD HORGAN BMH WS 1644, 5

31 January 1920

Capt Michael O'Sullivan, O/C Mitchelstown Company, together with Volunteers Seán Keane and William J Ryan, were arrested and sent to Cork jail, and later to Wormwood Scrubs. Along with several others, they went on hunger strike for eighteen days, finally being released in May.

MICHAEL O'SULLIVAN BMH WS 1186, 12

James Brennock, OC Rathcormac Company, began arrangements to carry out an attack on Aghern RIC barracks. A small patrol of RIC was arrested and disarmed, but the IRA having discovered that a large motorised British military presence was in the vicinity, the idea of taking the barracks was abandoned.

JAMES BRENNOCK BMH WS 1113, 3

January 1920 (no date available)

Volunteer Daniel Daly and five others from Rathcormac Company lay in wait at Castlelyons for Sergeant O'Shea and two constables. The patrol failed to appear, however, and the volunteers disbanded.

DANIEL DALY BMH WS 743, 4

Jim Lordan and William Desmond, officers in Newcestown Company, transported fifteen hundredweight of guncotton, seized by the Bantry Volunteers, from Coppeen to Newcestown.

WILLIAM DESMOND BMH WS 832, 8

A meeting of the Third Cork Brigade was held in the house of Patrick O'Brien, Adjutant Dunmanway Battalion, where a decision to attack Mount Pleasant RIC barracks was made.

PATRICK O'BRIEN BMH WS 812, 8

Newcestown Company carried out raids for arms in the Newcestown and Enniskeane districts. In the house of a Mr Woods of Castlelands, an ex-Dublin Military Police man, a girl was accidentally injured by shotgun fire.

WILLIAM DESMOND BMH WS 832, 8

Five members of Araglin Company, First Battalion, Second Cork Brigade – Volunteers Patrick Donovan, Matt Mahony, Paddy Buckley, Batt Joyce and Con Leddy, company OC – were arrested and imprisoned for three months in Wormwood Scrubs. They were released after a twenty-one day hunger strike.

CON LEDDY BMH WS 756, 8

Intensive raiding followed the attack on Carrigtwohill RIC barracks on 3 January; Daithí O'Brien, OC, and the Stack brothers of Cobh Company were arrested. John P O'Connell was appointed company captain following O'Brien's arrest around the middle of January.

JOHN P O'CONNELL BMH WS 1444, 5

Captain White and a party of British military broke in the door of Christopher O'Keeffe, QM Newmarket Company, and took him off to the local barracks. O'Keeffe was later released unharmed.

CHRISTOPHER J O'KEEFFE BMH WS 761, 10

The RIC barracks in Crosshaven was evacuated, the policemen moving to Fort Camden. A week later it was burned by IRA men from the city.

EDWARD SISK BMH WS 1505, 1

A company of Volunteers was formed in Carrigaline in January of 1920. Edward Sisk was elected captain of this sixty-man company; John Barry and Edmund Cogan became first and second lieutenants respectively. Raids were made for arms, while a British soldier stationed at Templebreedy Fort contributed a rifle and two hundred rounds of ammunition.

EDWARD SISK BMH WS 1505, 1

February 1920

1 February 1920

Three policemen, one sergeant and two constables, were held up and disarmed by members of Fermoy Battalion. They were held for some hours and released near Aghern.

DANIEL DALY BMH WS 743, 4; JJ BRENNOCK BMH WS 1113, 4

Due to intense activity of Crown forces, a planned attack on Aghern RIC barracks was postponed.

PATRICK AHERN BMH WS 1003, 14

A mock attack was planned for Freemount RIC barracks in the Charleville Battalion area, the object being to draw British military from Buttevant. Due to a misunderstanding, some trenching of roads was not completed on time, and the attack was called off. The village was encircled the following evening by Crown forces, and the garrison abandoned the police barracks the following month.

THOMAS CULHANE BMH WS 831, 3; DENIS MULLANE BMH WS 789, 11; PATRICK O'BRIEN 764, 10

5 February 1920

Barryroe Company made plans to attack Timoleague RIC barracks.

MICHAEL COLEMAN BMH WS 1254, 4

9 February 1920

Castlemartyr RIC barracks was attacked. Sergeant O'Brien and Constable Collins were arrested by IRA Fourth Battalion members on the way from the fair at Midleton to their barracks. Diarmuid Hurley, OC Midleton Company, had a plan to take the police post by using the two RIC men to effect entry, but despite argument and then threats, the policemen refused to cooperate. Hurley used a different strategy, knocking on the door and answering in Sergeant O'Brien's voice when challenged. Constable Lee opened the door, but a security chain barred entry, and a huge struggle ensued, with Hurley and Lee exchanging shots. Hurley broke the chain with the butt of his now-empty revolver, and the garrison was taken after Lee received a bad eye injury. A haul of arms was secured for the IRA. Hurley shook hands with O'Brien and Collins, telling them he admired their loyalty to their comrades.

JOSEPH AHERNE BMH WS1367, 9; MICHAEL KEARNEY 1418, 8; THOMAS HOURIHANE BMH WS 1366, 1; PATRICK J WHELAN BMH WS 1449, 15

12 February 1920

An attack lasting five hours against Allihies RIC barracks was made by approximately twenty volunteers of the Castletownbere Battalion, with twenty more engaged in scouting and blocking roads. Having blown a large hole in the back wall of the building, the attackers called on those within to surrender, but the reply was a burst of rifle fire. After many hours the IRA withdrew. The garrison vacated the barracks the next day. Members of Bere Island Company who took part were James Sullivan (OC),

Michael Sullivan, Florence Sullivan and Tim Harrington; also William O'Neill, Christopher McGrath, Con Sullivan, and Christy O'Connell. Perhaps unknown to the attacking party, Constable Michael Neenan, from Co Clare, died in this incident.[5]

JAMES SULLIVAN BMH WS 1528, 4; WILLIAM O'NEILL BMH WS 1536, 2; CHRISTOPHER O'CONNELL BMH WS 1530, 7, 9

Timoleague RIC barracks was attacked on this date. As with many such attacks, a mine set against the door failed to explode, and after an exchange of gun fire the IRA withdrew.

MICHAEL COLEMAN BMH WS 1254, 4

16 February 1920

A second attempt was made to capture Aghern RIC barracks. Volunteers from several companies in Fermoy Battalion surrounded the building, some attempting to lay a charge of gelignite, while the garrison dropped Mills bombs from above, injuring Volunteer Michael Condon seriously. In the confusion to withdraw, Condon was arrested.

PATRICK AHERN BMH WS 1003, 14; JJ BRENNOCK BMH WS 5

18 February 1920

According to Jeremiah Keating, intelligence officer with the Second Battalion of the First Cork Brigade, a spy called Quinlisk was shot by members of his battalion a few miles outside the

---

[5] Keane, p111, Abbot, p60; Kingston, 138.

city. He had been seen previously acting suspiciously near the Thomas Ashe Hall, the battalion headquarters.[6]

JEREMIAH KEATING BMH WS 1657, 3; MICHAEL MURPHY BMH WS 1547, 12; DANIEL BREEN BMH WS 1739, 28; RICHARD WALSH BMH WS 400, 102; JOSEPH O'SHEA BMH WS 1675, 7

20 February 1920

About twenty volunteers from Donoughmore Company lay in wait at Tullig, on the Donoughmore-Coachford road, about two miles from the former village. They expected a party of RIC to return from an enquiry in Coachford, but the police chose a different route.

JOHN MANNING BMH WS 1720, 12

25 February 1920

Captain Daniel Canty, OC Newcestown Company, along with volunteers from Crosspound under Captain Tom Kelleher and from Tinker's Cross, opened an attack on Mount Pleasant RIC barracks. Explosives were to be deployed by the IRA on this occasion, but there would seem to be some confusion as to why they were not used. Fire lasting twenty minutes was opened by the IRA, but with ammunition scarce and knowing there would be no fruitful outcome, the volunteers withdrew.

DANIEL CANTY BMH WS 1619, 7

---

[6] Keane, p111

Timoleague RIC barracks was attacked on this night by IRA men from five companies in the Bandon Battalion under its OC, Commandant Tom Hales: Ballinadee, Clogagh, Timoleague, Kilbrittain and Barryroe. Under a covering fire from across the street, a mine was placed against the door. Failing to explode, hay and straw were lit near the mine, again with no result. Rifle fire lasted from midnight until five o' clock in the morning, when the IRA withdrew. Extensive searching and questioning by Crown forces in the following days resulted in some volunteers quitting their jobs and going on the run.

DANIEL DONOVAN BMH WS 1608, 3; WILLIAM FOLEY BMH WS 1560, 4

28 February 1920

John P O'Connell, OC, and several others from Cobh Company accosted a British Army corporal and three privates at Bunkers Hill and disarmed all but one soldier, who tried to run away; he was shot dead. He was Private William Newman.[7]

JOHN P O'CONNELL BMH WS 1444, 5; MICHAEL BURKE BMH WS 1424, 13; SÉAMUS FITZGERALD BMH WS 1737, 33.

---

[7] Keane, p112

February 1920 (no date available)

On his release from Cork Prison, Liam O'Dwyer, OC Castletownbere Battalion, was re-arrested and sent to Wormwood Scrubs. He, along with a group of over ninety IRA men, went on strike, being released under a general amnesty in May of 1920.

LIAM O'DWYER BMH WS 1527, 9

First Lieutenant Michael Bowler of C Company, First Battalion, First Cork Brigade, was arrested by Crown forces at his home in Clogheen. His company arrived, opening fire to prevent him being taken to Blarney, to no avail.

DANIEL HEALY BMH WS 1656, 5

Volunteers from Bandon Battalion opened fire on Farnivane RIC barracks in the early hours of the morning, withdrawing after an hour. The barracks was evacuated the next day.

SEÁN MURPHY BMH WS 1445, 5; CHARLES O'DONOGHUE BMH WS 1607, 2

Volunteers P Crowley and D Crowley of Kilbrittain Company were arrested by Crown forces and later interned in Wormwood Scrubs until June of 1920. John J O'Mahony was arrested and sent uncharged to Cork prison.

JAMES O'MAHONY/ DENIS CROWLEY/ JOHN FITZGERALD BMH WS 560, 7

March 1920

2 March 1920

Capt Daniel Canty, OC Newcestown Company, purchased a service rifle (for £5) and collected some small arms from a volunteer source in Bandon. He dumped them and went to his home in Farnalough, Newcestown. During the night his house was surrounded by police and by military from the Essex Regiment and he was arrested. Volunteer John Allen, also of the local company, along with Volunteers John O'Mahony of Kilbrittain and Frank Hurley of Tinker's Cross, were also arrested that night, eventually being sent to Wormwood Scrubs, where they went on hunger strike.

DANIEL CANTY BMH WS 1619, 9

7 March 1920

A second attempt was made to attack Inchegeela RIC barracks by a combined effort of the First Cork Brigade. Explosives were to be used to breach the wall, but it was observed that a barbed wire cordon surrounded the barracks to the depth of ten yards, and the IRA withdrew.

DANIEL HARRINGTON BMH WS 1532, 5

Five youths of Na Fianna raided a house in Douglas belonging to a retired British Army colonel. They were arrested that night by the RIC. The colonel's household was threatened by the IRA not to attend an identification parade, and all five Fianna members were released.

CHARLES MEANEY BMH WS 1631, 3

10 March 1920

Two members of Donoughmore RIC garrison were driven to a local point-to-point race by a shopkeeper from the village. An ambush was laid for their return journey, but a different route was taken. A two-month boycott was placed on the shopkeeper, as well as two farming brothers who worked at the garden plot at the barracks. Both boycotts were lifted when public apologies were read out at the church gates after mass.

MAURICE BREW BMH WS 1695, 13; JOHN MANNING BMH WS 1720, 13

11 March 1920

Volunteers from Riverstown Company of the IRA held up three RIC men near Glanmire police barracks. Constable Scully was shot dead when he resisted arrest. He was a native of Adrigole, Co Cork. [8]

JOSEPH CASHMAN BMH WS 1466, 2

12 March 1920

Police and British military raided the Thomas Ashe Hall in Charlotte Quay in Cork, headquarters of the Cork City Battalion, First Cork Brigade. Several were arrested and subsequently imprisoned.

JEROME COUGHLAN BMH WS 1568, 7

---

[8] Keane, p112; Abbot, p 63.

15 March 1920

Three members of the Manchester Regiment were held up by four unarmed volunteers at the gates of Mount Massey House, Macroom. The four were members of B Company, Macroom Battalion, and four rifles were secured. Volunteer Dick Browne was subsequently recognised, arrested and imprisoned for three months.

CHARLES BROWNE BMH WS 873, 14

Captain Daniel Canty of Newcestown Company, in Cork Prison since the 3 March, was transferred with three other prisoners to Wormwood Scrubs in England. After going on hunger strike, they were released in May 1920.

DANIEL CANTY BMH WS 1617, 9

16 March 1920

Despite warnings from IRA intelligence, all except two officers of the IRA in the Cobh area were arrested by Crown forces and sent to Wormwood Scrubs Prison.

SÉAMUS FITZGERLD 1737, 22

Several members of Dunmanway Company were arrested on this date, being sent to Belfast Prison where they were involved in a 'smash up' directed by Austin Stack, then to Wormwood Scrubs where they went on hunger strike for eighteen days. They were finally released.

EDWARD YOUNG BMH WS 1402, 9

19 March 1920

Constable Murtagh of the RIC was shot dead at Pope's Quay in Cork by Volunteers Christy McSwiney and O'Connell of C Company, First Battalion, First Cork Brigade. The two IRA men fled to the house of Captain Peg Duggan, an officer in the Tomás Ceannt branch of Cumann na mBan, in Blackpool.[9]

PEG DUGGAN BMH WS 1576, 9; PATRICK A MURRAY BMH WS 1584, 11; MAURICE FORD AND OTHERS BMH WS 719, 5; MICHAEL MURPHY BMH WS 1547, 18

20 March 1920

District Inspector Swanzy left King Street (now Mac Curtain Street) RIC barracks with a group of men. Arriving at the house of Lord Mayor Tomás Mac Curtain in Blackpool, they were admitted by his wife. Mac Curtain, OC First Cork Brigade, was shot outside his bedroom, and died where he fell some time later.[10]

MICHAEL J FEELEY BMH WS 68, passim; PEG DUGGAN BMH WS 1576, 9; MICHAEL MURPHY BMH WS 1547, 18; MAURICE FORDE AND OTHERS BMH WS 719, 5; SEÁN CULHANE BMH WS 746, 7; SEÁ HEALY BMH WS 1479, 9; TIMOTHY SEXTON BMH WS 1565, 6; SEÁN O'CONNELL BMH WS 1706, 2

---

[9] Keane, p25; Abbott, p64.
[10] Keane, p25.

21 March 1920

Séamus Fitzgerald, an officer in Cobh Company, received a death threat in the post, promising immediate assassination if any RIC man was shot as a reprisal for the killing of Lord Mayor Tomás Mac Curtain the previous day.

SÉAMUS FITZGERALD BMH WS 1737, 22

23 March 1920

Twelve men from G Company, First Cork Brigade, were ordered to guard all entrances to Cork city hall, where a meeting of brigade officers was taking place under Vice-Brigadier Terence Mac Swiney. Although it was a day after Tomás Mac Curtain's funeral and a time of heightened tension, no raid took place.

JEREMIAH KEATING BMH WS 1657, 4

31 March 1920

Volunteers from Durrus, Caheragh and Bantry Companies, under the command of Ted O'Sullivan, OC Bantry Battalion, opened fire on Durrus RIC barracks. The adjoining house was commandeered and an attempt made to fire and bomb the outpost. Two of the garrison were severely wounded. The attacking party retreated at daylight, and the building, now greatly damaged by fire, was abandoned by the police the next day.

SEÁN COTTER BMH WS 1493, 8; TED O'SULLIVAN BMH WS 1478, 12

March 1920 (no date available)

An attempt was made to ambush a police patrol at Airhill, near Glanworth. In the same month the RIC sergeant at Glanworth was held up and his revolver and ammunition captured. Liam Lynch, OC Second Cork Brigade, aware that attacks on houses in the name of the IRA were taking place, ordered a temporary halt to legitimate IRA raids. Despite this, volunteers from the Brigade raided the house of Charlie Oliver, 'an Imperialist', near Kildorrery.

THOMAS BARRY BMH WS 430, 6

Several arrests were made in east Cork of men suspected of taking part in the attack on Aghern RIC barracks in February by Rathcormac Company.

JAMES BRENNOCK BMH WS 1113, 5

James Brennock, OC Rathcormac Company, and Volunteer Dan Daly lay in wait near Rathcormac RIC barracks, their intention being to shoot Sergeant Burns, whom Brennock claimed had given the family of Volunteer Michael Condon 'a bad time'. Volunteer Condon had been badly wounded and captured in the attack on Aghern RIC barracks on the 16 February 1920.

JAMES BRENNOCK BMH WS 1113, 6

John P O'Connell, OC Cobh Company, was arrested by British Army and RIC personnel and taken to Cork prison, from there to Belfast, and finally to Wormwood Scrubs in England, where he went on hunger strike for twelve days. He was hospitalised and released in June of 1920.

JOHN P O'CONNELL BMH WS 1444, 5

Members of Charleville Battalion IRA lay in wait for a British military lorry on the Milford-Charleville road, but their enemy failed to appear.

MICHAEL O'DONNELL BMH WS 1145, 4

Charles O'Donoghue, a member of Farnivane Company and quartermaster of Bandon Battalion, was sworn in to the Irish Republican Brotherhood by Liam Deasy.

CHARLES O'DONOGHUE BMH WS 1607, 2

The parish priest of Timoleague was warned by the IRA not to deliver any sermons denouncing them. A local press reporter, J O'Mahoney, was also warned not to report the priest's sermons.

JOHN O'DRISCOLL BMH WS 1250, 3

Patrick O'Leary and Denis J Long, OC and second lieutenant respectively of Kilmurry Company, were arrested, eventually being sent to Wormwood Scrubs, where they were released after a hunger strike lasting twenty-two days.

JOHN O'MAHONY BMH WS 1662, 7

Charleville Battalion staff and some company officers attended a brigade convention at Dromahane schoolhouse; Liam Lynch, OC Second Cork Brigade, presided.

MICHAEL GEARY/ RICHARD SMITH BMH WS 754, 10

April 1920

1 April 1920

George Power of Fermoy Company, intelligence officer with the Second Cork Brigade, was arrested by Crown forces at his parents' house. He received permission from the officer in charge to go upstairs to collect a change of clothes, whereupon he escaped out the window and got away.

GEORGE POWER BMH WS 451, 5

2 April 1920

Seán Cotter, adjutant of Bantry Battalion and a member of its flying column, was arrested by Crown forces at Scart, Bantry, as a result of his involvement in the Durrus RIC barracks attack on 31 March 1920. He was imprisoned at Wormwood Scrubs, where he went on hunger strike for twenty-one days, and was then hospitalised before finally being released.

SEÁN COTTER BMH WS 1493, 10

3 April 1920

Charlie Hurley, OC Third Cork Brigade, and senior officers including Liam Deasy, Con Crowley and Con Lehane (Bandon Brigade armourer) narrowly avoided arrest at Hatter's Cross, between Ballineen and Rossmore, when they ran into a British cycle patrol.

PADDY O'BRIEN BMH WS 812, 8

3-4 April 1920

Easter Saturday and Easter Sunday 1920 saw a huge spate of attacks on RIC barracks throughout Ireland. The following is a list of some barracks mentioned in the witness statements.

Ballyhooley and Glanworth: THOMAS BARRY BMH WS 1585, 5

Courtmacsherry: DANIEL DONOVAN BMH WS 1608, 4; CORS CALNAN BM WS 1317, 4

Glashakinleen: JAMES CASHMAN BMH WS 1270, 4; DANIEL FLYNN BMH WS 1240, 4

Kenneigh: PHILIP CHAMBERS BMH WS 738, 1; SEÁN MURPHY BMH WS 1445, 6

Rathcoole: CON MEANY 787, 7; DANIEL COAKLEY BMH WS 1406, 3

Ballinspittle: DENIS COLLINS BMH WS 827, 3

Goleen: RICHARD COLLINS BMH WS 1542, 3

Adrigole: EUGENE DUNNE BMH WS 1537, 5

Liscarroll: MICHAEL GEARY BMH WS 754, 10

Tarelton: CORNELIUS KELLEHER BMH WS 1654, 6

Castletownsend: DANIEL KELLY BMH WS 1590, 3

Mitchelstown: PATRICK LUDDY BMH WS 1151, 9

Rylane: JOHN MANNING BMH WS 1720, 14

Eyeries: JAMES MCCARTHY BMH WS 1567, 11

Lombardstown: MICHAEL MCCARTHY BMH WS 1238, 3

Blackrock, Mallow: JOHN C MURPHY BMH WS 1217, 3; JOHN BOLSTER BMH WS 808, 16

Ballingurteen: PATRICK O'BRIEN BMH WS 812, 8; EDWARD YOUNG BMH WS 1402, 9

Ballingeary: CORNELIUS CRONIN BMH WS 1726, 5

Freemount: DENIS MULLANE BMH WS 789, 12

Baltimore and Ballydehob: DENIS CROWLEY BMH WS 560, 8

Farnanes, Tarelton and Ballinagree: CHARLES BROWNE BMH WS 873, 14

Togher: MICHAEL MURPHY BMH WS 1547, 21

5 April 1920

Members of B and G Companies, First Battalion, First Cork Brigade under battalion OC Daniel Donovan burned the income tax office at South Mall, Cork.

PATRICK J DEASY/ MAURICE FITZGERALD/ JOHN J LUCEY/ MARK WICKHAM BMH WS 558, 2

9 April 1920

Cobh Urban Council passed a resolution pledging allegiance to Dáil Éireann.

SÉAMUS FITZGERALD BMH WS 1737, 21

12 April 1920

Volunteer Patrick Morrissey of Gortroe, Youghal, was arrested by Crown forces. The following night he was admitted to hospital with pellet wounds from a shotgun. He died of septicaemia.[11]

---

[11] Keane, p113.

16 April 1920

Members of D Company, Fourth Battalion, First Cork Brigade raided the Cork to Youghal train at 5.45 am at Carrigtwohill station, taking three horseloads of mail for censoring. An hour later the village was cordoned off by two hundred British troops, who carried out futile searches for enemy personnel and arms.

FRANCIS HEALY BMH WS 1694, 13

22 April 1920

Constable Michael McCarthy, a member of the Dublin Metropolitan Police, was on leave at his home at Lackenalooha, near Clonakilty, when unknown IRA men approached him and fired several times; he died of his injuries.[12]

24 April 1920

Six civilian men were arrested by members of the Second Cork Brigade; they were accused of taking part in the theft of £18,000 of National Bank money at Ballydaly.

CORNELIUS MEANY BMH WS 787, 8

26 April 1920

Cornelius O'Sullivan, OC Innishannon Company, recalls an attack on a police patrol on the road between Upton and Innishannon, resulting in the deaths of Sergeant Cornelius

---

[12] Keane, p114; Abbot p73; Kingston, 95.

Crean and Constable Patrick McGoldrick. Sergeant Crean was a brother of the famous Antarctic explorer Tom Crean. [13]

CORNELIUS O'SULLIVAN BMH WS 1740, 4; RICHARD RUSSELL BMH WS 1591, 4; FRANK NEVILLE BMH WS 443, 3; JAMES O'MAHONY AND OTHERS 560, 8; MICHAEL J CROWLEY BMH WS 1603, 5

28 April 1920

First Lieutenant Michael Riordan of Kilpatrick Company, along with Dick Barrett (Third Cork Brigade quartermaster) and Tom Kelleher (OC Crosspound Company), marched with others from Crosspound to Kinsale Junction railway station, where a mail train bearing coded messages between Crown forces was raided.

MICHAEL RIORDAN BMH WS 1638, 10

---

[13] Keane, p114; Abbot, p73; Kingston, 71.

May 1920

6 May 1920

John J O'Sullivan, an officer in Bantry Battalion, received an order from his battalion OC to destroy the income tax offices in Bantry. Accompanied by two others, he set the building alight.

JOHN J O'SULLIVAN BMH WS 1578, 9

8 May 1920

Cloyne RIC barracks was successfully attacked by volunteers from Cobh and Midleton Companies under Commandants Leahy and Hurley, the building being destroyed by fire and its garrison surrendering; some arms were captured.

JOSEPH AHERNE BMH WS 1367, 16

9 May 1920

Most of the volunteers who had taken part in the successful attack on Cloyne RIC barracks the previous night attended a concert in the village, Dan Hobbs being the guest artist. The programme of music ended with the Soldier's Song.

JOSEPH AHERNE BMH WS 1367, 16

10 May 1920

A patrol of four RIC men was ambushed at Ahawadda, one mile from Timoleague, by members of the Barryroe Company; Charlie Hurley, later OC Third Cork brigade, was the senior officer in command. Sergeant John Flynn, Constable William Brick and Constable Edward Dunne were shot dead.[14]

DENIS O'BRIEN BMH WS 1306, 4; MICHAEL COLEMAN BMH WS 1254, 4; DENIS CROWLEY BMH WS 560, 8; JAMES MOLONEY BMH WS 1310, 6; JOHN O'DRISCOLL BMH WS 1250, 9

11 May 1920

Members of the Cork city active service unit (the urban name for flying column) shot dead Sergeant Garvey and Constable Harrington, and seriously wounded Constable Doyle, at the Lower Road in Cork. Garvey had figured prominently in the inquest into the death of Lord Mayor Tomás Mac Curtain.[15]

DANIEL HEALY BMH WS 1656, 6; PATRICK MURRAY BMH WS 1584, 13; SEÁN HEALY BMH WS 1479, 16

Volunteer Charles O'Donoghue of Farnivane Company was arrested by a British cycle patrol in the command of Lieutenant Hotblack, afterwards killed at Crossbarry. O'Donoghue was imprisoned at Wormwood Scrubs and Pentonville, being eventually released at the end of August 1920.

CHARLES O'DONOGHUE BMH WS 1607, 2

---

[14] Kingston, pp96, 99; Keane, p114; Abbott, p75.
[15] Keane, p115; Abbott, p76.

12 May 1920

Following the shooting dead of two RIC men the previous night, a detachment of seventeen IRA men from Cork city guarded the dwelling house of Terence Mac Swiney, OC First Cork Brigade and Lord Mayor of Cork.

DANIEL HEALY BMH WS 1656, 7

13 May 1920

First Lieutenant Daniel McCarthy of Lombardstown Company, along with two volunteers, arrested two men wanted by the IRA in connection with the robbery of a bank at Millstreet. The two men were taken to Dromahane Company area.

DANIEL MCCARTHY BMH WS 1239, 4; MICHAEL MCCARTHY BMH WS 1238, 4

17 May 1920

A detachment of the King's Liverpool Regiment landed at Bantry and were billeted at the Bantry workhouse.

THOMAS REIDY BMH WS 1422, 7

23 May 1920

Twelve IRA men from Ballyvourney, Ballingeary and Kilnamartra Companies gathered at Ballingeary village to attack the local RIC barracks. Fearing something was afoot, the garrison rushed indoors and barricaded the door, and the operation was called off.

PATRICK J LYNCH BMH WS 1543, 7

28 May 1920

Members of Charleville Volunteers took part in the attack on Kilmallock RIC barracks in Co Limerick.

THOMAS CULHANE BMH WS 831, 4; PATRICK O'BRIEN BMH WS 764, 11; MICHAEL SHEEHY BMH WS 989, 8

31 May 1920

A large quantity of guncotton, detonators and wireless equipment was seized by members of Bantry Battalion when they raided the Mizen Head fog station.

TED O'SULLIVAN BMH WS 1478, 15

May 1920 (no date available)

Volunteers from A Company in Macroom raided the office of solicitor T P Grainger, Macroom; they were seeking arms. A Webley and a Colt revolver were taken. While the raid was in progress, armed British military came to the door, but did not attempt to enter.

CHARLES BROWNE BMH WS 873, 16

Schull workhouse was destroyed by fire by members of Schull Company under OC Jerry McCarthy. They probably thought the building was to be used by Crown forces.

CHARLIE COTTER BMH WS 1519, 3

The recently abandoned Ballingeary RIC barracks was burned down by the local company.

CORNELIUS CRONIN BMH WS 1726, 5

About fourteen members of the Bandon Battalion lay in wait at Killowen, four miles west of Bandon on the road to Enniskeane, for a British Army cycle patrol. The IRA, under the command of Tom Hales, withdrew after dark when the enemy failed to show.

WILLIAM DESMOND BMH WS 873, 12

Five members of Kilpatrick Company lay in ambush at Brother's Fort, two miles from Innishannon, awaiting an RIC patrol; it never turned up.

MICHAEL RIORDAN BMH WS 1638, 11

Farnivane RIC barracks, recently evacuated by its garrison, was destroyed by fire by volunteers from Newcestown company.

WILLIAM DESMOND BMH WS 832, 12

Six members of H Company, First Battalion, First Cork Brigade, lay in wait at Ballincarriga Bridge, on the old Cork-Ballincollig road, for a motorised patrol of RIC. To the surprise of the IRA, two lorries full of British troops also arrived, and after an exchange of shots the volunteers, now hopelessly outgunned, withdrew.

EDWARD HORGAN BMH WS 1644, 6

Rockchapel post office was robbed by civilians; the Freemount Volunteers helped in the apprehending of the culprits.

DENIS MULLANE BMH WS 789, 12

Members of Burnfort and other companies in the Mallow Battalion area raided the home of Hugh and Dan O'Brien at Inchmay; they were suspected of robbing £18,000 from a bank in Millstreet.

TADHG MCCARTHY BMH WS 965, 5; TADHG LOONEY BMH WS 1196, 5

A British military lorry broke down at Faunkill, near Eyeries, on its way from Castletownbere to Kenmare. Christopher O'Connell, OC Eyeries Company, mobilised some men to go to the scene, but the lorry was repaired and was gone by the time they reached Faunkill.

JAMES MCCARTHY BMH WS 1567, 11

A section of volunteers from Freemount Company was mobilised to attack the police guard on the mail car of the Charleville to Ballagh train.

DENIS MULLANE BMH WS 789, 12

Ballydehob Company demolished the local courthouse stone by stone, and burned all documents.

SEÁN O'DRISCOLL BMH WS 1518, 3

Newmarket courthouse was destroyed by fire through the efforts of Freemount Company.

DENIS MULLANE BMH WS 789, 12

Killeagh RIC barracks was evacuated by its garrison.

JOSEPH AHERNE BMH WS 1367, 16

The bakery of Alfred Cotter of Enniskeane was boycotted because it supplied the Crown forces. Following this, eighty British military arrived in the village and took over the house of Dr Fehily.

PADDY O'BRIEN BMH WS 812, 8

The British military established a garrison in Charleville.

MICHAEL GEARY/ RICHARD SMITH BMH WS 754, 9

The house of Eugene Sweeney at Toormore, in the Schull Battalion area, was raided for arms, three rifles and some ammunition were taken.

PATRICK WILCOX BMH WS 1529, 10

A raid for arms was made on Atkins, gun dealers, of Dunmanway, by the local company. Some ammunition was taken, but no arms found.

EDWARD YOUNG BMH WS 1402, 10

June 1920

1 June 1920

Captain John Manning, OC Donoughmore Company, marched his unit to Healy's Bridge on the Leemount Road. A tree was felled to block access to Blarney. A lorry carrying British military engaged the IRA for some time before eventually retreating. Donoughmore RIC barracks was burned down the same night.

JOHN MANNING BMH WS 1720, 15

Blarney RIC barracks was attacked and destroyed by explosives, the attacking party being drawn mainly from the Cork city companies. The building was evacuated the next day.

MORTIMER CURTIN BMH WS 1679, 6

Believing that the Glebe House in Inchegeela was about to be occupied by the British military, it was burned down by Michael O'Sullivan and two others of Ballyvourney Battalion.

MICHAEL O'SULLIVAN BMH WS 793, 6

Members of Bantry Company IRA lay in wait near Glengarriffe for an entire week; they were waiting for a patrol of RIC, but it never came as far as the intended ambush site.

TED O'SULLIVAN BMH WS 1478, 16

5 June 1920

The Essex Regiment was replaced in Midleton by the Cameron Highlanders. Later that evening they were shown the local countryside by Constable O'Connor of the RIC by cycle patrol. They came across a number of men bowling at Mile Bush, west of the town. At the signal of a revolver shot fired by Tadhg

Manley, the men, members of Midleton Volunteers, rushed the Crown forces, seizing twelve rifles and twelve hundred rounds of ammunition. The regiment caused destruction in Midleton that night by way of retaliation.

JOHN KELLEHER BMH WS 1456, 13; MICHAEL LEAHY BMH WS 1421, 28; PATRICK J WHELAN BMH WS 1449, 27; JOSEPH AHERNE BMH WS 1367, 18

Farran RIC barracks was attacked by members of the Second and Third Battalions, First Cork Brigade. The garrison within sent up Verey lights after the building was bombed, and the volunteers, fearing the arrival of reinforcements, withdrew. The police abandoned the building the following day.

JIM AHERN BMH WS 810, 11

6 June 1920

A number of local volunteers gathered across the road from Ballingeary RIC barracks. Suspecting an attack, the garrison, fourteen in number, retreated indoors.

MICHAEL O'SULLIVAN BMH WS 793, 6

About twenty volunteers from the Fourth Battalion, First Cork Brigade, gathered near Ballycotton RIC barracks with a view to capturing it. Finding it strongly guarded by a detachment of Cameron Highlanders, some of whose members had been disarmed the previous evening at Mile Bush near Midleton, the IRA withdrew.

MICHAEL LEAHY BMH WS 1421, 28

7 June 1920

John O'Mahony, QM Kilmurry Company, relates that Kilmurry RIC barracks was evacuated by its garrison on the morning of the 7 June 1920. It was burned later that day by members of the Company under its OC, Jack O'Connell.

JOHN O'MAHONY BMH WS 1662, 8

9 June 1920

Carrigadrohid RIC barracks was attacked by volunteers from the Seventh Battalion of the First Cork Brigade. Despite the building being fired, the garrison within fought on, sending up Verey lights to no avail. The IRA withdrew at 3 am, and the garrison abandoned the building the following day, but returned within a week to occupy O'Donoghue's house nearby.

MAURICE BREW BMH WS 1695, 16; WILLIAM POWELL BMH WS 1699, 6; CHARLES BROWNE BMH WS 873, 17

12 June 1920

Farran RIC barracks, which had been abandoned by its garrison on 6 June, was burned by the IRA.

JIM AHERN AND OTHERS BMH WS 810, 12

At Anagashel, on the Bantry-Glengarriff road, Constable Thomas King was shot and killed by members of the Third Cork Brigade. Constable King, from Co Galway, had previously served in the Royal Navy.[16]

---

[16] Kingston, p125; Keane, p115; Abbott, p88.

TED O'SULLIVAN BMH WS 1478, 16; MICHAEL O'DRISCOLL BMH WS 1297, 1; SEÁN COTTER BMH WS 1493, 10; JOHN J O'SULLIVAN BMH WS 1578, 10

13 June 1920

Con Murphy, an IRA man who was friendly with one of the policemen at Inchegeela RIC barracks, hatched a plan to bring a drugged bottle of poitín to the garrison. One of the constables having got violently sick after tasting it, the others became suspicious, and a plan by the IRA to seize the barracks was cancelled.

DANIEL HARRINGTON BMH WS 1532, 6

19 June 1920

Jim Brislane, local Battalion OC, and a group from Charleville Company raided a mail train some distance from the town, taking seven mailbags destined for Crown forces.

MICHAEL GEARY/ RICHARD SMITH BMH WS 754, 11; PATRICK O'BRIEN BMH WS 764, 12; THOMAS CULHANE BMH WS 831, 4

Volunteers from Ballinadee, Kilbrittain and Newcestown assembled at Ballinadee Feis in hopes of capturing arms and ammunition from a British military cycle patrol. The patrol, however, never materialised.

DANIEL CANTY BMH WS 1619, 12; WILLIAM FOLEY BMH WS 1560, 5

20 June 1920

Members of Newcestown Company under its OC, Daniel Canty, took part in the destruction of the evacuated RIC barracks at Farnivane, narrowly missing a British military cycle patrol afterwards.

DANIEL CANTY BMH WS 1619, 11

21 June 1920

A cycle patrol of RIC was fired on at Clonee Wood, near Bantry. The attacking party of IRA, under the command of Bantry Battalion Vice-OC Maurice Donegan, killed Constable James Brett, a native of Waterford, and seriously injured two others.[17]

SEÁN COTTER BMH WS1493, 11; MAURICE DONEGAN BMH WS 639, 3; TED O'SULLIVAN BMH WS 1478, 16

Members of Freemount Company IRA took part in the burning of Drumcollogher courthouse, Co Limerick. An unexplained explosion took place while the attacking party were inside, resulting in the deaths of three local men, Volunteers Buckley, Dave Brennan and Billy Danagher.

DENNY MULLANE BMH WS 789, 12

24 June 1920

Pat Harte, quartermaster Third Cork Brigade, was in charge of a party of IRA men awaiting the appearance of Crown forces at Derrigra, near Ballineen. They failed to appear.

SEÁN MURPHY BMH WS 1445, 7

---

[17] Kingston, p127; Keane, p116; Abbott, p89.

24 June 1920 saw the destruction by burning of the previously evacuated Blackrock RIC barracks in Cork, a job carried out by men of B Company Second Battalion, First Cork Brigade.

MICHAEL MURPHY BMH WS 1547, 21

A detachment of fifty soldiers of the East Kent Regiment took over the house of Miss Webb in Castletownroche.

DAVID O'CALLAGHAN BMH WS 950, 7

Following the death of Constable Brett on 21 June 1920, masked men raided the houses of IRA men in Bantry. Three houses were burned, and two more wrecked. Cornelius Crowley, a member of Sinn Féin, and described as 'a cripple', was shot dead in his bed.[18]

TED O'SULLIVAN BMH WS 1478, 16; MAURICE DONEGAN BMH WS 639, 3; SEÁN COTTER BMH WS 1493, 13; JOHN J O'SULLIVAN BMH WS 1578, 14

An RIC barracks 'about two miles east of Cork city' was evacuated by its garrison on this date. It was burned some days later by men from C Company, Second Battalion, First Cork Brigade.

MICHAEL WALSH BMH WS 1521, 9

26 June 1920

Following the destruction of Ballygurteen RIC barracks, along with the postbox nearby, Timothy Warren, captain Ballineen Company (a postman), was ordered to attend Clonakilty courthouse. . He refused.

---

[18] Keane, p117.

TIMOTHY WARREN BMH WS 1275, 5

Brigadier General Cuthbert Henry Tindall Lucas was the most senior British Army officer captured by the IRA during the War of Independence. Along with two other officers, he was accosted and forced to surrender while fishing near Fermoy. The IRA group of five, which included Brigade OC Liam Lynch and Newmarket Battalion OC Seán Moylan, drove from the scene in two cars with the captured men. A conversation which they later discovered was in Arabic between Lucas and one of his officers, a Colonel Danford, precipitated a vicious struggle between the general and Lynch. During this altercation, the car in which they were travelling crashed; Lynch got the upper hand. A second struggle was halted when Lynch shot Colonel Danford in the face. Lucas was kept in various locations until he was released by the IRA.

GEORGE POWER BMH WS 451, 5

29 June 1920

In the wake of the capture of General Lucas, OC British forces at Fermoy, the Volunteers heard rumours that the town was to be burned in retaliation. Liam Lynch, OC Second Cork Brigade, compelled General Lucas to write a despatch to the acting OC forbidding this. Volunteer Michael McCarthy of Lombardstown Company bore the message to Fermoy.

MICHAEL MCCARTHY BMH WS 1238, 5; MICHAEL O'CONNELL BMH WS 1428, 5; WILLIAM BUCKLEY BMH WS 1009, 6; JAMES HACKET BMH WS 1080, 2; DANIEL MCCARTHY BMH WS 1239, 5

Volunteer Philip Chambers, later captain of Coppeen Company, attended a Volunteer sports day at Kilnadur. A British military plane, flying low over the sports field, lost altitude and made a forced landing nearby.

PHILIP CHAMBERS BMH WS 738, 1

Brigadier General Lucas, OC British forces in Fermoy, having been captured some days before, was transferred to the West Limerick Brigade area under orders of Liam lynch, OC Second Cork Brigade IRA.

MICHAEL O'CONNELL BMH WS 1428, 6

June 1920 (no date available)

Having observed British officers and RIC frequenting the house of Sir George Bowen-Colthurst in Ballyvourney, the local IRA company burned it down, fearing it was about to be garrisoned.

PATRICK O'SULLIVAN BMH WS 784, 6

Several raids by the IRA took place in the Innishannon area, yielding a quantity of shotguns and rifles.

RICHARD RUSSELL BMH WS 1591, 6

An armed gang of thieves, numbering about twenty, were operating in the area of Kilmallock, Co Limerick. Eleven members of Charleville Company captured eighteen of them, including their leader. Two of them were deported, the rest being released after a few days.

MICHAEL GEARY/ RICHARD SMITH BMH WS 754, 11

Six members of Dunmanway Company under the command of vice-OC Michael McCarthy lay in wait near Drimoleague for an armed patrol of RIC. The patrol did not show up.

EDWARD YOUNG BMH WS 1402, 10

Members of B Company, Second Battalion of the First Cork Brigade were at revolver practice at Skehard, in the city suburb of Blackrock, when they were surprised by a number of Black and Tans. During an exchange of gunfire, Volunteer John Cotter was wounded in the shoulder.

MICHAEL WALSH BMH WS 1521, 10

A small gang of IRA men carried out armed robberies in the Schull Battalion area. They were disciplined by the IRA, some of them being deported and others made to work on farms where sons of the house were on active service with the IRA.

PATRICK WILCOX BMH WS 1529, 5

Crown forces dressed in civilian clothes raided the house of the Rice family of Strawhall, Fermoy, a meeting-place for the Fermoy Company, leaving the house partially burned. The local IRA traced the supply of civilian clothing to Mr Longhurst, an Englishman living in Fermoy. He was deported.

PATRICK AHERN BMH WS 103, 16

The Machine Gun Corps, who had replaced the East Lancs at Mallow barracks in the early months of 1920, were in turn replaced by the Seventeenth Lancers in June.

RICHARD WILLIS/ JACKIE BOLSTER BMH WS 808, 16

Sinn Féin set up Donoughmore Parish Court in June of 1920. The court registrar was David Mullane.

MAURICE BREW BMH WS 1695, 16

A patrol of two RIC and one British soldier came on foot from Ballincollig to Donoughmore. Maurice Brew, second lieutenant Donoughmore Company, and about a dozen volunteers gathered at Crean's Cross to intercept them, but the patrol went back to Ballincollig by another route.

MAURICE BREW BMH WS 1695, 17; JOHN MANNING 1720, 16

Four volunteers from Mitchelstown Company travelled to Ballindangan railway station to attack a patrol of RIC expected on the train from Cork. The patrol never turned up.

PATRICK CLIFFORD BMH WS 946, 3

Howes Strand coast guard station was raided by Kilbrittain Company and its garrison of seven coast guards was arrested and disarmed.

JAMES O'MAHONY/ DENIS CROWLEY/ JOHN FITZGERALD BMH WS 560, 8

The house of two officers of the British garrison in Kinsale was raided near the Old Head, but no weapons were discovered.

DENIS COLLINS BMH WS 827, 3

Two Black and Tans stationed at Elizabeth Fort in Cork were set upon and disarmed at Crosse's Green by Patrick Collins, captain G Company, Second Battalion of the First Cork Brigade, and Volunteer Seán Mitchell.

PATRICK COLLINS BMH WS 1707, 5

Members of Cullen Company were involved in blocking roads and cutting communications on the night Rathmore RIC barracks was attacked.

TIMOTHY CONDON BMH WS 1374, 4

Following information that Kilbrittain Castle was to be billeted with Crown forces, Kilbrittain Company IRA set fire to it, destroying it completely.

JAMES O'MAHONY/ DENIS CROWLEY/ JOHN FITZGERALD BMH WS 560, 8

An unsuccessful attempt was made to shoot Sir John French, commander-in-chief of British forces, while he was on a short visit to Cobh. The local IRA waited for him to exit the admiral's house, but he left early by a back door to Cushkinny pier and from there to the ship in which he had arrived.

SÉAMUS FITZGERALD BMH WS 1737, 23; MICHAEL J BURKE BMH WS 1424, 16; JOHN P O'CONNELL BMH WS 1444, 6; MICHAEL LEAHY BMH WS 1421, 29

James Whelton and his wife were arrested by the IRA on suspicion of giving information to British military at Timoleague castle. They were released with a warning.

WILIAM FOLEY BMH WS 1560, 5

Volunteers from Timoleague and Barryroe Companies attended mass in Timoleague with the intention of disarming a party of British soldiers sent to guard two RIC men who were attending the service. The soldiers never appeared.

WILLIAM FOLEY BMH WS 1560, 5

During a strike at Mallow railway station, the stationmaster was kidnapped by the IRA and detained in the Lombardstown area.

JOHN MOLONEY BMH WS 1036; JOHN C MURPHY BMH WS 1217, 3

Ring coastguard station was attacked by selected men from Clonakilty, Shannonvale and Ardfield Companies. A small amount of arms and ammunition was captured.

JAMES 'SPUD' MURPHY BMH WS 1684, 3

Captain John P O'Connell of Cobh Company was released from a London hospital, to which he had been admitted following a hunger strike at Wormwood Scrubs prison.

JOHN P O'CONNELL BMH WS 1444, 5

Two Black and Tans reinforced the RIC garrison at Ballineen. A number of attempts were made to ambush them on the road to Manch but they failed to show.

PATRICK O'BRIEN BMH WS 812, 9

Detective Maylor of the RIC was shot dead near the courthouse in Cork.

MICHAEL V O'DONOGHUE BMH WS 1741, 60

Clonakilty Battalion headquarters was established at Knockea in the Lyre Company area around this time.

MICHAEL DINNEEN BMH WS 1563, 7

July 1920

1 July 1920

King Street (now Mac Curtain Street) RIC barracks in Cork was attacked. A charge of gelignite was exploded in an adjoining house, and it was the intention of the IRA to rush the barracks. The element of surprise, however, was lost when a volunteer fired a revolver at an RIC man outside the barracks.

MICHAEL MURPHY BMH WS 1547, 21; EDWARD HORGAN BMH WS 1644, 8; PATRICK J DEASY BMH WS 558, 2; PA MURRAY BMH WS 1584, 14

2 July 1920

Volunteers from Leap and other companies, each with two rounds of ammunition, ambushed a party of RIC and Black and Tans at Brade; a policeman was slightly wounded.

STEPHEN HOLLAND BMH WS 649, 1; PATRICK O'SULLIVAN BMH WS 1481, 5

7 July 1920

Members of Ballyvourney Company, along with men from Kerry Third Brigade, lay in wait on the Loobridge road for a British military supply lorry which never materialised.

PATRICK J LYNCH BMH WS 1543, 8

9 July 1920

A raid was made on the mails at Banteer railway station by Captain Denny Mullane of Freemount Company and four others.

DENNY MULLANE BMH WS 789, 12

10 July 1920

Ballineen Company adjutant Jack Hennessy was arrested at his home in Ballineen by a party of the Essex Regiment under a Captain Davis. Hennessy's house was burned, he was beaten and subjected to a mock execution. He managed to escape.

JACK HENNESSY BMH WS 1234, 2

Mortimer Curtin, OC Grenagh Company, and seven others lay in wait at Grenagh for a police patrol to pass. The IRA opened fire and as a result a policeman was injured.

MORTIMER CURTIN BMH WS 1679, 7

Liscarrol Company IRA were called upon to police the Cahirmee horse fair; the effectiveness of the RIC was considerably diminished in that part of the county, according to Lieutenant Patrick O'Brien.

PATRICK O'BRIEN BMH WS 764, 13

11 July 1920

A party from the East Kent Regiment broke up an aeraíocht (a nationalist open-air cultural gathering) at Ballinvoher near Castletownroche, during which they attempted to remove a Tricolour. Two volunteers, O'Neill and Shinnick, were obliged to go on the run when they attempted to disarm a British officer.

DAVID O'CALLAGHAN BMH WS 950, 7

The RIC barracks at King Street (now Mac Curtain Street), was damaged by a gelignite explosion on 1 July; it was now entered and set alight. The fire service intervened and outed the blaze, but another fire was started the following evening and the brigade forced to turn back, resulting in the complete destruction of the building.

PATRICK J DEASY BMH WS 558, 2

Captain Timothy Warren of Ballineen Company was taken from his bed by a party of the Essex Regiment in the command of Corporal Davis. After much manhandling, he managed to escape.

TIMOTHY WARREN BMH WS 1275, 2

12 July 1920

An abortive attack was made on a British military lorry at Main Street, Macroom.

CHARLES BROWNE BMH WS 873, 19

14 July 1920

Blackrock Road RIC barracks in Cork city was evacuated and burned under the instruction of Michael Murphy, OC active service unit of the First Cork Brigade.

MICHAEL MURPHY BMH WS 1547, 22

A broken-down British military lorry was burned at Barracharraig on the Cork-Banteer road, according to Volunteer John Manning of Donoughmore Company.

JOHN MANNING BMH WS 1720, 17; DAN MCCARTHY BMH WS 1697, 9

15 July 1920

Lieutenant Edward Horgan of H Company, First Battalion, First Cork Brigade recounts how two armed British soldiers guarding two broken-down lorries at Dennehy's Cross were held up and disarmed; the lorries were burned.

EDWARD HORGAN BMH WS 1644, 10

16 July 1920

Members of Donoughmore Company raided 'Kilmurry railway station' (probably Dooniskey station), removing a quantity of petrol in tins.

JOHN MANNING BMH WS 1720, 17

17 July 1920

Divisional Commissioner Gerald Smyth of the RIC was shot dead at the County Club at the South Mall in Cork. He had gained notoriety the previous month by giving the RIC a carte blanche to shoot on sight, a speech which precipitated the Listowel Mutiny.[19]

STEPHEN FOLEY BMH WS 1669, 6; DANIEL HEALY BMH WS 1656, 9; SEÁN CULHANE BMH WS 746, 5; PA MURRAY BMH WS 1584, 15

---

[19] Keane, p118; Abbott, p96.

18 July 1920

Ballineen RIC barracks was evacuated on this date; that night it was burned by local volunteers.

PATRICK O'BRIEN BMH WS 812, 9

Volunteer Jackie Brien of E Company, Second Battalion, First Cork Brigade was killed by enemy machine-gun fire in King Street (now MacCurtain Street).[20]

THOMAS DALY AND SEVEN OTHERS BMH WS 719, 6

James Bourke, an ex-British soldier, died as result of an unprovoked attack by a patrol of British military in Shandon Street, Cork. He was bayoneted in the stomach.[21]

William Mc Grath, ex-British soldier, was fatally wounded as a result of indiscriminate firing by British soldiers in North Main Street, Cork.[22]

20 July 1920

Tom Hales and Pat Harte, OC and quartermaster respectively of the Third Cork Brigade, were captured at Lauragh and brought to Bandon military barracks. They were struck with rifles and tortured, their fingernails being pulled off. Harte received a blow from a rifle that led to his death in 1925.

PATRICK O'BRIEN BMH WS 812, 9; TED O'SULLIVAN BMH WS 1478, 18

---

[20] Keane, p118.
[21] Keane, p118.
[22] Keane, p118.

The Cork-Macroom train was held up at Dooniskey and mails taken.

CHARLES BROWNE BMH WS 873, 19; DANIEL J MCSWEENEY BMH WS 1651, 7

Men of Macroom Battalion fired on a British military lorry at Geata Bán, just east of Ballymakeera. Captain James O Airy and Private Ernest F Barlow, both of the Manchester Regiment, died of wounds received, Captain Airy the following day, Private Barlow on 1 August 1921.[23]

PATRICK J LYNCH BMH WS 1543, 9; MICHAEL O'SULLIVAN BMH WS 793, 9; PATRICK O'SULLIVAN BMH WS 794, 6; PATRICK O'SULLIVAN BMH WS 878, 13; DANIEL HARRINGTON BMH WS 1532

22 July 1920

About ten members of Kilbrittain Company entered Howes Strand coastguard station and removed an amount of arms and ammunition in early July. It was raided for a second time on 22 July, twenty-five rifles being captured by men from Kilbrittain and Ballinadee Companies. The arms were dumped at Ballinadee and Clonbuig.

DENIS O'BRIEN BMH WS 1353, 4; CON FLYNN BMH WS 1621, 10

---

[23] Keane, p120.

Volunteers Daniel Mc Grath and Thomas McDonnell were shot dead by British military at Corracunna Cross, one and a half miles from Mitchelstown on the road to Cahir.[24]

PATRICK J LUDDY BMH WS 1151, 10

24 July 1920

John Crowley of Upton, suspected of informing on the IRA at the Upton ambush, was arrested and executed by them.[25]

FRANK NEVILLE BMH WS 443, 4; TADHG O'SULLIVAN BMH WS 79

25 July 1920

Detective Sergeant William Mulherin, an RIC intelligence officer, was shot dead in Bandon on this date.[26]

MICHAEL RIORDAN BMH WS 1638, 11

Second Lieutenant James McCarthy of Eyeries Company gives an account of an attack on Ballycrovane coastguard station. After a prolonged gunfight, in which two officers of the garrison were killed, the remainder surrendered. The IRA took possession of some Ross rifles and other arms. Men from the following companies were involved: Eyeries, Inches, Ballycrovane, Ardgroom and Kilcatherine. The attack at Ballycrovane resulted in the deaths of Coastguard Philip Snewin and Coastguard Charles Brown.[27]

---

[24] Keane, p119.
[25] Keane, p121.
[26] Keane, p121.
[27] Keane, p373.

LIAM O'DWYER BMH WS 1527, 10; JAMES MCCARTHY BMH WS 1567, 12; CHRISTOPHER O'CONNELL BMH WS 1530, 12

At the same time as the attack on Ballycrovane was proceeding, twelve members of Castletownbere Company moved in on Castletownbere coastguard station. They were repulsed under a heavy fire; four IRA men were injured, three by gunshot wound, while the fourth, who had broken a leg in a fall, was later captured.

WILLIAM O'NEILL BMH WS 1536, 4

A party of the Seventeenth Lancers, forty in all, occupied Liscarroll Castle, in the Newmarket Battalion area, until October 1920.

DENIS MULLANE BMH WS 789, 14

Constable James Murray, newly arrived in Clonakilty, was seen firing at a number of unarmed civilians in the town.

JAMES 'SPUD' MURPHY BMH WS 1684, 3

27 July 1920

A party of volunteers from Kilmurry Company took part in the demolition of Shandangan courthouse.

JOHN O'MAHONEY BMH WS 1662, 9

Ted Hayes, intelligence officer of Clonakilty Battalion, relates that Constable James Murray was shot dead in Clonakilty. Some days previous to this, Murray had fired shots at a group of unarmed civilians. From Co Offaly, he had seen service with the Irish Guards in the First World War.[28]

TED HAYES BMH WS 1575, 6; JAMES 'SPUD' MURPHY BMH WS 1684, 3

On the night of Detective Sergeant Mulherin's funeral (see shooting of William Mulherin, 25 July), Major Percival, OC Essex Regiment Bandon, and Lance Corporal Maddox, IO Bandon military barracks, went, under cover of darkness, to the home of Seán Buckley, IO Bandon Battalion IRA. Volunteers Michael Doyle and John Coveney of Kilpatrick Company, and possibly others, were on sentry duty. Lance Corporal Maddox was killed by a single shot; Major Percival fled.[29]

JAMES DOYLE BMH WS 1640, 7; MICHAEL RIORDAN BMH WS 1638, 11

29 July 1920

Captain Timothy Warren of Ballineen Company and fellow volunteers raided a train at Ballineen station, removing the mails for censoring.

TIMOTHY WARREN BMH WS 1275, 6

John Ahern, a civilian from White's Cross, was shot dead by British Military. They claimed that he was wearing a Republican Army officer's uniform, but he does not appear in any Republican Roll of Honour.[30]

---

[28] Kingston, p97; Keane, p123; Abbott, p106.
[29] Keane, p122.
[30] Keane, p124.

July 1920 (no date available)

Men from Coomhola and Glengarriff Companies laid a mine at Holly Hill near Glengarriff, but the two expected lorries arrived two hours earlier than expected, and Volunteers Denis O'Driscoll and Flor O'Sullivan were taken prisoner.

TED O'SULLIVAN BMH WS 1478, 18

Charlie Hurley, at the time vice OC Bandon Battalion, was in charge of twenty men from Kilpatrick, Crosspound and Innishannon Companies awaiting a convoy of British lorries at Brothersfort, on the Cork-Bandon road. The expected enemy patrol did not turn up.

MICHAEL RIORDAN BMH WS 1638, 12

Michael McCarthy, vice OC Dunmanway Battalion, and Ned Young, OC Dunmanway Company, disarmed a British soldier at Kilbarry, west of Dunmanway, taking a Lee-Enfield service rifle from him.

EDWARD YOUNG BMH WS 1402, 10

Volunteers from Bere Island Company captured some small-calibre rifles in a raid on a British military stores on the island.

JAMES SULLIVAN BMH WS 1528, 5

Thirteen volunteers from the Third Battalion, First Cork Brigade, raided Colonel Onslow's at Inchigaggin near Carrigrohane but were repulsed under fire; their intention was to commandeer his car. They were successful the following week.

TIM HERLIHY AND SIX OTHERS BMH WS 810, 37

An attempt was made to ambush a patrol of RIC and Black and Tans at Rockmills, near Kildorrery, 'but we were given away', according to Thomas Bray, Mallow Battalion adjutant.

THOMAS BARRY BMH WS 430, 7

Following an IRA attack on King Street (now Mac Curtain Street) RIC barracks, volunteers from D Company, Second Battalion of the First Cork Brigade guarded the house of Steve Riordan, a city councillor.

WILLIAM BARRY BMH WS 1708, 4

Volunteer Danny Shinnick attempted to disarm a British officer at a feis in Castletownroche. When other officers came to his aid, Shinnick disappeared into the crowd.

THOMAS BARRY BMH WS 430, 7

Captain Daniel Canty, OC Newcestown Company, gives an account of two occasions where ambushes were planned in anticipation of British military patrols, but both times the enemy travelled by different roads.

DANIEL CANTY BMH WS 1619, 12

Volunteers from Glanmire Company opened fire on a British military lorry being driven from Fermoy to Cork at Bleach Hill, Sallybrook. A number of British military were wounded.

JOSEPH CASHMAN BMH WS 1466, 3

Members of Second Battalion, First Cork Brigade in charge of their OC, Seán O'Hegarty, attacked Farran RIC barracks. An explosive charge was set against the wall of an adjoining house. This explosion, however, was insufficient to cause serious damage, and the garrison within put up a stiff resistance, firing at the enemy and sending up flares. The IRA withdrew.

MICHAEL MURPHY BMH WS 1547, 22; PATRICK COLLINS BMH WS 1707, 6

Kanturk, Banteer and Dromtarriffe Volunteers blocked the Mallow-Killarney road and cut telegraph wires on the night of a planned attack on Rathmore RIC barracks.

DENIS MULCHINOCK/ MICHAEL COURTNEY/ JEREMIAH MURPHY BMH WS 744, 5

The mother and son of 'an Imperialist family' were engaged in a dispute. Despite their perceived allegience she sought redress through the Republican courts. The son was ordered to pay £300.

MAURICE NOONAN BMH WS 1098, 5; JOHN D CRIMMINS BMH WS 1039, 5

Two broken-down British lorries were burned at Túirín Dubh, Ballingeary, and a number of rifles captured. Twelve British soldiers surrendered; they were fed by the local Cumann na mBan and then ordered to walk to the military post at Inchegeela.

CORNELIUS CRONIN BMH WS 1726, 5; DANIEL HARRINGTON BMH WS 1532, 12

'Two men of B 1 Company shot an RIC man in Bandon.' No other information is given, but it may be a reference to the shooting of Detective Sergeant William Mulherin on 25 July.[31]

DENIS CROWLEY AND OTHERS BMH WS 560, 8

Following an ambush by Grenagh Company during which an RIC man was injured on 10 July, Rathduff RIC barracks was evacuated by its garrison shortly after.

MORTIMER CURTIN BMH WS 1679, 8

Under the command of Seán Hales, OC Bandon Battalion, men from Clogagh, Timoleague Companies lay in wait for an RIC cycle patrol near Killavarig, on the Timoleague-Ballinascarthy road. The patrol did not pass that day.

DAN DONOVAN BMH WS 1608, 5

Members of Kiskeam Company travelled to Newmarket on two occasions to attack a British curfew patrol; on both evenings the patrol never materialised.

DANIEL FLYNN BMH WS 1240, 4

The trial began at Cork County court sessions of those accused of taking part in what became known as the Wesleyan raid at Fermoy, 7 September 1919.

JOHN J HOGAN BMH WS 1030, 10

A feis was held sometime in July of 1920 in Ballinadee, the object being to to lure Crown forces to the event and disarm them, but none showed.

---

[31] Kingston, p72; Keane, p121; Abbott, p105.

DAN DONOVAN BMH WS 1608, 5

Members of H Company, First Battalion of the First Cork Brigade took part in an attack on a British motorcycle dispatch rider at Carrigrohane. Captain Tom Dennehy of H Company was arrested and sentenced to penal servitude for his involvement in this incident.

EDWARD HORGAN BMH WS 1644, 9

Several Cork city companies took part in the ambush of a British lorry at White's Cross; according to the witness statement, the driver was killed and several soldiers wounded. No record exists of British fatalities in that part of the county in July 1920. This incident probably took place on 31 July 1920.[32]

PA MURRAY BMH WS 1584, 16

While looking for Head Constable Ferris of the RIC, Volunteers Pat Collins and George Burke of G Company, Second Battalion of the First Cork Brigade came upon two armed Black and Tans having a drink in Turner's Hotel in Oliver Plunkett Street. The Black and Tanswere soon disarmed.

JEREMIAH KEATING BMH WS 1657, 6

Three civilians arrested in connection with a bank robbery in Millstreet were held prisoner in the Mourneabbey area. They were tried by Second Brigade staff and deported to England, according to lieutenant Jack Looney of Analeentha Company.

JACK LOONEY BMH WS 1169, 5

---

[32] Keane, pp124, 125.

A daylight attack was planned on Ballycotton RIC barracks by Midleton Company. When a party of Cameron Highlanders were seen at the barracks, the IRA, realising their limited supply of ammunition, withdrew.

JOHN KELLEHER BMH WS 1456, 15

About thirty men from Donoughmore Battalion lay in wait at Clonmoyle, on the Donoughmore to Coachford road, for an enemy patrol. The volunteers, armed with shotguns, withdrew after waiting a number of hours.

MICHAEL MULLANE BMH WS 1689, 5

August 1920

2 August 1920

Captain Peg Duggan, an officer in Cumann na mBan whose house at 49 Thomas Davis Street in the Cork suburb of Blackpool was a frequent meeting place for Republicans, tells of a meeting held in her home to organise a raid on 2 August on British military lorries at White's Cross, Tom Crofts being the senior IRA officer involved.

PEG DUGGAN BMH WS 1575, 11

3 August 1920

Members of Bantry Battalion carried out a raid on the lighthouse at Mizen Head. Hundredweight boxes of guncotton were captured and carried away by lorry to an arms dump.

MAURICE DONEGAN BMH WS 639, 4

4 August 1920

Volunteer Timothy Sexton, newly arrived in the Carrignavar area, was at pains to point out to the local company captain John Manning the necessity of posting scouts when company meetings were in progress. His advice was not acted on, leading to the arrest of two volunteers.

TIMOTHY SEXTON BMH WS 1565, 5

Captain Timothy Warren, OC Ballineen Company, a postman, had his house raided by a party of the Essex Regiment under Sergeant Tilly. They searched in vain for his postman's uniform. His house was raided several times in the following days.

TIMOTHY WARREN BMH WS 1275, 6

7 August 1920

Volunteers from the East Limerick flying column, with Commandant Thomas Barry of Glanworth and men under his command, attacked an RIC-Black and Tan patrol on the Kildorrery-Rockmills road, killing two, according to Volunteer Séamus O'Mahony of Mitchelstown Company. One policeman was killed that day. He was Constable Ernest Watkins, from Monmouth in Wales.[33]

SÉAMUS O'MAHONY BMH WS 730, 6; DAVID O'CALLAGHAN WS 950, 8; EDWARD TOBIN BMH WS 1451, 51; THOMAS BARRY BMH WS 430, 7

8 August 1920

A huge crowd awaited Archbishop Mannix of Melbourne as his ship Baltic approached Cobh. Five miles out to sea, however, his vessel was boarded by British agents; Mannix was arrested and taken by destroyer to England.

SÉAMUS FITZGERALD BMH WS 1737, 24

12 August 1920

A raid by Crown forces on Cork City Hall saw the arrest of Terence Mac Swiney, Lord Mayor and OC First Cork Brigade; Seán O'Hegarty, vice-OC First Cork Brigade, and others in the Republican movement.

---

[33] Keane, p125; Abbott, p110.

MICHAEL MURPHY BMH WS 1547, 26; TED O'SULLIVAN BMH WS 1478, 20; SEÁN HEALY BMH WS 1339, 3

For nine nights in a row volunteers from Donoughmore Company lay in wait in vain for the approach of a British military lorry at Kilcullen, on the Rylane-Donoughmore road.

MAURICE BREW BMH WS 1695, 17; DAN MCCARTHY BMH WS 1697, 9

14 August 1920

Daniel Canty, OC Newcestown Company, relates that the company was mobilised on this date; three volunteers were selected for an operation in Brinny the next day.

DANIEL CANTY BMH WS 1619, 12

British soldiers from Kanturk garrison formed a guard at the site of a forced aeroplane landing at Drominagh. Volunteers from Millstreet Battalion moved in to attempt an arms capture. A sentry on duty was shot dead, leading to a gun battle in which two of the volunteers were wounded. The soldier killed was Private Albert Nunn.[34]

MICHAEL COURTNEY/ DENIS MULCHINOCK/ JEREMIAH MURPHY BMH WS 744, 6; CORNELIUS HEALY BMH WS 1416, 7; CON MEANY BMH WS 787, 11; HUMPHREY O'DONOGHUE BMH WS 1351, 5

Captain Timothy Warren, OC Ballineen Company, took possession of a vanload of bread belonging to Cotter's bakery of

---

[34] Keane, p126.

Ballineen, a company which, despite many threats from the IRA, continued to supply the RIC and British military with its products. (Two pages of Captain Warren's witness statement have been abstracted, the reason given thus: '[That they] would or might cause distress or danger to living persons on the grounds that they might contain information about individuals, or would or might be likely to lead to an action for damages for defamation'.)

TIMOTHY WARREN BMH WS 1275, 3

John Coughlan of Cobh was abducted by the IRA because two of his daughters were 'keeping company' with the British military. While in IRA custody, he committed suicide by hanging himself.[35]

15 August 1920

Charleville Company IRA prevented the local cattle fair being held in the town, owing to the 'Baron of the Fair' applying to the British military for a permit. This was seen as bowing to British authority, something the IRA wished to disencourage in society.

THOMAS CULHANE BMH WS 831, 5

Volunteers from Lisgriffin, Dunmanus and Goleen Companies – described later in a British House of Commons debate as 'Irish Bolshevik anarchists' – captured a British fortified post at Brow head. Arms, ammunition, wireless and binocular equipment were carried off.

---

[35] Keane, p33.

RICHARD COLLINS BMH WS 1542, 4; PATRICK WILCOX BMH WS 1529, 3

Thomas Roche, an ex-RIC man and training officer with Newmarket Battalion, tells of a planned attack on a curfew patrol of Crown forces near Newmarket creamery. The patrol failed to turn up. An unsuccessful attempt was made next day to burn down the creamery.

THOMAS DELARUE BMH WS 1224, 15; THOMAS ROCHE BMH WS 1222, 9

Mitchelstown Company, in command of Captain Michael O'Sullivan, their OC, took up position at Kilyglas with the intention of attacking a cycle patrol of the Green Howards. They waited in vain, as the cycle patrol took another route.

MICHAEL O'SULLIVAN BMH WS 1186, 12

Tadhg O'Sullivan, QM Bandon Battalion, was arrested by Crown forces at Kinsale bridge; he had on his person a telegram from America from Diarmuid Lynch saying he intended to resign his Dáil seat. O'Sullivan was detained and beaten at Bandon military barracks. After two days, he was driven out the Innishannon road at night and released. Remaining hidden until daylight, he walked six miles to a safe house.

TADHG O'SULLIVAN BMH WS 792, 5

Paddy Clancy and Jack O'Connell, vice-OC Second Cork Brigade and OC Kanturk Battalion respectively, were arrested at Derrygallon, Kanturk by a party of British military guided by Sergeant Dennehy of the RIC; they were shot 'shot out of hand'. A sister of O'Connell woke the two men to tell them the house was surrounded. Both men made a run for it but were cut down less than fifty yards from the front door. Large crowds attended both funerals, O'Connell being buried in Dromtariffe and Clancy in Kilfinane.[36]

DENIS MULCHINOCK/ MICHAEL COURTNEY/ JEREMIAH MURPHY BMH WS 744, 7; DENIS MULLANE BMH WS 789, 4; MICHAEL O'CONNELL BMH WS 1428, 7; PATRICK MCCARTHY BMH WS 1163, 10; SEÁN MOYLAN BMH WS 838, 97; JOHN WINTERS BMH WS 948, 2; MICHAEL O'CONNELL BMH WS 1428, 7

17 August 1920

Third Cork Brigade Adjutant Liam Deasy prepared an ambush on the Ballineen-Clonakilty road. They lay in wait in vain for an Essex Regiment cycle patrol.

TIMOTHY WARREN BMH WS 1275, 6

18 August 1920

The Slippery Rock at Knockanure, near Ballyvourney, was where members of the Eight (Ballyvourney) Battalion lay in ambush for a cycle patrol of the Manchester Regiment to pass by. They were called on to surrender but rode ahead. Lieutenant Sharman, their officer, was shot dead, and four were wounded. Arms, ammunition and other equipment was captured.[37]

---

[36] Keane, p127.
[37] Keane, p128.

MICHAEL O'SULLIVAN BMH WS 793, 10; PATRICK O'SULLIVAN BMH WS 794, 8; DANIEL HARRINGTON BMH WS 1532, 10; PATRICK J LYNCH BMH WS 1543, 10; TIMOTHY DINNEEN BMH WS 1585, 7; TIMOTHY BUCKLEY BMH WS 1641, 13

20 August 1920

Members drawn from several companies in the Bandon Battalion area under the command of Seán Hales, battalion OC, lay in wait at Brinny for a bicycle patrol of the Essex Regiment, based at Bandon, to pass by. The volunteers were surprised, however, by a burst of gunfire, and fearing encirclement the IRA withdrew. Lieutenant Tim Fitzgerald, an IRA officer, was shot dead, his body being claimed by relatives the next day at Bandon military barracks. According to Tadhg O'Sullivan, QM Bandon Battalion, the position of the IRA was given away by a man called Dwyer, a spy.[38]

JAMES DOYLE BMH WS 1640, 7; CHARLES O'DONOGHUE BMH WS 1607, 3; DANIEL CANTY BMH WS 1619, 12; FRANK NEVILLE BMH WS 1403, 4; TADHG O'SULLIVAN BMH WS 792, 5; MICHAEL RIORDAN BMH WS 1638, 12; WILLIAM DESMOND BMH WS832, 18; LAURENCE SEXTON BMH WS 1290, 6; MICHAEL J CROWLEY BMH WS 1603, 7

---

[38] Keane, p129.

James Herlihy, an ex-British soldier, was known by the IRA 'to be in touch with the British military'. He was executed at Pouladuff, on Cork city's southside.[39]

PATRICK COLLINS BMH WS 1707; DANIEL HEALY BMH WS 1656, 12; JEREMIAH KEATING BMH WS 1656, 6

21 August 1920

Sergeant Daniel Maunsell of the RIC was ambushed and killed in the Inchegeela area on the night of 21 August.[40]

WILLIAM POWELL BMH WS 1699, 8; CHARLES BROWNE BMH WS 873, 20; DANIEL HARRINGTON BMH WS 1532, 6; TIMOTHY DINNEEN BMH WS 1585, 5; JOHN O'MAHONEY BMH WS 1662, 11

Captain William Powell of Crookstown Company noticed movement of British military lorries heading west through Lissarda at regular intervals. Dan Corkery, Macroom Battalion OC, sanctioned an attack at Lissarda. About thirty-five men lined both sides of the road, waiting from morning to eight o'clock at night, but withdrew when the convoy did not turn up.

WILLIAM POWELL BMH WS 1699, 10

Nine members of Innishannon Company, under command of Third Cork Brigade OC Charlie Hurley, lay in wait for an RIC cycle patrol at Curranure. During a short gunbattle, a police

---

[39] Keane, p128.
[40] Kingston, p147; Keane, p130; Abbott, p111.

rifle was captured. Another ambush was prepared in the same district some days later, but it came to nothing.

JEREMIAH DEASY BMH WS 1738, 8; CORNELIUS O'SULLIVAN BMH WS 1740, 6; RICHARD RUSSELL BMH WS 1591, 6

22 August 1920

Volunteers from Kilmurry and other companies again assembled at Lissarda on the afternoon of Sunday 22 August. They opened fire on a patrol coming from the west. Quickly dismounting, the patrol sought cover on the northern side of the road. During the ensuing gun battle Volunteer Michael Galvin was killed and a second volunteer wounded. The IRA believed they had inflicted casualties on the RIC.[41]

WILLIAM POWELL BMH WS 1699, 8; JAMES MURPHY BMH WS 1633, 10; CHARLES BROWNE BMH WS 873, 21; JOHN O'MAHONY BMH WS 1662, 11; MOLLIE CUNNINGHAM BMH WS 1681, 3; DANIEL CORKERY BMH WS 1719, 12

District Inspector Oswald Ross Swanzy was fired on and killed by Seán Culhane of B Company, First Battalion, First Cork Brigade and Michael Murphy, OC Second Battalion, as he left a church service in Lisburn, Co Antrim. Swanzy had been accused by the members of the official inquiry into the death of Lord Mayor Tomás Mac Curtain of being instrumental in the Corkman's assassination. The two IRA men were sheltered in Belfast by Joe McKelvey. According to Timothy Sexton, OC Ahadillane Company, the house of McCarthy of Carrignavar in Co Cork was raided by the IRA; a search yielded up the

---

[41] Keane, p130.

Lisburn address of District Inspector Swanzy. Much violence and arson directed at the Catholic population of Lisburn occurred subsequently.[42]

SEÁN CULHANE BMH WS 746, 7; TIMOTHY SEXTON BMH WS 1565, 6; MICHAEL MURPHY BMH WS 1547, 19

Séamus Fitzgerald of Cobh Company narrowly missed being killed by Crown forces when a bedroom he had recently vacated in the Clarence Hotel in Dublin was raided.

SÉAMUS FITZGERALD BMH WS 1737, 23

23 August 1920

Mrs Mary O'Keeffe of Masseytown, Macroom knocked out a soldier of the Manchester Regiment by attacking him with a hurley. Mrs O'Keeffe, whose husband was a volunteer, took the soldier's rifle.

CHARLES BROWNE BMH WS 873, 23

24 August 1920

Ballingeary Company were in the Keimcoraboula district when they received news that they were in imminent danger of being surrounded by a combined force of British military, RIC and Black and Tans, 'but, knowing the locality, we managed to by-pass the enemy'.

CORNELIUS CRONIN BMH WS 1726, 7

Members of Bantry Battalion entered Glengarriff at about 4 pm; three of them, armed with revolvers, entered O'Shea's public

---

[42] Abbott, p113.

house. Inside were three RIC men. The three constables upon leaving the premises, found themselves the target of an outbreak of gunfire on the street outside. Constable Mc Namara was shot dead and Constable Cleary wounded; a third RIC man escaped. A gun battle ensued between the rest of the garrison, called to the scene, and the IRA, the latter withdrawing to Coomhola across mountainous terrain. This incident led to the evacuation of the RIC post the next day.[43]

SEÁN COTTER BMH WS 1493, 12; MICHAEL O'DRISCOLL BMH WS 1297, 1; JOHN J O'SULLIVAN BMH WS 1578, 13; MAURICE DONEGAN BMH WS 639, 5; EUGENE DUNNE BMH WS 1537, 6

25 August 1920

Four members of Bantry Company, under their OC Ralph Keyes, fired on a number of RIC men in Bantry, killing Constable Matthew Haugh, while Constable Power escaped uninjured.[44]

MAURICE DONEGAN BMH WS 639, 4; SEÁN COTTER BMH WS 1493, 13; JOHN J O'SULLIVAN BMH WS 1578, 14

Members of Cobh Company disarmed a party of Cameron Highlanders at a place known as the Quarry in Cobh. Some British soldiers who resisted arrest were wounded in the attack.

MICHAEL LEAHY BMH WS 1421, 28; SÉAMUS FITZGERALD BMH WS 1737, 25; MICHAEL BURKE BMH WS 1424, 16

---

[43] Kingston, p129; Keane, p132; Abbott, p116.
[44] Kingston, 129; Keane, p131; Abbott, 117.

26 August 1920

The place known as Whiterock, in the townland of Churchtown North, three miles east of Midleton on the road to Youghal, was the scene of an ambush against the Cameron Highlanders regiment. Members of Midleton Company tried to fell a tree in the path of their lorry, but it got through and away to safety. The IRA believed they had wounded the driver, having seen the lorry career wildly away from them. Private Charles Edward Hall was the British fatality; Lieutenant Biggs was injured.[45]

PATRICK J WHELAN BMH WS 1449, 32; DANIEL CASHMAN BMH WS 1523, 1; JOHN KELLEHER BMH WS 1456, 17; MICHAEL KEARNEY BMH WS 1418, 17; JOSEPH AHERNE BMH WS 1367, 25

James Hurley, an IRA officer in charge of supply and transport in the Clonakilty Battalion area, was arrested by a combined force of British Army and RIC at his home at Kilkerrinmore, Clonakilty. He served a sentence of three months at Cork and Kilkenny.

JAMES HURLEY BMH WS 135

27 August 1920

Volunteer Seán Buckley, a member of Midleton Company, and his brother Batt were arrested at their home by the Cameron Highlanders and brought by lorry to Cork. During the journey both brothers were shot several times, Seán proving a fatality.

---

[45] Keane, p133.

The British gave the explanation of 'tried to escape', a frequent excuse when prisoners were shot out of hand.[46]

JOHN KELLEHER BMH WS 1456, 17; SÉAMUS FITZGERALD BMH WS 1737, 30; JOSEPH AHERNE BMH WS 1367, 23; MICHAEL KEARNEY BMH WS 1418, 18

28 August 1920

George Walker, a civilian who had served in the Boer War and the First World War in the British Army, was shot and bayoneted to death by a patrol of Cameron Highlanders at Cobh. Walker was totally innocent.[47] This regiment of the British Army were nototiously unruly.

31 August 1920

Lieutenant Maurice Brew of Donoughmore Company tells of an attack on Crown forces on the Inniscarra to Dripsey road. IRA men from Courtbrack and Donoughmore fired on the westbound military lorry, but its speed, and the fact that a tree was not felled in time to block the roadway, ensured a harmless exchange of gunfire.

MAURICE BREW BMH WS 1695, 17; JOHN MANNING BMH WS 1720, 17; DAN MCCARTHY BMH WS 1697, 10

---

[46] Keane, p134.
[47] Keane, p134.

August 1920

Volunteer Cornelius Calnan tells of how Barryroe Company lay in ambush for three or four days on the Courtmacsherry-Lislevane road; they were expecting to encounter a cycle patrol of one policeman and twelve soldiers. The patrol did not turn up.

CORNELIUS CALNAN BMH WS 1317, 4; JAMES MOLONEY BMH WS 1310, 6; DENIS MURPHY BMH WS 1318, 4

A gun battle between Bandon Battalion of the IRA and lorries of British military happened at Manch, on the Balineen to Dunmanway road. The IRA crossed the Bandon river to safety. There were no casualties on either side.

SEÁN MURPHY BMH WS 1445, 7; PADDY O'BRIEN BMH WS 812, 10; TIMOTHY WARREN BMH WS 1275, 5; JACK HENNESSY BMH WS 1234, 3; NED YOUNG BMH WS 1402, 10; PHILIP CHAMBERS BMH WS 738, 2

Members of Mitchelstown Company lay in wait for a cycle patrol of Black and Tans from Galbally. The patrol, however, returned to its base by a different route.

PATRICK CLIFFORD BMH WS 946, 3

Bandon Battalion council demoted the captain of Barryroe Company for repeated non-attendance at council meetings; he was reduced to the rank of quartermaster.

MICHAEL COLEMAN BMH WS 1254, 6

Tim Condon, QM Millstreet Battalion, was appointed clerk to Cullen parish court, the sittings being held every month in the old church.

TIM CONDON BMH WS 1374, 4

About a dozen members of Kilbrittain Company lay in wait at Granfeen, Kilbrittain for a party of Black and Tans seen observing the local countryside. Despite the IRA waiting for three days, the patrol never showed.

JAMES O'MAHONY/ DENIS CROWLEY/ JOHN FITZGERALD BMH WS 560, 12

The house of Robert Saunders, 'who was most hostile to the IRA', was raided by members of Charleville Company; a number of shotguns were taken.

THOMAS CULHANE BMH WS 831, 5

A feint attack was made on Milford RIC barracks by Charleville Company; its purpose was to draw out the British military from the town of Charleville, thus exposing them. Spotting a volunteer in a field and sensing an attack, the enemy were forewarned, and the episode ended without an engagement.

MICHAEL GEARY/ RICHARD SMITH BMH WS 754, 12

Courtbrack Company, Donoughmore Battalion, First Cork Brigade waited twelve nights at Turpin's Rock on the Shournagh road for a British military patrol. None came, and the volunteers had a very lucky escape when the military raided a Sinn Féin meeting at Matehy.

THOMAS J GOLDEN BMH WS 1680, 16

Volunteer John J Hogan, a member of Ballynoe Company, together with a number of other prisoners went on hunger-strike at Cork prison. He was later transferred to Winchester prison in England, and finally to the Curragh when the Truce came into effect.

JOHN J HOGAN BMH WS 1130, 11

Men from Clonakilty and other companies held up a mail train travelling from Clonakilty at Kilnagross, Shannonvale. They searched the train for Inspector O'Connor of the RIC. He was not on board, but his car, loaded on a goods wagon, was removed.

TED HAYES BMH WS 1575, 6

Griffin, a prison warder in Cork jail, was detained for six weeks by the IRA in the Donoughmore Battalion area, later being transferred to Cork. Prison Officers were seen as instruments of the Crown forces and therefore subject to the same tactics as RIC.

JOHN MANNING BMH WS 1720, 18

Farnanes Company, believing that Ryecourt House and Crookstown House were to be billeted by Crown forces, burned both.

JEREMIAH O'CARROLL BMH WS 706, 6

Seán O'Driscoll, OC Ballydehob Company, tells of a raid for arms at the home of R J Wood, about two miles from Ballydehob. Some shotguns and rifles, as well as two revolvers, were removed.

SEÁN O'DRISCOLL BMH WS 1518, 4

Officers of the Third Cork Brigade met with Tom Barry at the Camden Hotel in Cork to discuss his offer to join the IRA. Barry, because of his membership of the British Army during the First World War, was regarded with suspicion by the IRA. He became OC of the Third Cork Brigade flying column, commencing to train them in September of 1920.

TED O'SULLIVAN BMH WS 1478, 22

Lieutenant Patrick O'Brien of Liscarroll Company relates details of a meeting with a Lieutenant Honeywood at Liscarroll military post. During this exchange, Lieutenant Honeywood threatened Lieutenant O'Brien with dire consequences if any attacks were made on the RIC. Lieutenant O'Brien was arrested the following week; he went on hunger-strike.

PATRICK O'BRIEN BMH WS 764, 15

Pa Murray, OC of C Company, First Battalion, First Cork Brigade, tells that he met Michael Collins in Dublin. At the time, Lord Mayor Terence Mac Swiney was on hunger-strike. Collins's plan, according to Murray, was to have members of the British cabinet assassinated should Mac Swiney die. Murray was sent to London to investigate that possibility..

PATRICK A MURRAY BMH WS 1584, 17

Seán Murphy, OC Aultagh Company, and several others took positions near Drimoleague to ambush an RIC patrol. They waited in vain for several hours.

SEÁN MURPHY BMH WS 1445, 7

The garrison of Clonakilty RIC barracks, erroneously believing they were under attack, fired into the night air for several hours.

JAMES 'SPUD' MURPHY BMH WS 1684, 4

Members of Eyeries Company helped to prevent the arrest of Volunteer Con O'Dwyer by the RIC at Eyeries. Following this disturbance, a party of the King's Own Yorkshire Light Infantry were billeted in a local house. Several IRA men were arrested.

LIAM O'DWYER BMH WS 1527, 6

Section Leader James 'Spud' Murphy and two others lay in wait at Clonakilty for Inspector O'Connor of the RIC. Some civilians appeared, and they withdrew.

JAMES 'SPUD' MURPHY BMH WS 1684, 4

Several companies of Bandon Battalion planned a surprise attack on Innishannon RIC barracks. They were in the act of surrounding the building when a member of Kilbrittain Company accidentally discharged a shot. The element of surprise now gone, the IRA returned to their home areas.

JEREMIAH DEASY BMH WS 1738, 7; RICHARD RUSSELL BMH WS 1591, 6

Millstreet, Derrynagree and Drishane Companies raided the income tax office at Millstreet, destroying papers and carrying away a rifle and a revolver.

WILLIAM REARDEN BMH WS 1185, 4

Members of Mallow Battalion were joined by the flying column of the East Limerick Brigade in a vain wait for Crown forces at Carrig, near Mallow.

WILLIAM C REGAN BMH WS 1069, 1

Members of Carrigaline Company, in command of Captain Edward Sisk, waited for a patrol of about ten British military headed by an RIC man near Crosshaven. Due to a leakage of information regarding the IRA's intentions, the patrol took a different route.

EDWARD SISK BMH WS 1505, 2

Tim Buckley, OC Clondrohid Company, and others were selected to disarm three RIC men at fair day in Millstreet. The patrol returned to barracks early and no attack was made.

TIM BUCKLEY BMH WS 1641, 13

September 1920

3 September 1920

Members of the First Cork Brigade raided the American Oil Company's store at Victoria Quay in Cork. They came away with large supplies of petrol during the eleven-hour operation.

MICHAEL MURPHY BMH WS 1547, 27

4 September 1920

Jack Hennessy, an officer in Ballineen Company, tells of a training camp at Shanacrone, Togher, in command of Liam Deasy, Cork Third Brigade adjutant.

JACK HENNESSY BMH WS 1234, 3

5 September 1920

Miss Nora Cunningham of Macroom Cumann na mBan anticipated enemy reprisals following the disarming by Macroom B Company of a British soldier of the Masseytown House garrison. She and her colleagues in Cumann na mBan were engaged in watching enemy movements and dumping IRA small arms.

NORA CUNNINGHAM BMH WS 1690, 3

British military abandoned a lorry close to Ballyvourney. Local volunteers approached, and were fired on by British soldiers secreted inside. Volunteer Section Leader William Hegarty and a civilian named Michael Lynch were killed. Military honours were accorded to Volunteer Section Leader Hegarty at Kilgarvan graveyard.[48]

PATRICK LYNCH BMH WS 1543, 11; PATRICK O'SULLIVAN BMH WS 794, 9; DANIEL HARRINGTON BMH WS 1532, 9

7 September 1920

Following the disarming of a British soldier of the Masseytown House garrison, both Macroom IRA companies, fearing reprisals, lay in wait for six nights in a row at the approaches to the town. The Crown forces were confined to barracks.

DANIEL MCSWEENEY BMH WS 1651, 7

15 September 1920

Members of the Second Cork Brigade formed a flying column and trained for a week at Badger's Hill, Glenville, under Brigade OC Liam Lynch and Ernie O'Malley. Training consisted of musketry, marksmanship and field signals, according to Lieutenant Patrick O'Brien of Liscarrol Company.

PATRICK O'BRIEN BMH WS 764, 19

The IRA 'had ample evidence' that John O'Callaghan, a civilian, 'was conveying information to the enemy' in Cork city. He was executed.[49]

PATRICK COLLINS BMH WS 1709, 9; JEREMIAH KEATING BMH WS 1657, 5

---

[48] Keane, p135.
[49] Keane, p136.

19 September 1920

Liam Lynch, OC Second Cork Brigade, ordered JJ Brennock, OC Rathcormac Company, to Moulane, on the Glenville-Rathcormac road. Having cut telegraph wires, the local flying column waited in vain for an RIC patrol to pass by.

JJ BRENNOCK BMH WS 1113, 7

21 September 1920

Captain Timothy Warren, OC Ballineen Company, relates that a battalion council meeting took place at the house of James Coakley, the purpose being to organise dispatch routes in the Dunmanway Battalion area.

TIMOTHY WARREN BMH WS 1275, 7

25 September 1920

Commandant Michael Murphy, OC Second Battalion First Cork Brigade and OC brigade active service unit (a name given to a flying column in an urban area), tells that General Sir Peter Strickland, OC British forces at Victoria barracks, was sometimes observed leaving the barracks, under armed escort, in a car. After a wait of two weeks, the IRA finally got a chance to ambush him near King (now Mac Curtain) Street, but after an exchange of shots Strickland's car sped away to safety.

MICHAEL MURPHY BMH WS 1547, 27

26 September 1920

Liam Lynch, OC Second Cork Brigade, convened a meeting at Sheehan's of Mourneabbey. A plan to attack the British military barracks at Mallow was discussed.

JOHN BOLSTER/RICHARD WILLIS BMH WS 808, 20

Lombardstown Company mobilised at Barrett's Cross, Glantane, with a plan to take part in an ambush at Mourneabbey. The Second Cork Brigade OC, Liam Lynch, ordered the operation to be called off due to the planned attack on Mallow barracks two days later.

MICHAEL O'CONNELL BMH WS 1428, 7; JOHN (JACK) O'CONNELL BMH WS 1211, 6

27 September 1920

Members of Analeentha Company under Captain Jerome Buckley engaged in felling trees and cutting telegraph wires in preparation for the IRA capture of Mallow barracks.

JEROME BUCKLEY BMH WS 1063, 7

Volunteers from Mallow Company took up positions in Mallow town hall in preparation for the capture of Mallow barracks the following day.

JOHN C MURPHY BMH WS 1217, 4

28 September 1920

Daniel O'Driscoll, OC Drimoleague Company, and First Lieutenant Paddy Sullivan fired at and wounded Sergeant Dee of the RIC at Drimoleague.

DANIEL O'DRISCOLL BMH WS 1352, 5

As part of the preparations for the capturing of Mallow barracks, First Lieutenant (later Captain) Daniel McCarthy and eleven others were ordered at 4 a.m. to block the Mallow to Killarney road by felling trees.

DANIEL MCCARTHY BMH WS 1239, 5

The flying column of the Third Cork Brigade under its OC, Tom Barry, took up positions at Fanlobbus, on the Dunmanway to Ballineen road. They waited from 11 am to nightfall, with no sign of an enemy approach. They later withdrew to billets at Newcestown and Dunmanway.

SEÁN MURPHY BMH WS 1445, 8; PATRICK O' BRIEN BMH WS 812, 10; JACK HENNESSY BMH WS 1352, 5

Mallow barracks was captured by members of Mallow Battalion in command of Liam Lynch, OC Second Cork Brigade. The local flying column took over the house across the road from the barracks – headquarters of the Seventeenth Lancers – and the following morning saw Ernie O'Malley work a successful ruse to effect entry. Most of the garrison were away exercising the horses, and the remainder were soon overpowered. Sergeant William Gibbs, ignoring the 'hands up' order, was shot; he died of his wounds shortly after, despite first aid being administered by the IRA. An unsuccessful attempt was made to burn the building. This action, which yielded much in the way of arms and ammunition, was singular in that it was the only capture of a British Army barracks during the War of Independence.[50]

WILLIAM C REGAN BMH WS 1069, 2; JOHN O'SULLIVAN BMH WS 1376, 6; RICHARD WILLIS/ JOHN BOLSTER BMH WS 808, 7; LEO CALLAGHAN BMH WS 978, 7; DANIEL DALY BMH WS 743, 6; JEREMIAH DALY BMH WS 1015, 2; GEORGE POWER BMH WS 451, 11; SEÁN MOYLAN BMH WS 838, 108; TADHG MCCARTHY BMH WS 965, 6; OWEN HAROLD BMH WS 991, 11; JOHN C MURPHY BMH WS 1217, 7

29 September 1920

Following the wounding of Sergeant Dee of the RIC at Drimoleague by Captain Daniel O'Driscoll and Lieutenant Paddy Sullivan of Drimoleague Company, the home of the latter and that of his uncle were burned by Crown forces.

DANIEL O'DRISCOLL BMH WS 1352, 5

Anticipating reprisals in the form of an attack on Lombardstown creamery following the successful capture of Mallow barracks by Mallow Battalion IRA, Lombardstown Company, along with sections of the battalion flying column, placed a guard on the creamery.

MICHAEL O'CONNELL BMH WS 1428, 9; JACK O'CONNELL BMH WS 1211, 6

---

[50] Keane, p137.

30 September 1920

On the 30 September 1920, two days after the capture of Mallow barracks by the IRA, the Second Cork Brigade flying column moved from Lombardstown to Ardglass, in the Charleville area.

MICHAEL O'CONNELL BMH WS 1428, 9

September 1920 (no date available)

A man named Brady was overheard giving information on IRA billets to the Auxiliaries in Macroom. He was ordered out of the country and complied, but returned shortly after. He was next seen at Union Quay barracks in Cork; that night he was shot dead by the IRA at Tory Top Lane on the outskirts of the city.[51]

CHARLES BROWNE BMH WS 873, 26

Captain Daniel Canty, OC Newcestown Company, relates that the company planned an attack on an RIC-Black and Tan convoy that frequently made its way from Bandon to Macroom. The wife of an RIC man who lived on the route ensured that the Crown forces were informed in advance.

DANIEL CANTY BMH WS 1619, 13

Volunteers from Midleton Company spotted General Strickland at Midleton and lay in ambush for his return journey. His car returned to Cork by another route, and the volunteers survived a heavy fire from a separate Crown convoy at the Mile Bush.

DANIEL CASHMAN BMH WS 1523, 4

A flying column was formed in September 1920 in the Second Cork Brigade area. It was assembled in Glenville, with Ernie O'Malley as the training officer. Two ambushes were organised in the Fermoy area at this time, neither of them successful.

GEORGE POWER BMH WS 451, 9; JOHN RONAYNE BMH WS 1269, 6; OWEN HAROLD BMH WS 991, 9; SEÁN HEALY BMH

---

[51] Keane, p137

WS 1339, 3; JACK LOONEY BMH WS 1169, 6; PATRICK MCCARTHY BMH WS 1163, 11

Longhurst, an English shopkeeper living in Fermoy, was court-martialled by the IRA on the grounds that he aided Crown forces in burning the the property of Republican sympathisers. He was banished from the country for life.

GEORGE POWER BMH WS 451, 10

Paddy O'Brien, QM Second Cork Brigade, was the principal IRA officer in charge when a group of IRA took ambush positions awaiting a patrol of RIC near Milford police barracks. The RIC patrol never materialised.

TOM ROCHE BMH WS 1222, 9

Bandon Battalion OC Seán Hales organised a large force of volunteers to attend Ballinadee feis, the idea being to rush and disarm an expected patrol of British military. The patrol did not put in an appearance.

RICHARD RUSSELL BMH WS 1591, 11

Carrigaline RIC barracks was burned down by volunteers of the local company under the command of their captain, Edward Sisk.

EDWARD SISK BMH WS 1505, 3

James O'Sullivan, OC Bantry Company, and forty of his men lay in wait at Donemark for a British Army convoy. The IRA men, convened at thirty minutes' notice, were themselves awaiting arms from a nearby dump, and so the convoy was allowed to pass by.

JAMES O'SULLIVAN BMH WS 1455, 7

Bantry Company set up a 'listening-in' station between Bantry and Glengarriff at this time. A second telephone had been installed at the house of the Local Magistrate, the fact of which he was unaware. This telephone was for the use of an employee, a member of Cumann na mBan.

JAMES O'SULLIVAN BMH WS 1455, 7

A flying column of the IRA was set up in the Charleville Battalion area in September of 1920.

MICHAEL GEARY/RICHARD SMITH BMH WS 754, 17

Volunteers from the Bantry Battalion flying column lay in wait on two successive Sundays at Drimoleague, but the expected RIC patrol did not show, according to Seán Cotter, Adjutant Bantry Battalion.

SEÁN COTTER BMH WS 1493, 15

Clonbuig, east of Kilbrittain, was one of the first training camps set up for the flying column of the Third Cork Brigade. Under the command of Column OC Tom Barry, up to sixty volunteers trained here. Drilling, rifle and bayonet practice were taught.

DENIS COLLINS BMH WS 827, 4; DAN DONOVAN BMH WS 1608, 6; MICHAEL COLEMAN BMH WS 1254, 16; JEREMIAH DEASY BMH WS 1738, 11

Commandant Brislane of Charleville Battalion was in charge of an IRA firing party of eight men that opened fire on a convoy of Crown forces at Lisgriffin, near Buttevant. When called on to surrender, the British refused, and a soldier was wounded.

THOMAS CULHANE BMH WS 831, 5

William Desmond, lieutenant and later captain of Newcestown Company IRA, tells how a billet for fifteen men of Tom Barry's flying column was prepared at Corcoran's of Bengour.

WILLIAM DESMOND BMH WS 831, 17

Towards the end of September 1920, officers from Crosspound, Tinkers' Cross, Quarries Cross and and Newcestown companies took part in a week-long training camp at Ballymurphy. The camp, under the command of OC Third Cork Brigade flying column Tom Barry, consisted of drill, care and use of arms and the use of cover.

JAMES DOYLE BMH WS 1640, 8; WILLIAM FOLEY BMH WS 1560, 5

Members of the newly-formed Second Cork Brigade flying column took up position on the Keam-Glenville road in order to engage a lorry of British military, but rifle fire and a Mills bomb did not stop the lorry's progress and it got away to safety.

SEÁN HEALY BMH WS 1339, 4

Captain Patrick J Lynch of Ballyvourney Company relates that about forty members of Macroom Battalion lay in ambush in vain for six successive days on the Macroom-Inchegeela road.

PATRICK J LYNCH BMH WS 1543, 11

Second Lieutenant David O'Callaghan of Castletownroche Company relates that Carrig, on the Castletownroche to Mallow Road, was the planned scene of ambush of an expected British military convoy. Despite their waiting for two successive days, the convoy never showed.

DAVID O'CALLAGHAN BMH WS 950, 9

Late September 1920 saw Captain John P O'Connell of Cobh Company leave Cobh fearing his arrest following the abortive assassination attempt on Lord French; he fled to Midleton. He left the town soon after hearing from Father Dominic, chaplain to Lord Mayor Terence MacSwiney, that a document linking O'Connell to an incident at Bunkers Hill, Cobh had been found on the Lord Mayor at the time of his arrest on the 12 August 1920.

JOHN P O'CONNELL BMH WS 1444, 7

McCarthy, an RIC man formerly stationed in Ballineen, was arrested by Commandant Tom Barry in September 1920. He was released the next day.

PATRICK O'BRIEN BMH WS 812, 11

In late September 1920, eight members of the Second Cork Brigade flying column lay in wait for a British convoy of mule-drawn wagons at Lisgriffin. On hearing the IRA open fire, the British immediately offered to surrender, but the animals took fright and stampeded, bearing the Crown forces away to safety.

MICHAEL O'DONNELL BMH WS 1145, 5; MICHAEL GEARY /RICHARD SMITH BMH WS 754, 13

Early in September 1920 the Fourth Battalion of the First Cork Brigade formed a flying column. Numbering between twelve and fifteen men, Diarmuid Hurley was its OC.

MICHAEL KEARNEY BMH WS 1418, 19

October 1920

1 October 1920

Captain John Fanning, OC Fermoy Company, joined the flying column of the Second Cork Brigade at Freemount. Remaining there for two weeks, he moved to Araglin to train volunteers in the use of small arms.

JOHN FANNING BMH WS 990, 14

Lieutenant John Connolly, an officer in Bandon Battalion, was arrested in late September and taken to the Essex Regiment barracks in Bandon, 'where he was brutally tortured and interrogated for a full week'. On 1 October 1920, he was taken to Bandon Park and executed. A memorial records where he fell.[52]

CHARLES O'DONOGHUE BMH WS 1607, 10

Timothy J Warren, captain Ballineen Company, relates that the Black and Tans made a night time raid on Ballineen village, searching for him. He managed to slip away into the darkness.

TIMOTHY J WARREN BMH WS 1275, 7

3 October 1920

A patrol of Black and Tans was fired on in Patrick Street in Cork. Three were injured, one of whom died of his wounds some hours later. He was Constable Clarence Chave.[53]

---

[52] Keane, p138.
[53] Keane, 138; Abbott, p129.

4 October 1920

Seán Lehane, OC Schull Battalion, was in charge of the operation to capture and destroy Schull RIC barracks. The IRA had discovered the password of the day – 'Kilmallock' – and easily effected entry. Thirteen rifles and twenty-six revolvers, along with documents and a haul of ammunition, were captured. The barracks was set on fire.

CHARLIE COTTER BMH WS 1519, 4; SEÁN O'DRISCOLL BMH WS 1518, 7; EDWARD O'SULLIVAN BMH WS 1501, 3

The first Schull Sinn Féin parish court was held on this day.

WILLIAM LANNIN BMH WS 1520, 3

5 October 1920

Members of the Third Battalion of the First Cork Brigade lay in wait near the Chetwynd Viaduct for a party of British military travelling by lorry. The British, however, knew of their plan and surrounded their enemy. Volunteer Jeremiah O'Herlihy was captured. He was ordered to run, and was promptly shot in the back of the neck. O'Herlihy was mortally wounded; he died on the 14 October 1920 at the Mosphere private hospital in Dyke Parade.[54]

MICHAEL O'REGAN BMH WS 1524, 4; JEREMIAH O'CARROLL 706, 4; PATRICK CRONIN 710, 4; TIMOTHY HERLIHY AND OTHERS BMH WS 810, 15 & 25

A group of Auxiliaries involved in the Chetwynd Viaduct engagement later arrested some civilians and incarcerated

---

[54] Keane, p139.

them in a shed near Waterfall. They set fire to some hay within 'and stood some distance away to enjoy the sport'. A British Army officer came upon the scene, and following 'a bitter show-down' with the Auxiliaries the locals were released.

TIMOTHY HERLIHY AND SEVEN OTHER WITNESSES BMH WS 810, 15

6 October 1920

Francis Healy, section commander D Company, First Battalion, First Cork Brigade, was arrested at Carrigtwohill railway station for being a member of an illegal organisation. He was released from Victoria barracks after a month.

FRANCIS HEALY BMH WS 1694, 16

8 October 1920

Members of D Company, Second Battalion, First Cork Brigade ambushed a British Army lorry making its way from Victoria barracks to Elizabeth Fort at the foot of Barrack Street, Cork. The IRA claimed one soldier killed and several wounded when grenades were hurled at the lorry. The casualty was Private John Squibbs of the Hampshire Regiment. The ensuing gun battle lasted fifteen minutes.[55]

WILLIAM BARRY BMH WS 1708, 4; MICHAEL MURPHY BMH WS 1547, 28; CORNELIUS O'REGAN BMH WS 1200, 8

The flying column of the Third Cork Brigade, under its OC Tom Barry, took up positions at both sides of the road at Fanlobbus,

---

[55] Keane, p140.

about two miles east of Dunmanway. The expected enemy did not show.

EDWARD YOUNG BMH WS 1402, 12; CON FLYNN BMH WS 1621, 11; JEREMIAH DEASY BMH WS 1738, 12

Volunteer Dick Cotter, who narrowly escaped being captured at the Chetwynd Viaduct ambush on the 5 October, was surrounded by British military near Ballymurphy and led away to Ballincollig where he was tried under martial law.

JIM HERLIHY AND SEVEN OTHER WITNESSES BMH WS 810, 26

9 October 1920

Daniel Canty, OC Newcestown Company, was given instructions to arrange billets for a party of IRA volunteers from Kilbrittain. It was later that day that these men attacked a two-lorry British Army patrol just outside Newcestown village.

DANIEL CANTY BMH WS 1619, 13

Corcoran's house, about a mile from Newcestown, was the location of an IRA training camp in October 1920. Lieutenant William Desmond, later captain Newcestown Company, relates that Seán Hales, OC Bandon Battalion, rushed from the village to Corcoran's with the news that two lorries of Essex Regiment soldiers stationed at Bandon were in Newcestown. The IRA men made their way to the village. Fire was opened on the lorries close to the national school, the leading lorry being the first target. Fearing that it was the intention of those in the second lorry, now dismounted, to outflank and surround the IRA, Hales ordered a withdrawal of his men. Two officers of the Essex died, Lieutenant

Robert Robertson at the scene, and Lieutenant Gurth Richardson of his wounds on 13 October 1920. The IRA conceded no casualties. Three of the Essex Regiment, one of them being their OC Major Percival, were subsequently awarded medals for this engagement.[56]

WILLIAM DESMOND BMH WS 832, 21; DANIEL CANTY BMH WS 1619, 14; JAMES DOYLE BMH WS 1640, 10; DAN DONOVAN BMH WS 1614, 7; CORNELIUS O'SULLIVAN 1740, 11; JEREMIAH DEASY BMH WS 1738, 12; FRANK NEVILLE BMH WS 443, 5; CON FLYNN BMH WS 1621, 11; PHILIP CHAMBERS BMH WS 738, 5; TED O'SULLIVAN BMH WS 1478, 23; RICHARD RUSSELL BMH WS 1591, 12

A party of forty from the Seventeenth Lancers occupied Liscarroll Castle from July to October 1920. On the 9 October they raided the house of Denny Mullane, captain of Freemount Company, taking away with them historical notes on the castle dating from the seventeenth century.

DENNY MULLANE BMH WS 789, 14

11 October 1920

Maurice Griffin, a civilian who was deaf and dumb, was shot in the back during a police raid in Cork city. Griffin, aged fifty-two, died the following day.[57]

---

[56] Keane, p140; Crowley, Seán, *From Newce to Truce: a story of Newcestown and its hinterland from earliest times to the troubled birth of our new state*; published privately; no date, p307.
[57] Keane, p141.

Ballydrochane, one mile from Kanturk on the Kanturk-Newmarket road, was the scene of an ambush by the Newmarket Battalion on 11 October 1920. Under the command of Liam Lynch, OC Second Cork Brigade, the attackers occupied the northern side of the road. A cart was used to block the way, and in the ensuing gun battle an enemy lorry was fired on, the driver being killed and four others wounded. There were no IRA casualties. A haul of guns and ammunition was captured. Private Edward Cowin of the Royal Army Service Corps was the soldier killed; he was the driver of the lorry.[58]

DANIEL FLYNN BMH WS 1240, 5; DANIEL GUINEY BMH WS 1347, 6; JOHN BOLSTER BMH WS 808, 24; DANIEL BROWNE BMH WS 785, 7; PATRICK O'BRIEN BMH WS 764, 25; JAMES J RIORDAN BMH WS 1172, 6; THOMAS ROCHE BMH WS 1222, 10; MICHAEL COURTNEY BMH WS 744, 11; JAMES O'CONNELL BMH WS 949, 7; JAMES CASHMAN BMH WS 1270, 6; DENNY MULLANE BMH WS 789, 16

Liscarroll Castle, billet to the Seventeenth Lancers since July 1920, was abandoned by its garrison.

DENNY MULLANE BMH WS 789, 15

Following the successful Newcestown ambush, members of the flying column stayed for a day in the vicinity of Greenhill, marching to Crosspound on Monday 11 October.

JEREMIAH DEASY BMH WS 1738, 13

---

[58] Keane, p141.

13 October 1920

Samuel Shannon of Lissaclarig, near Ballydehob, was fired on at his home. He died of his injuries. The day previous to his being shot, a raid for arms, presumably conducted by the IRA, finished with Philip Shannon, the dead man's father, fighting off the raiders with a blackthorn stick.[59]

14 October 1920

Jeremiah O'Herlihy, OC signals Third Battalion, First Cork Brigade, died on this date as a result of wounds received at the Chetwynd Viaduct (see 5 October 1920).[60]

MICHAEL O'REGAN BMH WS 1524, 4; TIMOTHY HERLIHY AND SEVEN OTHER WITNESSES BMH WS 810, 15 & 25

Volunteer Liam O'Connell, killed in an attack on Crown forces in Dublin, was buried in his native Glantane. Volunteers from Mallow Battalion fired a salute over his grave.

TADHG MCCARTHY BMH WS 965, 7

15 October 1920

John Brennan, Freemount Company QM, was arrested and tried for his part in the Ballydrochane ambush of 11 October 1920.

DENNY MULLANE BMH WS 789, 30

The Black and Tans raided houses in Ballymakeera, shooting wildly and indiscriminately as they searched for IRA volunteers.

---

[59] Keane, p142.
[60] Keane, p139.

Finding none, they happened upon James Lehane, a civilian, at the local forge. He was dragged to a byroad and shot repeatedly.[61]

PATRICK J LYNCH BMH WS 1543, 12; DANIEL HARRINGTON BMH WS 1532, 11

Hugh O'Brien was arrested by the IRA on the suspicion of robbing a bank at Millstreet. He was deported.

JACK O'CONNELL BMH WS 1211, 7

16 October 1920

Ballyvourney RIC and military barracks was evacuated on this date.

PATRICK J LYNCH BMH WS 1543, 12; DANIEL HARRINGTON BMH WS 1532, 11

17 October 1920

On the 16 October 1920, Second Lieutenant Patrick Ahern of Fermoy Company was ordered to Cork prison to ascertain if Michael Fitzgerald, OC Fermoy Battalion, wished to send any message. Ahern was posing as the brother of Fitzgerald, who had been on hunger strike for several weeks. At 9 pm the following evening, 17 October 1920, as the Rosary was being led by three nuns and a priest, one of the nuns declared to Ahern, 'He's gone'. Shortly after, *Wrap the Green Flag Round Me* was played by the Volunteer Pipe Band outside the prison walls.[62]

PARTICK AHERN BMH WS 1003, 18; GEORGE POWER BMH WS 451, 5; CON LEDDY BMH WS 756, 8; JOHN FANNING

---

[61] Keane, p142.
[62] Keane, p143.

BMH WS 990, 15; JAMES COSS BMH WS 1065, 8; JAMES HACKETT BMH WS 1080, 2

19 October 1920

Michael Fitzgerald, OC Fermoy Battalion, having died on hunger strike at Cork prison, was buried at Kilcrumper cemetery near Fermoy. Huge crowds turned up for the funeral at the church in Fermoy, but British military blocked the bridge in the town, allowing only a small number of mourners on to Kilcrumper. Shortly after Crown forces moved away from the scene of the burial, members of the local battalion fired revolver shots over Fitzgerald's grave.

PATRICK AHERN BMH WS 1003, 20; JAMES HACKETT BMH WS 1080, 2; JAMES COSS BMH WS 1065, 8

20 October 1920

On this date Ballyvourney RIC barracks, evacuated four days previously by its garrison, was set on fire by the local IRA company. Just as the flames were beginning to take hold, two lorryloads of Black and Tans came into view. A gun fight ensued, although no casualties were reported.

PATRICK J LYNCH BMH WS 1543, 12; DANIEL HARRINGTON BMH WS 1532, 11

21 October 1920

A number of Black and Tans were fired on by members of Leap Company, five in number. The next morning the police raided Glandore seeking reprisal, believing the IRA men had come from that village. One of their number, in a drunken condition, was killed by his own grenade, though this casualty cannot be confirmed. It seems the IRA was not aware that they had caused two fatalities when they opened fire. They were:

Constable Bertie Rippingale, from Essex

Constable Albert Rundle, from London[63]

STEPHEN HOLLAND BMH WS 649, 1; PATRICK O'SULLIVAN BMH WS 1481, 7

22 October 1920

Toureen, on the main road between Innishannon and Ballinhassig, was the scene of an ambush by the flying column of the Third Cork Brigade, under its leader Commandant Tom Barry, against an expected Essex Regiment convoy. At 8 am the leading lorry passed, but an IRA mine failed to explode and it managed to flee in an easterly direction. The remaining lorry halted, and following the death of an officer by gunfire, the rest of the men surrendered. There were three fatalities on the British side, and four men were wounded; the IRA suffered no casualties. The fatalities were listed as follows:

Captain William Dixon

Private Charles Reid

Private Thomas Bennett[64]

MICHAEL COLEMAN BMH WS 1254, 7; JAMES DOYLE BMH WS 1640, 11; MAURICE DONOVAN BMH WS 1736, 2; CON FLYNN BMH WS 1621, 13; MICHAEL RIORDAN BMH WS 1634,

---

[63] Kingston, p115, 116; Keane, p145; Abbott, p135.
[64] Keane, p144

15; RICHARD RUSSELL BMH WS 1591, 12; TED O'SULLIVAN BMH WS 1478, 22; DANIEL CANTY BMH WS 1619, 17

23 October 1920

Volunteer John C Murphy of Mallow Company was captured during curfew hours by British military at Mallow. He was charged some days later with the murder of Sergeant Gibbs at Mallow barracks.

JOHN C MURPHY BMH WS 1217, 6

Volunteers from Bantry Battalion IRA gathered in Bantry to disarm an RIC party on the streets of the town. Not seeing an advantageous position to rush the police patrol, the would-be attackers withdrew.

DENIS KEOHANE BMH WS 1426, 6; DANIEL O'DRISCOLL BMH WS 1352, 6

A group of British military from Bandon, 'dressed in a nondescript way, none in full uniform', carried out reprisals in Newcestown. The village was the scene of an attack on an Essex Regiment patrol on the 9 October 1920, in which two British officers died of their wounds. The public house of Richard O'Sullivan and his dwelling house were burned, and an attempt made to burn Lordan's of Coolenagh, as well as fodder belonging to the Corcoran family.

WILLIAM DESMOND BMH WS 832, 25; DANIEL CANTY BMH WS 1619, 17

25 October 1920

Terence Mac Swiney, Lord Mayor of Cork, died on this day in Brixton prison in London following a hunger strike of seventy-six days. His last days are chronicled in diary form by his sister Annie Mac Swiney; this diary came into the possession of Margaret Lucey, treasurer of Cumann na mBan in Cork city, and it details the daily visits to the Lord Mayor's bedside at Brixton, as well as the traumatic events as the coffin bearing his body made its way to Ireland.[65]

MARGARET LUCEY BMH WS 1561

Edward Meade, an ex-soldier who worked as a clerk in Victoria barracks in Cork, was accidentally shot dead by a soldier.[66]

Volunteer Joseph Murphy died on hunger strike in Cork, three hours after Terence MacSwiney's death in Brixton.[67]

JOHN JONES BMH WS 759, 67; MICHAEL V O'DONOGHUE BMH WS 1741, PART 1, 75; FRANK HYNES BMH WS 446, 67

26 October 1920

Daniel O'Driscoll, OC Drimoleague Company, planned an attack on a police patrol in Drimoleague. Possibly fearing an attack due to the death on hunger strike of Terence MacSwiney the previous day, the police did not leave the barracks.

DANIEL O'DRISCOLL BMH WS 1352, 7

---

[65] Keane, p35.
[66] Keane, p145.
[67] Keane, p35.

27 October 1920

A member of the Seventeenth Lancers stationed at Mallow searched the house of Denis Barter near Mourneabbey.

JOHN BOLSTER/RICHARD WILLIS BMH WS 808, APPENDIX 1, 3

28 October 1920

Patrick McCarthy, whose rank was OC Mallow Battalion at the end of the War of Independence, was arrested near Mallow on this date, finally being released two days after the Treaty of 6 December 1921 was signed.

PATRICK MCCARTHY BMH WS 1163, 17

On the night Terence Mac Swiney's coffin arrived in Cork, Seán Cotter, Adjutant Bantry Battalion, Third Cork Brigade, left the city for London with £100 to cover the purchase and transportation of arms to West Cork. A Lewis gun and some rifles, supplied by members of Irish regiments in the British Army, were obtained.

SEÁN COTTER BMH WS 1493, 15

30 October 1920

Patrick O'Brien, vice OC Charleville Battalion, Second Cork Brigade, was in charge of men at Doona, Milford, where they lay in vain all day for an RIC patrol to pass.

JOHN D CRIMMINS BMH WS 1039, 6; MICHAEL O'DONNELL BMH WS 1145, 6

31 October 1920

The funeral of Terence Mac Swiney, OC First Cork Brigade and Lord Mayor of Cork, took place in his native city. Mass was said in the North Cathedral, and a huge crowd of civilians and IRA took part in the procession to St Finbarr's Cemetry.

MICHAEL V O'DONOGHUE BMH WS 1741, 75

Volunteer Michael O'Brien of Kilbrittain Company died of diphtheria on 31 October 1920. He was buried at Murragh cemetery, where a full parade of several companies gave military honours.

DENIS CROWLEY BMH WS 560, 14; FRANK NEVILLE BMH WS 443, 6; RICHARD RUSSELL BMH WS 1591, 12; CORNELIUS O'SULLIVAN BMH WS 1740, 12

Lieutenant Rutherford and Lieutenant Brown of the British Army, both armed and in civilian dress, were arrested near Coachford as they travelled by motorcycle. They were shot as spies and buried at Laharn, near Rusheen.[68]

CHARLES BROWNE BMH WS 873, 29; NED NEVILLE BMH WS 1665, 5

---

[68] Keane, p146.

October 1920 (no date available)

In early October 1920, Maurice Brew, an officer in Donoughmore Company, was charged with the task of guarding a prison officer named Griffin at a house in the company area. Griffin escaped, but he was recaptured the following day; he was held in the area for eight weeks.

MAURICE BREW BMH WS 1695, 20; JOHN MANNING BMH WS 1720, 19

Volunteer Denis Murphy, a member of the Third Cork Brigade flying column, received an order to transport Brigade OC Charlie Hurley by sea from Harbour View to Barryroe. The boat overturned in the rough sea, and Murphy's brother rescued them by rowing to their aid in a larger boat.

DENIS MURPHY BMH WS 1318, 5; MICHAEL COLEMAN BMH WS 1254, 8

On hearing that Crown forces had threatened to burn Dripsey woollen mills, Donoughmore Company placed a guard on the building early in October.

JOHN MANNING BMH WS 1720, 19

Early October saw a convoy of British military raid Murphy's farm in Bweeing. They enfiladed the haggard, scattering men working at the thrashing. Some men were cornered, and Volunteer Tom Walsh had his shoulder shattered by point-blank fire from an officer. Several volunteers were arrested and interned in Ballykinlar camp.

TADHG MCCARTHY BMH WS 965, 7

Michael O'Connell, whose rank was QM Fourth Cork Brigade, First Southern Division at the end of the war, awoke to find a British officer in his bedroom. Fearing the worst when he was ordered not to put on his boots, he saw the raiding party leave suddenly.

MICHAEL O'CONNELL BMH WS 1428, 10

A British military cycle patrol from Galbally passed regularly through Mitchelstown, and the local IRA company mobilised to give battle. Nothing materialised when the patrol took a different route back to barracks.

SÉAMUS O'MAHONY BMH WS 730, 5

An ambush, which proved abortive, was prepared at Farnahoe by members of Kilbrittain Company.

DENIS CROWLEY/JAMES O'MAHONEY/JOHN FITZGERALD BMH WS 560, 13

Second Lieutenant Patrick Ahern of Fermoy Company, IO Fermoy Battalion, was in a house in Barrack Hill in the town when it was raided by a party of British military. He managed to pass an incriminating document on to Volunteer McEvilly, who had already been searched, thus avoiding Ahern's detection by the British.

PATRICK AHERN BMH WS 1003, 18

Volunteers Michael O'Neill and John Fitzgerald were arrested by a party of British military. They were imprisoned in Ballykinlar camp until Christmas 1921.

DENIS CROWLEY/JAMES O'MAHONEY/JOHN FITZGERALD BMH WS 560, 13

Churchtown RIC barracks was fired on, 'but the attack was not pushed home'.

PATRICK O'BRIEN BMH WS 764, 24; MICHAEL GEARY BMH WS 754, 3

The IO of Kilbrittain Company arranged a meeting between Sergeant Kelby, OC Kilbrittain RIC barracks, and Charlie Hurley, OC Third Cork Brigade, to 'enlist his aid in the capture of the barracks'. The sergeant declined.

DENIS CROWLEY/JAMES O'MAHONY/JOHN FITZGERALD BMH WS 560, 13

A training camp in the Crosspound area under the command of Commandant Tom Barry having concluded, volunteers north of the River Bandon took up ambush positions at Farnahoe, Killountain, east of Innishannon, but the expected patrol did not materialise.

FRANK NEVILLE BMH WS 443, 5; JEREMIAH DEASY BMH WS 1738, 14

A training camp for officers of Clonakilty Battalion was arranged at Kilbree in late October of 1920. The use of small arms, the skills of scouting and the use of cover were some of the items taught.

TED HAYES BMH WS 1575, 7

When Paddy McCarthy, Mallow Battalion OC was arrested at the end of October 1920, he was replaced by Tadhg Byrne.

TIMOTHY LOONEY BMH WS 1196, 8

Lieutenant John Moloney of Mallow Company was billeted with two comrades in a house at Glenville for several days. They were awoken one morning by a British military search party in the yard. Possibly thinking they were at the wrong house, the British moved off, allowing the IRA men to flee.

JOHN MOLONEY BMH WS 1036, 7

Captain Timothy Warren, OC Ballineen Company, and company adjutant Jack Hennessy were arrested by the Essex Regiment at Ballineen; they were beaten and tortured before being released. Both men went on the run.

PATRICK O'BRIEN BMH WS 812, 13

Glenacurrane, three miles from Mitchelstown, was reconnoitred as a potential site for an ambush by Captain Daniel O'Keeffe, OC Mitchelstown Company. An engagement did take place there two months later.

DANIEL O'KEEFFE BMH WS 1587, 21

Macroom Battalion, under its OC Patrick O'Sullivan, lay in vain to ambush two lorryloads of Auxiliaries on the Ballyvourney to Macroom road. This was the same Auxiliary company that met the flying column of the Third Cork Brigade at Kilmichael on the 28 November 1920.

PATRICK J LYNCH BMH WS 1543, 13

Volunteers from several companies of Castletownbere Battalion took positions at Bealnalappa, on the Castletownbere to Eyeries road, for an expected convoy of Crown forces. They failed to show.

JAMES MCCARTHY BMH WS 1567, 16

Commandant Tom Barry was training officer at a camp at Kealkill for officers and men of Bantry and Skibbereen Battalions. Florence O'Donoghue, Skibbereen Battalion adjutant, was arrested on his way home from the camp.

PATRICK O'SULLIVAN BMH WS 1481, 6

Michael O'Leary's farmhouse at Knocknadulane, Kiskeam was used as a factory for making gunpowder and mines.

JAMES J RIORDAN BMH WS 1172, 8

Crown forces raided the house of Edward Sisk, OC Carrigaline Company, coming away empty-handed.

EDWARD SISK BMH WS 1505, 3

Liam Lynch, OC Second Cork Brigade, selected Volunteers Leo B Skinner and Dick Perrott of Mitchelstown Company to shoot District Inspector Walsh of the RIC, a man whom Skinner believed was 'rather harmless', but William O'Regan, vice OC Sixth Battalion, called off the action.

LEO B SKINNER BMH WS 940, 2

Mid-October 1920 saw an attack on Dunmanway RIC barracks by members of Dunmanway Company. A member of the garrison was injured.

EDWARD YOUNG BMH WS 1402, 12

The house of General Caulfield at Innishannon was raided by IRA members from Innishannon Company. Led by Second Lieutenant Jeremiah Deasy, they came away with a revolver.

RICHARD RUSSELL BMH WS 1591, 13

Two IRA officers from the Ballincollig area, Leo Murphy and Willie Cotter, were confronted by Sergeant Dodds of the RIC. He was knocked over, his head hitting the ground with such force that he was killed instantly. This event purportedly happened near the Mardyke Parade in Cork, but no evidence would appear to show the existence of a Sergeant Dodds.

TIM HERLIHY AND SEVEN OTHERS BMH WS 810, 16

November 1920

1 November 1920

Four members of Innishannon Company, including its OC Dan C Crowley, were arrested for taking part in the Toureen ambush. Con O'Sullivan now became company OC.

RICHARD RUSSELL BMH WS 1591, 13; CORNELIUS O'SULLIVAN BMH WS 1740, 12

2 November 1920

Volunteers from Third Battalion, Second Cork Brigade approached Milford RIC barracks at Doonagh after its garrison was seen to have departed, but some crown forces remained. Firing broke out from within and a volunteer was wounded; the remainder of the garrison fled, and the building was destroyed by fire a few days later. Some time after this incident, Milford co-operative creamery was burned in reprisal.

JOHN D CRIMMINS BMH WS 1039, 16; TIM CRIMMINS BMH WS 1051, 6; MICHAEL GEARY/RICHARD SMITH BMH WS 754, 14; PATRICK O'BRIEN BMH WS 764, 29

4 November 1920

Members of Dunmanway Company arrested James Mahony, alias Hawkes. A watchmaker, Mahony was accused of spying. He escaped his captors, but was later shot dead at the workhouse in Skibbereen.[69]

---

[69] Keane, p146.

EDWARD YOUNG BMH WS 1402, 12; JEREMIAH KEATING BMH WS 1667, 7; DANIEL C KELLY BMH WS 1590, 5

5 November 1920

The Hampshire Regiment carried out a raid in Youghal, during which Private William King was shot dead by the IRA.[70]

6 November 1920

T J Walsh, an Irishman whose rank was inspector in the RIC, was arrested by members of the IRA on a train at Blarney. While being led away, he bolted and evaded his captors. Frank Busteed, OC Blarney Company, and his men eventually recaptured him at 4 am. 'He was found guilty of being a traitor to his country and he paid the supreme penalty.'[71]

SEÁN HEALY BMH WS 1479, 31

8 November 1920

William Mulcahy, a civilian, was shot dead by Crown forces for failing to halt at Kyrls Quay, Cork.[72]

10 November 1920

Christopher Lucey, a former section commander of B Company of the IRA inthe city, was killed as he tried to escape from C Company of the Auxiliary Division Royal Irish Constabulary

---

[70] Keane, p147.
[71] Keane, p147.
[72] Keane, p148.

at Ballingeary. His company provided a firing party over his grave at the republican plot in Saint Finbarr's cemetery.[73]

WICKAM/LUCEY/DEASY/FITZGERALD BMH WS 558, 3; DANIEL HARRINGTON BMH WS 1532, 11; CORNELIUS CRONIN BMH WS 1726, 7

11 November 1920

Four volunteers from A Company, Macroom Battalion raided the railway in Macroom and came away with captured enemy stores.

CHARLES BROWNE BMH WS 873, 27

14 November 1920

Mount Massey house, less than a mile from the town of Macroom, was vacated by the British military; it was promptly burned by the IRA.

CHARLES BROWNE BMH WS 873, 27

15 November 1920

According to Michael O'Regan of Ovens, an officer in the local battalion, four unarmed British soldiers were arrested and held for a week in Farran Company area. They were shot dead on instructions of the brigade OC and buried near Aherla.

There would appear to be no evidence to support this statement, and O'Regan is very possibly confusing it with the arrests and

---

[73] Keane, p148.

executions of three British military bandsmen who had been stationed in Ballincollig barracks (see 5 June 1921).

MICHAEL O'REGAN BMH WS 1524, 5

Four British intelligence officers were taken at gunpoint from the Cork to Bandon train at Waterfall. One of them, Lieutenant Goode, was ordered to stand aside while the three others were taken to a field nearby and shot by men of the Second Battalion, First Cork Brigade. It is possible that the IRA believed that the officers they shot had been instrumental in the torture of IRA Third Brigade officers Tom Hales and Pat Harte. The fatalities were:

Captain Stewart Chambers

Captain Montague Green

Lieutenant William Watts[74]

MICHAEL MURPHY BMH WS 1547, 29; LAURENCE NUGENT BMH WS 907, 242; MICHAEL O'REGAN BMH WS 1524, 5

16 November

Two members of the Auxiliary Division Royal Irish Constabulary, Bertram Agnew and Lionel Mitchell, travelled from Macroom to Cork on 15 November. The next morning, while about to collect a car from Johnson and Perrott in the city centre, they were arrested by the IRA, taken outside the city and shot.[75]

---

[74] Keane, p149.
[75] Keane, p149.

MARK WICKHAM BMH WS 558, 3

Following a raid by Crown forces on five homes in the Cullen area, including his own, Matthew Murphy, Millstreet Battalion adjutant, went on the run.

MATTHEW MURPHY BMH WS 1375, 11

Charles Browne, adjutant Seventh (Macroom) Battalion, was summoned to O'Sullivan's of Kilnamartra, where an ambitious plan to storm and capture the Auxiliary quarters at Macroom Castle was discussed. The subsequent attack on the Auxiliaries at Kilmichael on 28 November 1920 rendered this plan redundant.

CHARLES BROWNE BMH WS 873, 27

17 November 1920

The 17 November 1920 saw four deaths in Cork city:

Sergeant James O'Donoghue, RIC

Patrick Hanley, Na Fianna

Eugene O'Connell

James Coleman

A man dressed as a policeman broke the door of 2 Broad Street, shot James Coleman as he lay in bed, then shot a seventeen year old youth, Patrick Hanley. A member of Na Fianna, Hanley's last words were, 'Don't shoot; I am an orphan and my mother's only support'. He died instantly. Another Fianna boy in Grattan Street was shot in the face, though he survived. Eugene O'Connell lived at 17 Broad Lane. Both O'Connell and Coleman were civilians. It was believed that these attacks were thought to be a reprisal for the shooting of Sergeant O'Donoghue at White Street earlier in the day. An IRA man suspected of giving information on O'Donoghue's death was later executed.[76]

GEORGE HURLEY BMH WS 1630, 4; LEO BUCKLEY BMH WS 1714, 5; MATTHEW O'CALLAGHAN BMH WS 561, 2

20 November 1920

Daniel McCarthy, First lieutenant Lombardstown Company, transported a supply of Lee-Enfield rifle ammunition from his company area to Kilcorney; it was used some nights later in an attack on the Black and Tans at Millstreet.

DANIEL MCCARTHY BMH WS 1239, 7

Selected volunteers from Castletownbere Battalion travelled to Togher, in the Dunmanway Battalion area, to join the flying column of the Third Cork Brigade.

CHRISTOPHER O'CONNELL BMH WS 1530, 13

The local Black and Tan garrison in Millstreet 'smashed up' the house of Mrs Lenihan in the town and attempted to destroy two other houses.

CORNELIUS HEALY BMH WS 1416, 8; WILLIAM REARDEN BMH WS 1185, 4

---

[76] Keane, p150; Abbott, p150.

21 November 1920

Volunteers from Leap Company opened fire on two Black and Tans in Leap; one was killed and the other, although wounded, kept firing from a concealed position. The dead man was named as Constable Harry Clement Jays, from Hampshire in England.[77]

PATRICK O'SULLIVAN BMH WS 1481, 7; STEPHEN HOLLAND BMH WS 649, 1

A meeting of the Third Cork Brigade council met at Gloun North, Dunmanway, where a decision was made to make the newly-formed flying column a regular feature of the War of Independence.

SEÁN MURPHY BMH WS 1445, 8

Members of the Third Cork Brigade flying column from Castletownbere, Clonakilty, Dunmanway and Schull Battalions assembled at Farrell's of Clogher, near Dunmanway.

TED O'SULLIVAN BMH WS 1478, 26; JAMES MURPHY BMH WS 1684, 6

Three horse cars were stopped by Macroom Auxiliaries at Coppeen; on board were senior officers of the Third Cork Brigade, including Charlie Hurley, Dick Barrett, Liam Deasy, Seán Hales and Jim Lordan. A sum of £2,400 for the Republican Arms Fund was hidden on one of the cars. All the above-mentioned were let go, leaving two others in custody.

PADDY O'BRIEN BMH WS 812, 13

---

[77] Kingston, p116; Keane, p150; Abbott, p151.

22 November 1920

Millstreet flying column entered the town after ten o'clock on Monday 22 November 1920. They took up positions at five locations, their objective being to give battle to the Black and Tan garrison. Volunteer Paddy McCarthy received a head wound and died instantly, his body being conveyed by car to Owen Sullivan's of Gortnavehy. Following his burial, the flying column visited the town several nights in a row in an attempt to engage the Crown forces in battle[78]

CORNELIUS HEALY BMH WS 1416, 8; WILLIAM REARDEN BMH WS 1185, 4; DANIEL BROWNE BMH WS 785, 8; SÉAMUS HICKEY BMH WS 1218, 7; JOHN BOLSTER BMH WS 808, 25; LEO CALLAGHAN BMH WS 978, 9; GEORGE POWER BMH WS 451, 13; CORNELIUS MEANY BMH WS 787, 13; JEREMIAH MURPHY AND OTHERS BMH WS 744, 12; DENNY MULLANE BMH WS 789, 16; RICHARD WILLIS AND JOHN BOLSTER BMH WS 808, 25; SEÁN MOYLAN BMH WS 838, 147; JOSEPH P MORGAN BMH WS 1097, 8; JAMES J RIORDAN BMH WS 1218, 7; THOMAS ROCHE BMH WS 1222, 11; DANIEL MCCARTHY BMH WS 1239, 7; JAMES CASHMAN BMH WS 1270, 6; SEÁN HEALY BMH WS 1339, 8

David O'Callaghan, Second lieutenant in Castletownroche Company, and Volunteer Thomas De La Rue of Mitchelstown Company were arrested on this date; they were transferred to Ballykinlar Camp in Co Down.

DAVID O'CALLAGHAN BMH WS 950, 9; THOMAS DE LA RUE BMH WS 1224, 16

---

[78] Keane, p151.

23 November 1920

The annual Manchester Martyrs parade, which had been banned by the RIC, was the scene of sustained rioting in Charleville, with the local volunteers throwing stones and bottles at members of the Black Watch Regiment.

MICHAEL GEARY/RICHARD SMITH BMH WS 754, 15

Volunteer Patrick McCarthy, killed in action on 22 November 1920 at Millstreet, was buried at night at Kilcorcoran graveyard. He was re-interred at Clonfert, Newmarket, in 1922.

DENNY MULLANE BMH WS 789, 16 & 30

Captain Joseph Thompson, IO Manchester Regiment garrisoned at Ballincollig barracks, was shot dead at Carrigrohane by Leo Murphy, OC Third Battalion and two other volunteers. Thompson had a reputation for terrorising civilians, including Murphy's mother. Thompson, whose motorcycle had crashed, tried in vain to save his life by concocting a story that a ceasefire was imminent and that Ireland was about to get limited freedom. Captain Vining succeeded him as IO.[79]

TIM HERLIHY AND OTHERS BMH WS 810, 13; MICHAEL O'REGAN BMH WS 1524, 5

A grenade exploded among five volunteers standing in a group in Patrick's Street in Cork. One witness statement says it was thrown by a Black and Tan in civilian dress, another that it was as a result of a grenade falling accidentally and exploding. Three fatalities resulted from this incident:

---

[79] Keane, p151.

Patrick Trahey, Vice Commandant Second Battalion, First Cork Brigade

Patrick O'Donoghue, QM Second Battalion

Volunteer James Mehigan[80]

MICHAEL MURPHY BMH WS 1547, 29; MICHAEL V O'DONOGHUE BMH WS 1741, PART 1, 80; GEORGE POWER BMH WS 451, 13; JEREMIAH MURPHY AND OTHERS BMH WS 744, 12; DANIEL BROWNE BMH WS 785, 8; CORNELIUS MEANY BMH WS 787, 13

24 November 1920

A boy named Denis O'Donnell was shot dead by the Black and Tans at Kildorrery. He was hit nine times in the presence of his family.[81]

THOMAS BARRY BMH WS 430, 9; SÉAMUS O'MAHONY BMH WS 730, 6; WILLIAM C REGAN BMH WS 1069, 3; PATRICK J LUDDY BMH WS 1151, 11

The flying column of the Third Cork Brigade left Farrell's of Clogher, north-west of Dunmanway, to Sullivan's of Ahilane, in the Kenneigh Company area.

PADDY O'BRIEN BMH WS 812, 14

Leap RIC barracks was abandoned by its garrison; the building was burned by the IRA that night.

STEPHEN HOLLAND BMH WS 649, 2

---

[80] Keane, p152.
[81] Keane, p152.

26 November 1920

Volunteers Christy Morrissey and Liam Mulcahy of E Company, First Battalion, First Cork Brigade were killed when they tampered with a bomb of IRA manufacture in a house in Blackpool, Cork. Volunteer Dónal Kelleher escaped with injuries.[82]

THOMAS DALY AND SIX OTHERS BMH WS 719, 6

The inquest into the death of Denis O'Donnell, a civilian who had been shot dead by the Black and Tans on the 24 November, began at Kildorrery. The Crown forces returning from the inquest were ambushed at Labbacally, on the Glanworth to Fermoy road. Shots were fired at the leading vehicle, a lorry, and a grenade exploded in the vehicle resulting in the deaths of Privates Walter Gammon and Ernest Hall. An officer was thrown from the cab into the ditch; he was relieved of his arms and sent on his way.[83]

PATRICK LUDDY BMH WS 1151, 11; WILLIAM C REGAN BMH WS 1069, 3; SÉAMUS O'MAHONY BMH WS 730, 6; THOMAS BARRY BMH WS 430, 10

Patrick Ahern, second lieutenant Fermoy Company, was arrested while on the run on this day. He was sent to Ballykinlar camp, being released on 8 December 1921.

PATRICK AHERN BMH WS 1003, 22; JAMES HACKETT BMH WS 1080, 3

---

[82] Keane, p153.
[83] Keane, p153.

27 November 1920

Patrick O'Brien, Girlough, on the orders of Commandant Tom Barry, went from Ahilane, where the flying column of the Third Cork Brigade were lodged, to Ballinacarriga Company area, where four more volunteers were recruited to the column.

PATRICK O'BRIEN BMH WS 812, 15

Timothy Warren, captain Ballineen Company, was with the flying column of the Third Cork Brigade at Ahilane on the eve of the Kilmichael ambush, when he was withdrawn by Liam Deasy, brigade adjutant. Warren was given the task of organising communications and dispatch routes in the seven battalions that formed the Third Cork Brigade.

TIMOTHY WARREN BMH WS 1275, 7

Captain Joseph Aherne, OC Midleton Company, gives an account of an outbreak of shooting in Castlemartyr in which Volunteer William Heffernan and Constable Timothy Quinn lost their lives. Seeing Joseph Aherne sitting in the back of a motor car, Sergeant Curley opened fire, killing Volunteer Heffernan who was sitting in the driver's seat. The constable was shot by Aherne, and he died of his wounds the next day. He was from Co Tipperary and had fourteen years' police service. Volunteer Heffernan, aged about 21, was a member of B Company, Fourth Battalion.[84]

JOSEPH AHERNE BMH WS 1367, 34

28 November 1920

---

[84] Keane, p154; Abbott, p155.

The flying column of the Third Cork Brigade set off from O'Sullivan's of Ahilnane in the early hours of the 28 November 1920, the men having had their confessions heard by Fr Patrick O'Connell, parish priest of Enniskeane. Tom Barry and Michael McCarthy, OC and vice OC respectively of the column, had chosen an ambush position in the townland of Haremount near Kilmichael, halfway between Macroom and Dunmanway. Rocky outcrops bounded the road in places, and trees, bushes and other vegetation were almost totally absent. Barry divided his men into several small groups, placing them at strategic points on either side of the road. A patrol of Auxiliaries based in Macroom had been observed on several previous Sundays driving in the direction of Gloun Cross, sometimes turning left for Coppeen, otherwise right for Dunmanway. Scouts were posted on the Macroom side of the ambush site, their job to inform the IRA of their enemy's approach and the number of lorries in the convoy. The column had been in position for about eight hours until after four o'clock when the approach of the Auxiliaries, in two lorries, was signalled by the scouts. Barry, dressed in Volunteer uniform, stood in the way of the first lorry, throwing a Mills bomb into the cab when it came to a halt. The IRA commenced firing from their positions at this first lorry. The second Crossley Tender, meanwhile, stopped a hundred yards back the road, its driver attempting in vain to reverse the vehicle. There now followed an intense gun battle, with the Auxiliaries seeking shelter behind and under the stricken lorry. Those of the IRA, including Barry, who had dealt with the first lorry now joined their comrades attacking the Auxiliaries at the remaining vehicle. Two witness statements – those of Jack Hennessy and Timothy Keohane – give details of a false surrender by the Auxiliaries. Altogether sixteen Auxiliaries were killed at Kilmichael, with one escaping from the scene only to be arrested and shot later. Three Irish soldiers were killed as a result of the ambush, two at the scene and one of his wounds later that night.

The Irish casualties were as follows:

Third Cork Brigade IRA Flying Column Vice-Commandant Michael McCarthy

Volunteer Pat Deasy

Volunteer Jim O'Sullivan

The Auxiliary casualties at Kilmichael were:

Colonel F W Craik, MC

Captain P N Graham

Major F Hugo, OBE, MC

Captain W Pallester

Captain C Wainwright

Cadet W T Barnes, DFC

Cadet L D Bradshaw

Cadet A G Jones

Cadet W Hooper-Jones

Cadet E W H Lucas

Cadet H O Person

Cadet F Taylor

Cadet B Webster

Temporary Cadet C D W Bayley

Temporary Constable A F Poole

Temporary Cadet JC Gleave

Lieutenant C J Guthrie (killed by IRA some distance from Kilmichael after the ambush)

Lieutenant H F Forde, MC, though seriously wounded, survived the Kilmichael ambush.[85]

JACK HENNESSY BMH WS 1234, 4; TIMOTHY KEOHANE BMH WS 1295, 6; EDWARD YOUNG BMH WS 1402, 13; PATRICK O'BRIEN BMH WS 812, 15; JAMES 'SPUD' MURPHY BMH WS 1684, 5; CHARLES BROWNE BMH WS 873, 29; MICHAEL O'DRISCOLL BMH WS 1297, 4; CORNELIUS KELLEHER BMH WS 1654, 10

Seán Cotter, an officer in Bantry Battalion, was arrested with three others – including Maurice Donegan, battalion OC – in the Donemark area by a strong force of the British Army. They were moved to Ballykinlar Camp until after the signing of the Treaty.

SEÁN COTTER BMH WS 1493, 16; DENIS KEOHANE BMH WS 1426, 9; MAURICE DONEGAN BMH WS 639, 6

---

[85] Kingston, p148-161; Keane, pp39, 155; Abbott, p156; Whyte, Louis, The Wild Heather Glen: The Kilmichael Story of Grief and Glory, Tower Books of Ballincollig, 1995.

Thomas Downey, otherwise Downing, who had been arrested as a spy by the IRA on the 23 November, was executed by them.[86]

29 November 1920

Volunteer Edward Young of Dunmanway, who had fought at Kilmichael the previous day, was, along with several other members of the flying column, ordered to fire at any Crown forces approaching Manch bridge on the 29 and 30 November.

EDWARD YOUNG BMH WS 1402, 16

Charles O'Donoghue, QM Bandon Battalion, was part of a group of forty men from the northern part of the battalion area who lay in wait at Quinn's farmhouse in anticipation of enemy lorries passing by. A mine was laid. When no lorries showed, they withdrew. On their way to billets they got word of the Kilmichael ambush the previous day.

CHARLES O'DONOGHUE BMH WS 1607, 5

Volunteers Con Crowley and John O'Mahony from Kilbrittain, who were detained in Macroom Castle, were given 'the unenviable job' of washing the corpses of the sixteen Auxiliaries killed by the flying column of the Third Cork Brigade at Kilmichael the previous day.

MICHAEL J CROWLEY BMH WS 1603, 12

Timothy Warren, captain Ballineen Company, relates that Tom Barry's flying column rested at Granure, in the Ballinacarriga

---

[86] Keane, p154.

Company area, for three nights following the Kilmichael ambush, moving to Coxtown near Ahiohill and Cahir, in the Lyre Company area, on subsequent nights.

TIMOTHY WARREN BMH WS 1275, 8

Men drawn from the First Battalion of the Third Cork Brigade, with Liam Deasy in command, lay in wait at Clashanimud, near Brinny, for a mixed patrol of Crown forces. Witness accounts vary, with another attempted ambush taking place in early December, but either way it would appear that no casualties were inflicted on either side. On their way to billets the volunteers got news of the Kilmichael ambush the previous day.

WILLIAM DESMOND BMH WS 832, 26; CON FLYNN BMH WS 1621, 14; DANIEL CANTY BMH WS 1619, 19; CHARLES O'DONOGHUE BMH WS 1607, 5

Volunteer Denis O'Riordan – known as Din-Din – was suspected of giving information to Crown forces. A trap was laid, and he was interrogated and executed by the IRA.[87]

James and Frederick Blemens, father and son, were kidnapped by the IRA and held for several days before being shot as spies. It appears the information that led to their abduction came from Josephine Marchment Browne, an employee in the office of Captain Kelly, chief of British intelligence in Cork.[88]

MICHAEL MURPHY BMH WS 1547, 33

---

[87] Keane, p58.
[88] Keane, p59.

Denis O'Sullivan, a civilian, was having a drink in Cronin's bar in Dromleigh, Kilmichael, when he was dragged out by a group of Auxiliaries from Macroom and shot dead. This being the day after the Kilmichael ambush, there is little doubt that this was a revenge killing.[89]

---

[89] Keane, p156.

November 1920 (no date available)

Henry O'Mahony, OC Passage West Company, relates that an attack was made on a patrol of RIC immediately as they left their barracks in the town; a policeman was wounded.

HENRY O'MAHONY BMH WS 1506, 4; JOHN BARRETT BMH WS 1538, 3

Both Ballineen courthouse and the abandoned RIC barracks nearby were demolished by the local IRA.

PHILIP CHAMBERS BMH WS 738, 5

A plan to ambush a convoy of Auxiliaries travelling from Fermoy to Cork was made at Blackstone Bridge, three miles from Rathcormac. About forty men from Fermoy Battalion were lying in wait for the five-lorry convoy when a funeral of almost forty horses and traps passed by. The Auxiliaries passed by unharmed.

JOHN FANNING BMH WS 990, 15

All companies of Schull Battalion sent representatives to a training camp at Dunmanus, moving on subsequent days to Dreemolane and Mount Kidd in the Ballydehob area. Five rounds of ammunition were allowed each man in musketry practice. Commandant Tom Barry was in charge.

RICHARD COLLINS BMH WS 1542, 5; SEÁN O'DRISCOLL BMH WS 1518, 11; EDWARD O'SULLIVAN BMH WS 1501, 3

Jeremiah Deasy, Second Lieutenant Innishannon Company, Bandon Battalion, spotted two men in British Army uniform near his home; following them for some distance, they were eventually arrested, whereupon they declared themselves deserters and asked for civilian clothing. They were Peter Monaghan, a Scotsman of Irish parentage who subsequently died in the service of the IRA at Crossbarry in March 1921, and Tom Clarke.

JEREMIAH DEASY BMH WS 1738, 16; CON FLYNN BMH WS 1621, 15

A party of the Essex Regiment stationed at Courtmacsherry opened fire on Michael O'Driscoll at Timoleague. They believed him to be Lieutenant William Foley of Timoleague Company, and O'Driscoll spent six months recovering from six bullet wounds at Victoria barracks in Cork. Having shot him, the Essex made a vain attempt to burn down his place of work later that night.

WILLIAM FOLEY BMH WS 1560, 6

Liam Lynch, OC Second Cork Brigade, and officers of Millstreet Battalion were appraising a stretch of road at Keam, three miles from Millstreet, as an ambush site. Two lorries full of Auxiliaries came into view and stopped six hundred yards from them. Lynch and his group moved off when the Auxiliaries dismounted.

CORNELIUS HEALY BMH WS 1416, 7

What was believed to be a senior military intelligence officer was kidnapped coming from mass at Glanmire church. It turned out to be Constable Ryan, who was released.

DANIEL HEALY BMH WS 1656, 11

The house of Con Leddy, OC Araglin Company, First Battalion, Second Cork Brigade, was visited by British military. Finding him absent, the officer in charge told his mother that their farm and property would be destroyed if he did not give himself up at Moorepark barracks.

CON LEDDY BMH WS 756, 10

Volunteer Tadhg McCarthy of Donoughmore Company was arrested in his own area and detained in Mallow; he was released after a fortnight.

TADHG MCCARTHY BMH WS 965, 8

A young man called Parsons was often near the house of Michael Murphy, OC First Cork Brigade flying column. According to Murphy, Parsons admitted to being a spy after interrogation, adding that it was he who told District Inspector Swanzy, the officer in charge of the party of police that shot Lord Mayor Tomás Mac Curtain, that Mac Curtain had arrived home on the evening of 19 March 1920, the date of his death. The brigade OC ordered Parsons to be shot. According to Barry Keane, it is more likely that William Edward Parsons, aged sixteen, was executed by the IRA in July of 1922.[90]

MICHAEL MURPHY BMH WS 1547, 33

Early November 1920 saw men from Rusheen and Ballinagree Companies lay in wait at Carrigadrohid for a patrol of Black and Tans. The volunteers were instructed to withdraw when the convoy failed to show.

EDWARD NEVILLE BMH WS 1665, 4

Towards the end of November 1920 an ambush was planned for Gortmore, in the Mallow Battalion area. The plan was

---

[90] Keane, p291.

abandoned when an inexperienced volunteer discharged a shot accidentally, thus warning the Crown forces.

MICHAEL O'CONNELL BMH WS 1428, 10

Ordnance was moved from Kilbrittain to Carhue, near Timoleague, in preparation for an ambush on the Courtmacsherry road, but for some unspecified reason the attack was not pressed home.

JOHN O'DRISCOLL BMH WS 1250, 7

Volunteer Paddy O'Keeffe, later director general of the GAA, was arrested by five Auxiliaries in civilian attire in Cork city centre. He was found to have a grenade in his pocket; he was arrested, tried and was sentenced to fifteen years' penal servitude.

MICHAEL V O'DONOGHUE BMH WS 1741, 86

Members of Bantry Company intercepted a despatch box dropped from a military airplane at West Park, Bantry.

JAMES O'SULLIVAN BMH WS 1455, 10

Skibbereen and Bantry Battalions sent officers to a training camp at Kealkil, Tom Barry OC brigade column in charge. The care and use of arms and all aspects of guerrilla warfare were taught, with lectures taking place at night.

JOHN J O'SULLIVAN BMH WS 1578, 15

Thomas Roche, training officer Newmarket Battalion, relates that positions were taken over two days at Kingwilliamstown (now Ballydesmond) by members of the Battalion, with a view to an attack on their enemy, but Crown forces failed to show.

THOMAS ROCHE BMH WS 1222, 11

Jeremiah Deasy, Second lieutenant Innishannon Company, was arrested in November 1920, his post being filled by Patrick Crowley.

RICHARD RUSSELL BMH WS 1591, 14

A Constable James Gordon was allegedly captured while drunk, and was executed. It was stated that he was responsible for the deaths of several nationalists in Tipperary. No record of the constable would appear to exist to back up the witness statement, and he is not mentioned in Richard Abbott's book.

MAURICE FORD BMH WS 719, 6

December 1920

1 December 1920

According to James Coss, IO Fermoy Company and Battalion, a group of Auxiliaries arrived at the Royal Hotel in Fermoy on this date. After they manhandled some customers, a man called Prendergast, an ex-captain in the Great War, remonstrated with them, whereupon he was set upon and beaten to death, his body dumped in the River Blackwater. The perpetrators then set a number of shops on fire.[91]

JAMES COSS BMH WS 1065, 8

Michael Murphy, commandant Second Battalion, First Cork Brigade, claims that 'about 20' Black and Tans raided the Thomas Ashe Hall in Cork city centre. A trap mine was exploded. Murphy does not give an accurate account of casualties, "but it is safe to assume that practically all the force was…either killed or wounded". There is no reference to back up this statement.

MICHAEL MURPHY BMH WS 1547, 31

A Norwegian sailor named Carl Johansen was shot in the back by a group of Auxiliaries at Customs House Quay in Cork. He died of his injuries.[92]

Having rested three nights at Granure following the Kilmichael ambush, the flying column of the Third Cork Brigade moved on to the Lyre Company area. It was at this time that

---

[91] Keane, p158.
[92] Keane, p157.

Commandant Tom Barry, OC of the flying column, fell ill with a cardiac complaint.

PATRICK O'BRIEN BMH WS 812, 17

2 December 1920

George Power, IO Second Cork Brigade, his health depleted from nervous exhaustion and a septic wound, entered Fermoy hospital on this date to recuperate. The hospital was raided twice, although he escaped detection.

GEORGE POWER BMH WS 451, 14

Clashanimud, between Killeady and Kilpatrick, was the scene of an attack on a motorised convoy of Crown forces by members of Bandon Battalion, Third Cork Brigade, in command of Charlie Hurley, Brigade OC. Fire was returned by Crown forces, who sped away. The IRA, numbering about thirty, then returned to their billet in Crowhill, where they were dismissed and ordered home. No combatants on either side were injured, but Captain Daniel Canty, OC Newcestown Company, says that a fifteen year old girl, a witness in an impending court case, having been dropped off one of the lorries, was inadvertently wounded by IRA fire. Newcestown, Quarries Cross, Crosspound and Kilpatrick Companies were represented in this attack.

DANIEL CANTY BMH WS 1619, 20; WILLIAM DESMOND BMH WS 832, 26; JEREMIAH DEASY BMH WS 1738, 17; MAURICE DONOVAN BMH WS 1736, 5; CORNELIUS O'SULLIVAN BMH WS 1740, 12; MICHAEL RIORDAN BMH WS 1638, 17

Percy Taylor, who claimed to be a British Army deserter formerly based at Bandon, arranged a clever ruse to draw out Tom Barry, OC Third Cork Brigade flying column. A rendezvous was arranged near Bandon where Barry was to receive intelligence that would lead to an IRA attack on Bandon military barracks. Barry, however, suffered a heart attack earlier that day, and three IRA men sent to guard him walked into a trap set by a detatchment of the Essex Regiment; all three were killed. They were:

Volunteer Joseph Begley

Lieutenant James Donoghue

Captain John Galvin[93]

CHARLES O'DONOGHUE BMH WS 1607, 10

3 December 1920

Barryroe and Timoleague Companies engaged in the destruction of the abandoned RIC barracks at Timoleague, as well as Timoleague Castle and the house of Colonel Travers.

LAURENCE SEXTON BMH WS 1290, 7; DAN DONOVAN BMH WS 1608, 8; CORNELIUS CALNAN BMH WS 1317, 5; JAMES MOLONEY BMH WS 1310, 7; DENIS MURPHY BMH WS 1318, 6

Laurence Condon, Second lieutenant Fermoy Company, was arrested at Clondulane railway station after an incriminating dispatch was found in his clothing. He was sentenced to two years in Kilkenny prison, from where he and over thirty other prisoners escaped by digging a tunnel.

LAURENCE CONDON BMH WS 859, 10

---

[93] Keane, p157.

A party of RIC from Youghal crossed over to the Waterford side of the River Blackwater, where they were fired on by the West Waterford Brigade. Constable Maurice Prenderville, a native of Kerry, was wounded; he died later that day.[94]

JAMES *PRENDERGAST BMH WS 1655, 6*

Private Percy Taylor and Private Thomas Watling, two deserters from the Essex Regiment in IRA captivity, attracted suspicion when three Bandon IRA men were ambushed and shot dead by the Essex Regiment outside Bandon (see 2 December 1920). The IRA believed that Taylor and Watling had been implicit in sending them to their deaths. The two British Army men were executed at Kilbree.[95]

5 December 1920

The flying column of the Third Cork Brigade was billeted in Knockea, in the Lyre Company area, around this time. Lyre Company were responsible for scouting the locality, providing provisions and arranging dispatch riders.

MICHAEL DINNEEN BMH WS 1563, 10

6 December 1920

Ballinguile, Tullylease was the location of a three-day training camp for members of Newmarket Battalion flying column.

DENNY MULLANE BMH WS 789, 16

A delegation of Labour party MPs from England, tasked with gathering information on the political and military situation in

---

[94] Keane, p158; Abbott, p163.
[95] Keane, p159.

Ireland, attended a commission in the council chambers of Cork City Hall. Organised by Séamus Fitzgerald, an officer in Cobh Company, approximately eighty witnesses of murders, shootings and other events gave evidence.

SÉAMUS FITZGERALD BMH WS 1737, 30

7 December 1920

In Timoleague, the public house and grocery store of William Foley, an officer in the Third Cork Brigade, was burned in reprisal for his activities and for the IRA's burning of the house of Colonel Travers.

WILLIAM FOLEY BMH WS 1560, 6

The body of Volunteer Denis Regan was found on the roadside between Clonakilty and Timoleague. It is believed that he was shot by Crown forces.[96]

8 December 1920

Blackstone Bridge, near Rathcormac, on the main Cork to Fermoy road, was the scene of an attempted ambush on the Auxiliary division of the RIC by the Second Cork Brigade flying column, under the command of brigade adjutant Moss Twomey. Having waited since dawn, the attackers received signals from scouts at 4 pm that their enemy was approaching. As the IRA prepared to fire, a large funeral party came upon the scene, and to prevent danger to civilian lives the convoy was allowed to pass through.

---

[96] Keane, p159.

JJ BRENNOCK BMH WS 1113, 9; LAURENCE CONDON BMH WS 859, 10; CON LEDDY BMH WS 756, 11; WILLIAM BUCKLEY BMH WS 1009, 7

Gaggin, on the main road from Bandon to Clonakilty, was the scene of an ambush by the flying column of the Third Cork Brigade on 8 December 1920. In command was brigade OC Charlie Hurley (Tom Barry was still recovering from his heart attack). As a lorryload of RIC was coming from a westerly direction, a shot was accidently fired by a member of the column. Several of the RIC, knocked off the swerving lorry, gave battle. The column moved off in the direction of Kilbrittain; coming under fire from the RIC, they replied. Some time after the firing had ceased, Lieutenant Michael McLean of Schull Company, who had been guarding the members of a nearby household, was shot dead 'by enemy reinforcements which had come out from Bandon', according to Edward Young, a member of the brigade column. The column rested in O'Callaghan's of Laravoultig that night; others went in the direction of Kilbrittain.[97]

WILLIAM DESMOND BMH WS 832, 26; MICHAEL DINNEEN BMH WS 1563, 10; TIMOTHY KEOHANE BMH WS 1295, 8; JACK HENNESSY BMH WS 1234, 8; EDWARD YOUNG BMH WS 1402, 16; JAMES MURPHY BMH WS 1684, 8; TIMOTHY WARREN BMH WS 1275, 8; FRANK NEVILLE BMH WS 443, 9; PATRICK O'BRIEN BMH WS 812, 17

Michael Murphy, a civilian, was shot dead by the Auxiliaries after curfew hour in Cork city centre.[98]

---

[97] Keane, p159.
[98] Keane, p160.

9 December 1920

Moss Twomey, Second Cork Brigade adjutant, was arrested on this date.

CON LEDDY BMH WS 756, 11

John Fleming, a civilian, was walking with three others at the Lower Road in Cork when Crown forces in a passing lorry opened fire. He died later that day.[99]

George Horgan, a civilian, was accused by the IRA of spying on them. He was shot, his body buried on the Douglas Road in Cork city.[100] Horgan's disappearance prompted dire warnings in the newspapers, the Crown forces promising death and destruction of property for 'the rebels of Cork' in the event of his death.

10 December 1920

Two days after the failed attack at Blackstone Bridge, the flying column of the Second Cork Brigade engaged the British Army at Leary's Cross, near Castlelyons. After a protracted firefight, the Crown forces surrendered in several stages, sustaining one dead and two wounded; the IRA had no casualties. The IRA retired to four different billets at Ballyard. Expecting enemy retaliation, shotgun men from Bartlemy and Castlelyons Companies prepared to move to Fermoy the next day. Four houses were burned by Crown forces in the aftermath of this attack. The soldier who died was Gunner Robert Cambridge of the Royal Field Artillery; he was a native of Surrey.[101]

---

[99] Keane, p161.
[100] Keane, p162.
[101] Keane, p162.

WILLIAM BUCKLEY BMH WS 1009, 9; JJ BRENNOCK BMH WS 1113, 10; CON LEDDY BMH WS 756, 11; GEORGE POWER BMH WS 451, 14; DANIEL DALY BMH WS 743, 7; CON LEDDY BMH WS 756, 11; LAURENCE CONDON BMH WS 859, 10

Lieutenant John Kelleher of Midleton Company, Fourth Battalion, First Cork Brigade relates that the battalion flying column waited for several days at Aghada in the vain expectation that British military would cross by water from Cobh to Fort Carlisle.

JOHN KELLEHER BMH WS 1456, 23; PATRICK J WHELAN 1449, 34

Sarah Medaile, a civilian, died of a heart attack brought on by the shock of her home being ransacked by Auxiliaries. She was around sixty years old.[102]

11 December 1920

Sixteen men from First Battalion, First Cork Brigade waited in vain at Dillon's Cross in the city on Friday 10 December for an expected patrol from Victoria barracks. The following evening, the attacking group, now reduced to six to minimise detection, opened fire with revolver and grenade on a two-lorry Auxiliary patrol. According to Lieutenant Seán Healy of A Company, First Battalion, 'Fifteen of the enemy were put out of action, which left an equal number to carry on the fight'. The alarm was soon raised in the nearby barracks, and the IRA withdrew. According to Lieutenant Healy, one man was killed and twelve wounded seriously. The man who died was Cadet Spenser Chapman.

---

[102] Keane, p163.

Following the attack on the Auxiliaries at Dillon's Cross, Crown forces took their revenge by burning much of Cork city centre. Public buildings, including the city hall and the Carnegie library, as well as shops, private houses and offices, were torched. Looting was rife.[103]

SEÁN HEALY BMH WS 686, 1/1479, 56; MICHAEL V O'DONOGHUE BMH WS 1741(1), 93

Two members of E Company, First Battalion, First Cork Brigade accompanied Volunteer Jeremiah Delaney to his house in Dublin Hill on the northern outskirts of Cork city. It was the 11 December, the night of the Dillon's Cross attack by the IRA on the Auxiliaries based in Victoria barracks, and the subsequent burning of Cork by Crown forces. In the early hours of the morning both Delaney and his brother Cornelius were shot in their beds by a party of masked men who broke into their house; Jeremiah died instantly, Cornelius a fortnight later. Their aged uncle was also shot and wounded.[104]

THOMAS DALY AND OTHERS BMH WS 719, 10; PATRICK O'BRIEN BMH WS 764, 33

12 December 1920

Daniel Coholan, the Catholic bishop of Cork, issued a decree excommunicating members of the IRA for bearing arms.

MICHAEL V O'DONOGHUE BMH WS 1741, 99

John O'Brien, a civilian teenager, was shot by members of the Cameron Highlanders regiment following a gun battle with the

---

[103] Keane, p51; Abbott, p164.
[104] Keane, p54.

east Cork flying column.The flying column was in danger of being trapped by their enemy, but they escaped thanks to a covering fire from Paddy Whelan and Jack Ahern. It was after the column's escape that O'Brien was shot by Sergeant Major Mackintosh using a Lewis gun.[105]

JOHN KELLEHER BMH WS 1156, 21; PATRICK J WHELAN BMH WS 1449

13 December 1920

Around this date, K Company Auxiliary Division RIC, the men responsible for the burning of Cork on the 11 December, were moved to new headquarters at the workhouse in Dunmanway; another company was billeted in the local model school. K Company was in command of an officer named de Havilland, with Brownie as intelligence officer. Lists were drawn up of friendly and hostile houses in the locality, with detailed descriptions of all suspects. All this effort came to naught, however, as a local man sympathetic to the nationalist cause, Florence J Crowley, was employed as a clerk in the workhouse. As well as Crowley, the local IRA was tipped off regarding planned raids by Cahill, an RIC man.

PATRICK O'BRIEN BMH WS 812, 6

14 December 1920

Charlie Hurley, OC Third Cork Brigade, was in charge of a party of men from the brigade flying column that raided the mails at Ballineen train station. The mail was scrutinised at

---

[105] Keane, p163.

O'Callaghan's of Laravoultig that night, being returned to the post office at Enniskeane the following morning.

WILLIAM DESMOND BMH WS 832, 26

15 December 1920

Dunmanway Battalion arranged a meeting at the Buttimer house of Ahakeera for the Third Cork Brigade council.

PATRICK O'BRIEN BMH WS 812, 6

Canon Thomas Magner, parish priest of Dunmanway, and a local man, Volunteer Timothy Crowley of Behigullane, met a patrol of K Company Auxiliary Division RIC, newly billeted at the workhouse outside Dunmanway. Both men were giving assistance to R S Brady, a resident magistrate from Bantry, whose car had broken down. Both Canon Magner and Volunteer Crowley were shot dead from point blank range by Cadet Hart, but the fleeing Brady, although fired at, managed to escape. The subsequent trial of Hart found him guilty but insane.[106]

PATRICK O'BRIEN BMH WS 812, 18; TED O'SULLIVAN BMH WS 1478, 27

17 December 1920

A three-vehicle British Army convoy was driving northwards at Glencurrane in Co Limerick, on the Mitchelstown-Tipperary road, when members of the Second Cork Brigade flying column, along with the East Limerick flying column, opened fire at four o'clock in the day. The driver of the first vehicle, an open touring car, was killed. When a second soldier was killed, the remainder

---

[106] Keane, p164.

surrendered; four had been wounded. This ambush was in the command of Donnchadh Hannigan, OC East Limerick Brigade. The casualties were Private Joseph Minchin and Sergeant Leonard Ellis, both of the Lincolnshire Regiment.

LEO CALLAGHAN BMH WS 978, 11; THOMAS BARRY BMH WS 430, 12; PATRICK LUDDY BMH WS 1151, 14; SÉAMUS O'MAHONY BMH WS 730, 8; PATRICK CLIFFORD BMH WS 946, 4; RICHARD WILLIS/JOHN BOLSTER BMH WS 808, 26; WILLIAM C REGAN BMH WS 1069, 5; LEO SKINNER BMH WS 940, 3

18 December 1920

The columns that had fought at Glencurrane on 17 December now assembled at Ballynacourty near Kilfinnane in Co Limerick, in the expectation that a convoy of three British military lorries would pass by. In the afternoon the parish priest of Glenroe, Fr Ambrose, drove into the ambush position and informed Donnchadh Hannigan, OC East Limerick Brigade, that the Crown forces were aware of their whereabouts.

PATRICK LUDDY BMH WS 1151, 15; WILLIAM C REGAN BMH WS 1069, 6

19 December 1920

On this date British military stationed in Fermoy combed the districts of Castlelyons, Bawnard and Rathcormac, in search of IRA members. Twenty-eight arrests were made, the majority of the prisoners being released on Christmas Eve.

WILLIAM BUCKLEY BMH WS 1009, 12

20 December 1920

Volunteers from Coolea and Ballyvourney Companies finally succeeded in burning the abandoned police barracks at Ballyvourney.

PATRICK J LYNCH BMH WS 1543, 13

Three British soldiers were arrested in Timoleague and held for some hours before being released unharmed.

DENIS O'BRIEN BMH WS 1306, 6; JAMES O'MAHONY/DENIS CROWLEY/JOHN FITZGERALD BMH WS 560, 14

Volunteers from Charleville Battalion flying column, Second Cork Brigade, raided the night mail train to Dublin at Charleville. Some Black and Tans came on the scene, firing and calling them to halt, but the IRA escaped.

MICHAEL GEARY/RICHARD SMITH BMH WS 754, 17

21 December 1920

An IRA raid on the General Post Office in Oliver Plunkett Street went badly wrong. Volunteer Patrick Tarrant, from Ballintemple in the city, was shot dead by undercover policemen. A civilian, Timothy Donovan, an ex-member of the Munster Fusiliers, was killed in the crossfire.[107]

22 December 1920

The flying column of the Third West Cork Brigade were demobilised on this date near Ballineen; their rifles were stored in the Kilmeen Company area.

---

[107] Keane, p164.

PATRICK O'BRIEN BMH WS 812, 19

24 December 1920

Christmas Eve 1920 found the East Cork flying column billeted in a farm outhouse in Ballymountain, east of Midleton. The column OC, Diarmuid Hurley, planned a post-Christmas attack on the Black and Tans in the town.

JOHN KELLEHER BMH WS 1456, 21

26 December 1920

The British military stationed at Castletownroche raided the home of the Healy brothers, local republicans, on Saint Stephen's Day. The brothers fled the scene as the enemy approached, and the remainder of the family were subjected to an interrogation before the military left the scene.

SEÁN HEALY BMH WS 1479, 40

Captain Timothy Warren of Ballineen Company and Jack Hennessy, another officer in the same company, were fired on by two lorryloads of Black and Tans, but they managed to escape.

TIMOTHY WARREN BMH WS 1275, 9

28 December 1920

The Third Cork Brigade of the IRA held a council meeting at Ballinacarriga on this date. Fearful that the morale of the IRA might be on the wane, Charlie Hurley, brigade OC, and other officers decided that the flying column, which had been demobilised for the Christmas, should reassemble in mid-January.

TED O'SULLIVAN BMH WS 1478, 27

The East Cork flying column, in the command of Diarmuid Hurley and numbering about twelve, made an attack on a patrol of Black and Tans in the main street in Midleton on 28 December 1920. Armed with revolvers, the flying column gave battle for about twenty minutes, some witnesses believing they had caused many deaths and injuries. One IRA man sustained a hand wound. This incident precipitated a series of 'official reprisals' in the locality. Those killed, or who died as a result of their wounds, were:

Constable Martin Mullen

Constable Ernest Dray

Constable Arthur Thorpe[108]

PATRICK J WHELAN BMH WS 1449, 43; JOHN KELLEHER BMH WS 1456, 22; DANIEL CASHMAN BMH WS 1523, 7; DIARMUID O'LEARY BMH WS 1589, 3; MICHAEL KEARNEY BMH WS 1418, 20; PATRICK J HIGGINS BMH WS 1467, 3; JOSEPH AHERNE BMH WS 1367, 40

The printing press of the Cork Examiner – 'decidedly pro-British in its outlook'- was broken up and smashed with sledgehammers by volunteers from First and Second Battalions, First Cork Brigade.

MICHAEL MURPHY BMH WS 1547, 34; WICKHAM/ LUCEY /DEASY/FITZGERALD BMH WS 558, 3

---

[108] Keane, p165; Abbott, 168.

29 December 1920

The home of Captain Timothy Warren of Ballineen Company, a member of the flying column of the Third Cork Brigade, was burned by the British Army on this date.

TIMOTHY WARREN BMH WS 1275, 9

31 December 1920

IRA men, mostly from Kilbrittain Company, carried out an attack on Kilbrittain RIC barracks. As often happened during the War of Independence, a mine placed at the barracks door failed to explode, and the IRA withdrew after an exchange of gunfire lasting three hours.

DAN HOLLAND BMH WS 1341, 7

Private George Lockyer of the King's Liverpool Regiment was killed by an accidental shot discharged by a member of his regiment while raiding a house at Mohonagh, Skibbereen.[109]

---

[109] Keane, p166.

December 1920 (no date available)

Hearing that the home of Volunteer Liam O'Dwyer was about to be raided by Crown forces, positions were taken up at Beel, one mile east of Eyeries, by Eyeries and Ballycrovane Companies. The RIC did not show.

JAMES Mc CARTHY BMH WS 1567, 17

British military from Mallow occupied the house of Volunteer Ned Waters at Glashabuidhe, in the Mallow Battalion area. The IRA approached in the morning and was on the receiving end of a fusillade of gunfire, one man sustaining a leg wound.

TADHG Mc CARTHY BMH WS 965, 8

As a result of arrests of IRA volunteers in the Fermoy area, Liam Lynch, OC Second Cork Brigade, made several new appointments to the command structure of the Fermoy Battalion.

CON LEDDY BMH WS 756, 13

Michael Murphy, commandant Second Battalion and OC active service unit (flying column) of the First Cork Brigade, received orders from Seán O'Hegarty, brigade OC, to go to London to purchase arms. Scouring the second-hand gunshops of London, he got 'two barrels of "stuff" 'shipped back to Cork, where the consignment ended up in the Cork Steampacket Company's store. Knowing the company would report the cargo to the authorities, Murphy, armed with a revolver, visited the warehouse and ensured the cargo was released.

MICHAEL MURPHY BMH WS 1547, 30

Frank Neville, QM Knockavilla Company, was arrested in open countryside by three British officers of the Essex Regiment, one of whom he discovered later to be Major Percival. He, along with other IRA men, was brought to Jagoe's farmyard at Knockavilla, and loaded on a lorry bound for Cork. Shortly into the journey, he was ordered to dismount by a corporal of the Essex. Being aware of the Essex Regiment's 'shot while trying to escape' policy, Neville made a dash to save his life and managed to escape, though under fire. Neville remarks that Jagoe, in whose farmyard the captured IRA men were assembled, had given information to the British, for which action he was forced by the IRA to leave the country. Another raid was carried out at this time in the Knockavilla area, resulting in the arrests of Volunteers John O'Sullivan and Patrick Cronin.

FRANK NEVILLE BMH WS 443, 7

Christopher O'Keeffe, QM Newmarket Company, was arrested with several comrades and subjected to 'an unmerciful hammering' and mock executions over four days. 'The Gestapo or Bolshies...had nothing on this crowd as regards inflicting punishment.' Volunteer Michael Brennan 'never got over the effects of the ill-treatment and died later as a result'.

CHRISTOPHER O'KEEFFE BMH WS 761, 13

The flying column of the First Battalion, Second Cork Brigade were billeted at Noonan's, Clancy's and Hennessy's while in the Kildorrery Company area in early December; fruitless efforts were made to engage the Black and Tans.

SÉAMUS O'MAHONY BMH WS 730, 8

Seán McCarthy, QM Schull Battalion, was court-martialled and removed from his position on the staff of the battalion for engaging in an unauthorised raid. Seán O'Driscoll was appointed in his place.

SEÁN O'DRISCOLL BMH WS 1518, 11

Ballydesmond was the location of an officer training camp, Tom Roche, an ex-RIC man from Tullylease, was the instructor. Each company in the battalion sent four officers for training.

DANIEL FLYNN BMH WS 1240, 7; JOHN JONES BMH WS 759, 6

Two intended ambushes against the RIC at Churchtown proved abortive. In the same month two British soldiers, possibly on a scouting mission, were captured and disarmed at Coolin, Charleville.

MICHAEL GEARY/RICHARD SMITH BMH WS 754, 16

Members of Fermoy Company IRA raided Fermoy railway station, seizing a quantity of 'Belfast goods' which were destroyed, including bales of cloth intended for Daniels' of Fermoy, a tailoring firm that made uniforms for the British Army.

JAMES HACKETT BMH WS 1080, 3

General Sir Peter Strickland, OC British Army in the Munster area, was reported to be on a tour of inspection in the IRA Donoughmore Battalion area. Iniscarra Company, under its OC Tim Twomey, waited in vain to ambush the convoy, it having taken a different route.

MICHAEL MULLANE BMH WS 1689, 7

Thomas J Golden, OC Donoughmore Battalion, relates that Turpin's Rock was the location where local IRA men lay in wait for about a week in December. The expected enemy patrol did not show up.

THOMAS J GOLDEN BMH WS 1680, 16

Tureen, Knocknagree was the location of a training camp, under the instruction of Tom Roche, for Newmarket Battalion, Second Cork Brigade.

JAMES CASHMAN BMH WS 1270, 6

William Foley, an officer in the Third Cork Brigade specialising in munitions, received orders from Charlie Hurley, brigade OC, to travel to Dublin to work in a bombmaking factory in Parnell street.

WILLIAM FOLEY BMH WS 1560, 6

Hallihan's Engineering Works in Midleton was burned by British military around this time.

PATRICK J WHELAN BMH WS 1449, 47

Liam Deasy, Adjutant Third Cork Brigade, travelled to Dublin to meet Michael Collins, Cathal Brugha, Liam Mellowes and others to arrange a shipment of arms from Italy, an enterprise that never materialised.

LIAM DEASY BMH WS 562, 1; FLORENCE O'DONOGHUE BMH WS 554, 1

A British soldier, not named, was arrested by the IRA at Grenagh; he claimed to be a deserter. He was executed. 'He died very bravely without the slightest flinching.'[110]

DENIS DWYER BMH WS 713, 4

---

[110] Keane, p166.

January 1921

1 January 1921

Captain Daniel Canty, OC Newcestown Company, and two fellow volunteers 'took a chance' and went to mass in Newcestown. Shortly after, a patrol of four lorries of Essex Regiment soldiers entered the village and arrested some civilians. Canty and his comrades got away.

DANIEL CANTY BMH WS 1619, 22

Liam Deasy and Tom Barry, adjutant and OC flying column respectively of the Third Cork Brigade, were lodged at O'Neill's house at Shanaway on the first day of 1921. Now in the company of Paddy O'Brien of Girlough and four comrades of his, the house was raided by two lorryloads of Auxiliaries from K Company based in Dunmanway. Barry, wishing to stand and fight, was dissuaded by the others, and they escaped before the Auxiliaries searched the house. The same group had earlier opened fire on and wounded an old man.

PATRICK O'BRIEN BMH WS 812, 19

What is believed to be the first official reprisals by Crown forces took place in Midleton on this date. McCarthy's, Carey's and O'Shea's shops were destroyed by mines set by British soldiers, and Midleton Garage and Engineering Works was destroyed by a fire started by the Black and Tans.

JOHN KELLEHER BMH WS 1456, 23

2 January 1921

Volunteers Daniel and Paddy Daly of Rathcormac Company were captured at their farm by the British Army and brought to Fermoy barracks, Paddy being interned shortly after at Ballykinlar in Co Down. Daniel was used as a human shield by the Crown forces, being tied to the front of their lorries as they went on patrol.

DANIEL DALY BMH WS 743, 8

A meeting of the Third Cork Brigade took place at Pat Hurley's of Granure, its intention to remobilise the brigade flying column, which had been demobbed before Christmas.

PATRICK O'BRIEN BMH WS 812, 21

Daniel Canty, OC Newcestown Company and six comrades were lodged in a house in the Newcestown area when it was surrounded by a British patrol. Volunteers Tom Lynch and Dan Walsh were arrested, while Canty and four comrades got away.

DANIEL CANTY BMH WS 1619, 22

Volunteers from Clogagh, Kilbrittain, Ballinadee, Barryroe, Timoleague and Ballinspittle Companies (all part of Bandon Battalion) were represented at Kilbrittain on this date when an attempt was made to capture the RIC barracks. Starting out from Ryan's of Clonbuig, they were in command of Seán Hales, OC Bandon Battalion (one witness says Tom Barry, OC flying column). Volunteer Peter Monaghan, a Scotsman who had deserted from the Cameron Highlanders Regiment based in Cobh, assembled a mine which was placed against the door. It failed to explode, and the IRA withdrew when they realised their efforts were futile.

CON FLYNN BMH WS 1621, 15; DANIEL DONOVAN BMH WS 1608, 9; DENIS COLLINS BMH WS 827, 7; CORNELIUS O'SULLIVAN BMH WS 1740, 13; RICHARD RUSSEL BMH WS 1591, 15; DANIEL HOLLAND BMH WS 1341, 7

Michael Leahy, vice OC First Cork Brigade, was summoned to Dublin on this date. Travelling on a false passport, he was sent to Genoa via France and Switzerland, there to meet with Dónal Hayes and arrange a shipment of arms to Ireland. No definite orders came from Ireland, and after several months in Italy and missing his contribution to the war effort at home, he finally returned just a few weeks before the Truce.

MICHAEL LEAHY BMH WS 555, 1

3 January 1920

A party of Auxiliaries from C Company based at Macroom Castle raided a house in the Ballingeary area. Volunteer Jeremiah Casey of A Company, Eighth Battalion, aged seventeen, was shot dead when he fled the house.[111]

PATRICK J LYNCH BMH WS 1543, 11

4 January 1921

The flying column of Newmarket Battalion attacked a convoy of two lorries carrying British troops on the Newmarket to Meelin road. The first lorry got away, leaving the second to

---

[111] Keane, p167.

come under a heavy attack. The IRA withdrew when enemy reinforcements arrived. The Crown forces retaliated by burning several properties in and near the village of Meelin, an action that received much publicity due to the presence of Countess Markievitz and a photographer. The Sinn Féin party saw the propaganda value of this publicity.

DANIEL BROWNE BMH WS 785, 1; TIMOTHY J CRONIN BMH WS 1134, 4; JOHN JONES BMH WS 759, 7; THOMAS ROCHE BMH WS 1222, 12; DENIS MULLANE BMH WS 789, 17

A patrol of Black and Tans left Union Quay barracks in Cork at six o'clock in the evening in the direction of Parnell Bridge, with the intention of moving off in several directions to patrol the city. Lewis machine gun fire was directed at them from Moore's Hotel by Michael Murphy, OC First Cork Brigade ASU, and several comrades; revolver fire and grenades were also used. The IRA were convinced that heavy casualties were inflicted: 'there must have been at least ten killed and as many wounded'. Two, in fact, died as a result of the attack:

Constable Francis Shortall

Constable Thomas Johnston (died of his wounds on 21 January 1921)[112]

PATRICK COLLINS BMH WS 1709, 9; MICHAEL MURPHY BMH WS 1547, 34; MICHAEL WALSH BMH WS 1521, 12; P J MURPHY BMH WS 869, 23; SEÁN O'CONNELL BMH WS 1706, 9

---

[112] Keane, p167; Abbott, p180.

5 January 1921

Brother Finbarr D'Arcy was arrested during a raid on the Imperial Hotel in Cork by the Hampshire Regiment. He was reported as having been shot while trying to escape, a common occurrence for anyone arrested by Crown forces.[113]

EOIN 'POPE' O'MAHONY BMH WS 1401, 4; ROBERT C AHERN BMH WS 1676, 13

Information that the Essex Regiment in Bandon knew the whereabouts of arms dumps in the Raheen area spurred Frank Neville, QM Knockavilla Company to build a new one elsewhere. The guns were removed just before the Essex raided.

FRANK NEVILLE BMH WS 443, 9

6 January 1921

At Jordan's Bridge, south of Mourneabbey on the Cork to Mallow road, members of the flying column of Mallow Battalion opened fire on a patrol of three lorries bearing British military. It appears that several of the attacked were wounded.

CORNELIUS O'REGAN BMH WS 1200, 9

Jeremiah Deasy, Second lieutenant Innishannon Company, Bandon Battalion was arrested outside Ballinadee church. He was eventually released from Ballykinlar camp, Co Down in December 1921.

JEREMIAH DEASY BMH WS 1738, 18

---

[113] Keane, p168.

John MacSweeney, a youth of fifteen, was shot in the back and killed when he attempted to run away from a British military patrol at Allenstown, Kanturk.[114]

JOHN JONES BMH WS 759, 7; DANIEL BROWNE BMH WS 785, 2; THOMAS ROCHE BMH WS 1222, 12

7 January 1921

The home in Cobh of Kevin Murphy, an officer in Na Fianna, was raided by the Cameron Highlanders. He was beaten and tortured. Transferred to Victoria barracks in Cork, he was used as a hostage by the Black and Tans as they drove through the streets of the city.

KEVIN MURPHY BMH WS 1629, 8

8 January 1921

The following volunteers were arrested in a joint British Army/RIC roundup: Denis O'Sullivan, C Connolly, M Hallissey, Jeremiah Fitzgerald. They were interned in Ballykinlar camp until December 1921.

JAMES O'MAHONY/DENIS CROWLEY/JOHN FITZGERALD BMH WS 560, 17

---

[114] Keane, p169.

11 January 1921

Glanworth was the venue for a meeting of brigades from Cork, Waterford, Tipperary and east Limerick, one of the main items for discussion being the import and distribution of arms from Italy.

FLORENCE O'DONOGHUE BMH WS 554, 3

12 January 1921

The flying column of the Third Cork Brigade remobilised at Kilmeen on the 12 January 1921; they rested that night in Bealad, then in Ballinard for two nights.

PATRICK O'BRIEN BMH WS 812, 21

14 January 1921

Liam Lynch, OC Second Cork Brigade, held a council meeting of Fermoy Battalion at Dooley's of Ballyard; several appointments, principally that of Tom Griffin, Ballynoe, as OC, were made.

WILLIAM BUCKLEY BMH WS 1009, 14

15 January 1921

Another attempt to capture the RIC barracks at Kilbrittain was made on this date. As with the attack of a fortnight previous, a mine was placed against the barbed wire surrounding the building; once again, it failed to explode. After an exchange of shots, the IRA withdrew. They were in the command of Liam Deasy, Third Cork Brigade adjutant.

DAN DONOVAN BMH WS 1608, 9; CON FLYNN BMH WS 1621, 16; DENIS COLLINS BMH WS 827, 9

Tom Griffin, OC Fermoy Battalion, was arrested in a roundup at Ballynoe. Volunteer David Kent was arrested at Boultha, as were three other volunteers.

WILLIAM BUCKLEY BMH WS 1009, 14

Gerald Pring, an unarmed civilian, was shot dead in an unprovoked attack by an RIC motor convoy while walking with some family members at the Western Road in Cork.[115]

16 January 1921

Members of Fermoy Battalion took positions to attack a Black and Tan patrol at Rathcormac. The appearance of an armoured car and two lorries full of British military at the last moment, however, changed their minds.

WILLIAM BUCKLEY BMH WS 1009, 13

Volunteer Patrick Donovan of Timoleague Company was shot dead by members of the Essex Regiment on this date. The British soldiers, who had come out from Bandon, attempted a round-up firstly at Barryroe. John Hayes, Second lieutenant Barryroe Company, was captured, and Volunteers James O'Hea and John Coleman, though wounded, managed to escape. Some volunteers were pursued for a distance of six miles before giving the enemy the slip.[116]

MICHAEL COLEMAN BMH WS 1254, 9; JOHN O'DRISCOLL BMH WS 1250, 20; CHARLES O'DONOGHUE BMH WS 1607, 9

---

[115] Keane, p169.
[116] Keane, p170.

17 January 1921

Denis Lordan, QM Third Cork Brigade flying column, writes that a brigade staff meeting took place in Kilbrittain at this time. 'To counteract the actions of the Pro British RC Clergy...it was decided to punish any member of the IRA, who refused duty because of pronouncements made by the local clergy.' The local Catholic clergy had been quite vociferous in their condemnation of IRA activities.

DENIS LORDAN BMH WS 470, 12

Daniel McCarthy, first lieutenant Lombardstown Company, Mallow Battalion, Second Cork Brigade, was arrested by Black and Tans on this date. He was given a sentence of twelve months for possession of seditious literature, but was released after the signing of the Treaty.

DANIEL McCARTHY BMH WS 1239, 8

Maliff and Ryan, two city-based RIC detectives noted for their brutal treatment of IRA men during interrogation, were traced to an inter-provincial rugby match at the Mardyke in Cork, then to Washington Street where they were shot in the head. Although badly wounded, they survived.

MICHAEL MURPHY BMH WS 1547, 35

19 January 1921

Volunteer Denis Hegarty was employed by John Good of Barryshall, Timoleague, and lived in a house in Good's farmyard.

He was found shot dead at the entrance to the farm on this date. It is not known who killed him.[117]

CHARLES O'DONOGHUE BMH WS 1607, 9; JOHN O'DRISCOLL BMH WS 1250, 20, 36

20 January 1921

A trap was laid for a suspected spy named Dan Lucey. He was tried by Sinn Fein court and executed by the IRA in the Millstreet Battalion area.[118]

EDWARD NEVILLE BMH WS 1665, 4; MATTHEW KELLEHER BMH WS 1319, 7

Shinanagh, on the main Buttevant-Charleville road, was the scene of an ambush on a party of the Machine Gun Corps by Newmarket Battalion IRA. The accidental discharge of a shot by an IRA man destroyed the element of surprise. The Crown forces stopped to give battle, while one account (Maurice Noonan, adjutant Milford Company) says that they fled through the fields immediately. Colonel Hope, OC Ballyvonare camp, was injured in this attack.

MICHAEL GEARY/RICHARD SMITH BMH WS 754, 18; MAURICE NOONAN BMH WS 1098, 7; SEÁN MOYLAN BMH WS 838, 164; THOMAS CULHANE BMH WS 831, 6

The flying column of Bandon Battalion, under its OC Seán Hales, were remobilised at Quarries Cross on this date; six volunteers from Newcestown Company were present, according to Captain

---

[117] Keane, p170.
[118] Keane, p170.

William Desmond, OC Newcestown Company. Each of the six had a rifle, fifty rounds of ammunition, a revolver and a grenade.

WILLIAM DESMOND BMH WS 832, 27

Tom Barry, OC the flying column of the Third Cork Brigade, and other officers came across 'a suspicious character' by the roadside at Mawbeg, between Bandon and Enniskeane. Believing the men with trenchcoats and bandoliers were of the Crown forces, the man soon let it be known that he was collecting information on the IRA, unaware that he was in fact speaking to the IRA. He was taken prisoner, tried and executed the following morning. He was Denis O'Dwyer of Castletown Kenneigh, an ex-British soldier. His body was left at Farnalough cross roads as a trap to induce the British military, but it was not removed until after the column had left.[119]

WILLIAM DESMOND BMH WS 832, 28; JAMES MURPHY BMH WS 1684, 9; MICHAEL RIORDAN BMH WS 1638, 19; DANIEL CANTY BMH WS 1619, 23; DENIS LORDAN BMH WS 470, 13; WILLIAM FOLEY BMH WS 1560, 7; JACK HENNESSY BMH WS 1234, 9; CHARLES O'DONOGHUE BMH WS 1607, 6; DENIS COLLINS BMH WS 827, 9

21 January 1921

Newcestown Company adjutant and a volunteer from the company were captured by British forces in the Quarries Cross area, as were four volunteers from Quarries Cross Company: Dave Keane, Bill Harte, Pat Hayes and John Murphy.

---

[119] Keane, p171.

DANIEL CANTY BMH WS 1619, 22; WILLIAM DESMOND BMH WS 832, 28; MAURICE DONOVAN BMH WS 1736, 5

Sergeant Henry Bloxham and Head Constable Larkin of the RIC cycled from their barracks at Ballincollig to Waterfall, where they were ambushed, Sergeant Bloxham (a Mayo man) was killed and Larkin wounded, although he managed to escape. Their attackers' names are given as Leo Murphy (OC Third Battalion, First Cork Brigade), and Volunteers J Murray, Dan Donovan and Jerry O'Shea.[120]

TIM HERLIHY AND OTHERS BMH WS 810, 12 & 33; MICHAEL O'REGAN BMH WS 1524, 6

Dunmahon, Glanworth was the scene of the remobilisation of the Mitchelstown Battalion flying column.

SÉAMUS O'MAHONY BMH WS 730, 11

22 January 1921

Patrick Rea, an ex-British soldier from Passage West, went missing on this date. Bearing in mind that his family was awarded £2,000 by the British government in compensation for his disappearance, it seems probable that he was killed by the IRA.[121]

23 January 1921

As happened on 20 January with Denis O'Dwyer, a spy was convinced by the clothing and arms carried by a detachment of

---

[120] Keane, p171; Abbott, p187.
[121] Keane, p172.

the Third Cork Brigade flying column that they were of the Crown forces. He 'unbosomed himself to them and gave all the information of rebels and rebel houses in the district'. He was Thomas J Bradfield of Carhue, and he was tried and executed that night.[122]

ANNA HURLEY O'MAHONEY BMH WS 540, 4; DANIEL CANTY BMH WS 1619, 23; WILLIAM DESMOND BMH WS 832, 28; DENIS LORDAN BMH WS 470, 14; CHARLES O'DONOGHUE BMH WS 1607, 6; JAMES MURPHY BMH WS 1684, 12

23 January 1921

Richard Morey, a boy aged ten, was shot dead when Crown forces fired into a crowd at the Shandon Street area.[123] It was 8pm on a Sunday evening, and the previous day had seen British military curfew hours extended from 5pm to 3am on Saturdays and Sundays.

24 January 1921

Barry's flying column took up positions at the start of the Dunmanway road in Bandon. In the early hours of the morning they opened fire on the Essex Regiment barracks, and this fire was swiftly returned. It resulted in the death of Volunteer Daniel O'Reilly of Kilbrittain Company.[124]

---

[122] Keane, p173.
[123] Keane, p172.
[124] Keane, p174.

DANIEL CANTY BMH WS 1619, 24; DENIS O'BRIEN BMH WS 1353, 8; PATRICK O'BRIEN BMH WS 812, 23

A section of the Third Cork Brigade flying column, under the command of Seán Hales, OC Bandon Battalion, was billeted at Knocknacurra on the night Bandon was attacked by the rest of the column. The following night they crossed the Bandon river by boat from Collier's Quay, where they were joined by the rest of their comrades, all moving off to be billeted at Rearour.

DENIS COLLINS BMH WS 827, 10

Frank Neville, OC Knockavilla Company, was sent with several other volunteers to raid for explosives at Castlemore castle, Crookstown. None was found.

FRANK NEVILLE BMH WS 443, 10

25 January 1921

Captain Mark Wickham, OC B Company, First Battalion of the First Cork Brigade, was arrested on this date; he was detained at Victoria barracks before he was interned at Spike Island.

MARK WICKHAM AND OTHERS BMH WS 558, 4

26 January 1921

The approach roads to Innishannon were blocked prior to an attack on the local RIC barracks. Members of the Third Cork Brigade flying column placed a mine against the front door of the steel-shuttered two-storey building, which was surrounded by barbed wire. As happened many times during the War of Independence, the IRA bomb failed to go off. Firing was returned from the upstairs windows. The element of surprise gone, the IRA withdrew.

TIMOTHY WARREN BMH WS 1275, 10; DENIS COLLINS BMH WS 827, 11; RICHARD RUSSELL BMH WS 1591, 16

27 January 1921

Michael Mullane, OC Inniscarra Company, Donoughmore Battalion, First Cork Brigade, received instructions from Jack O'Leary, battalion OC, to have twenty men ready at Peake. It was the eve of the Dripsey ambush, and Captain Mullane's duties included the digging of trenches and preparing of trees to act as roadblocks.

MICHAEL MULLANE BMH WS 1689, 8; JOHN MANNING BMH WS 1720, 21

28 January 1921

Members of Donoughmore Battalion flying column, in the command of its OC John O'Leary, took up positions along a 150-yard stretch of road from dawn near Dripsey on the 28 January 1921. Expecting a convoy of British military to pass in the morning, they waited until well into the afternoon, when a seventy-strong detachment from the Manchester Regiment based at Ballincollig took them by surprise, opening fire from the fields north of the IRA positions. The volunteers, seeking to escape encirclement, fought a rearguard action, most of them making a rendevous at Coachford before seeking a billet at Rylane. Five prisoners taken by the British – Volunteers Tadhg McCarthy, Patrick Mahoney, John Lyons, Dan O'Callaghan and Thomas O'Brien – were tried and executed the following month at Victoria barracks in Cork; Donoughmore Battalion QM James Barrett subsequently died of his wounds, while Volunteer Denis Murphy, who was seriously wounded, was tried after the Truce and sentenced to penal servitude. Volunteer Denis Dwyer, later a lieutenant in Grenagh Company, says that the scouts, who had been on duty for almost twenty hours, became careless and sought food in local houses, leaving no-one to observe the advance of the British troops.

DENIS DWYER BMH WS 713, 5; DANIEL McCARTHY BMH WS 1457, 6; JOHN MANNING BMH WS 1721, 21; DAN McCARTHY BMH WS 1697, 13

Seán Moylan, OC Newmarket Battalion flying column, was the officer in charge of an IRA attack on a Black and Tan patrol at Tureengarriffe, about a mile west of Ballydesmond (then known as Kingwilliamstown). This well-planned attack saw riflemen taking positions north and south of the roadway, together with a group of volunteers operating a Hotchkiss light machine gun. Shortly after midday two touring cars, bearing seven men, drove into the firing zone; they were forced to stop at a newly-dug trench. Called upon to surrender, they opened fire at the enemy, eventually surrendering when one of their number was killed outright, and their Divisional Commissioner Holmes wounded seriously. Most of the Crown forces sustained wounds, and these were dressed on the roadside by the volunteers, who sustained no injuries. The more seriously wounded were taken to Ballydesmond by a commandeered car. The fatalities were as follows:

RIC Divisional Commissioner Philip Armstrong Holmes, who died of his wounds the following day

Constable Thomas Moyles[125]

TIMOTHY J CRONIN BMH WS 1134, 6; DANIEL GUINEY BMH WS 1347, 8; JAMES CASHMAN BMH WS 1270, 7; DANIEL FLYNN BMH WS 1240, 8; SEÁN MOYLAN BMH WS 838, 167

29 January 1921

A party of British military arrived at Kingwilliamstown (now Ballydesmond) from Tralee. Seeking revenge for the deaths of RIC Divisional Commissioner Holmes and Constable Moyles (see Tureengarriffe ambush, 28 January), they burned the post office, a drapery shop and a grocery shop.

TIMOTHY J CRONIN BMH WS 1134, 7; DANIEL GUINEY BMH WS 1347, 11

30 January 1921

Patrick O'Driscoll, OC Myross Company and vice OC Skibbereen Battalion, gives an account of preparations made in his company area for the landing of arms from Italy. Ardra, Squince and Carrigillihy strands, all adjacent to Rabbit Island, were chosen as the landing-places. As detailed elsewhere in this book (see witness statement of Michael Leahy, 2 January 1921), the plan was never executed.

PATRICK O'DRISCOLL BMH WS 557, 1

---

[125] Keane, p174; Abbott, p189.

January 1921 (no date available)

All companies throughout the Mallow Battalion area received orders from headquarters to trench roads and destroy bridges, thus making communications as difficult as possible for Crown forces.

RICHARD WILLIS/JOHN BOLSTER BMH WS 808, 10

Daniel Lynch, accused of passing information to the Crown forces regarding the Brinny ambush, was shot as a spy.[126]

WILLIAM NORRIS BMH WS 595, 4; TADHG O'SULLIVAN BMH WS 792, 5; JOHN O'DRISCOLL BMH WS 1250, 21; WILLIAM MCCARTHY BMH WS 1255, 1; SEÁN MURPHY BMH WS 1445, 10

A consignment of eighteen rifles were transferred from Cork to Macroom in preparation for the establishment of a flying column in the Macroom Battalion area. A total of twenty-eight men were mobilised in Liscarrigane. Dances and sing-songs in the local farmhouses were an important social feature of the men's spare time.

CHARLES BROWNE BMH WS 873, 32; WILLIAM POWELL BMH WS 1699, 14

A planned attack on Rathcormac RIC barracks in mid-January did not materialise due to the arrival of a convoy of British military. About a fortnight later, members of Fermoy Battalion

---

[126] Keane, p368.

sniped the building for over an hour in a futile attempt to draw out the garrison from Fermoy.

WILLIAM BUCKLEY BMH WS 1009, 13 & 15

A brief encounter between the flying column of Newmarket Battalion and British military took place near Meelin. The IRA broke off when more British military personnel were sent to the scene.

JAMES CASHMAN BMH WS 1270, 7; DANIEL GUINEY BMH WS 1347, 8

Charlie Cotter, OC Schull Company, was given custody of Robert Lenihan, a suspected spy. Having been moved to several locations in the Schull area, Lenihan eventually escaped, returning with a convoy of nineteen British Army lorries three weeks later, though according to Cotter no IRA men were captured.

CHARLIE COTTER BMH WS 1519, 7

Sergeants Slack and Toohey, members of the Machine Gun Corps, had 'made themselves rather notorious' while stationed at Charleville. Michael Geary, OC Charleville Company, and others in the company attempted their capture near the town, but they only managed to secure Sergeant Slack.

MICHAEL GEARY/RICHARD SMITH BMH WS 754, 19

Members of Charleville Battalion, Second Cork Brigade, fired on Buttevant military barracks, the fusillade lasting for fifteen minutes.

MICHAEL GEARY/RICHARD SMITH BMH WS 754, 19; THOMAS CULHANE BMH WS 831, 6

John Fanning, OC Fermoy Company, and Moss Twomey, adjutant Fermoy Battalion, were captured by British military engaged in a roundup at Clondulane. They were taken to Fermoy military barracks and released after the signing of the Treaty.

JOHN FANNING BMH WS 990, 17; JAMES HACKETT BMH WS 1080, 3

An IRA bomb-making foundry was set up in a secluded ravine in the Knockraha area by members of the Fourth Battalion, First Cork Brigade. The foundry operated day and night from January until the end of March 1921.

SÉAMUS FITZGERALD BMH WS 1737, 32

Several members of the Donoughmore Battalion, including its ex-OC, Patrick P Twomey, were arrested in the Grenagh area.

THOMAS J GOLDEN BMH WS 1680, 17

Ballycrovane and Eyeries Companies were represented in the twenty-five men who took up ambush positions at Faunkil, east of Eyeries, at the end of January 1921. Despite their waiting all night, the enemy failed to show.

JAMES McCARTHY BMH WS 1567, 17

A flying column billeted in the Doneraile area assembled each morning before dawn and lay await until darkness in the Kilbrack area for a week in January 1921, 'but the enemy forces were not obliging'.

SÉAMUS O'MAHONY BMH WS 730, 12

The flying column of Mallow Battalion was formed in January 1921, Jack Cunningham its OC. Its first training camp was at Laharn, where musketry, scouting and other skills were taught.

TADHG McCARTHY BMH WS 965, 9; JOHN MOLONEY BMH WS 1036, 8; JOHN O'SULLIVAN BMH WS 1376, 8; DANIEL McCARTHY BMH WS 8

Donoughmore Battalion, First Cork Brigade, formed a flying column in early January 1921. Over the course of a month, sixty men were given basic training at Sweeney's house at Monatagart, although a lack of ammunition was a constant problem. Denis Dwyer, a lieutenant in Grenagh Company and an ex-British Army soldier, was in charge of training.

JOHN MANNING BMH WS 1720, 20; DAN McCARTHY BMH WS 1697, 13 CORNELIUS HORGAN BMH WS 1461, 4

A flying column of the First Cork Brigade was formed in early January, Seán Hegarty, OC First Cork Brigade, in command. Training was held in Ullanes in the Ballyvourney Company area; over a dozen Cork city volunteers, all of them on the run, took part.

DANIEL HARRINGTON BMH WS 1532, 12

Members of Midleton Company, about a dozen in all, opened fire on Midleton RIC barracks at night-time. According to Lieutenant Michael Kearney, 'it was more in the way of a nuisance attack, to keep the garrison...jittery'. A heavy fire was returned, but no casualties were inflicted on either side.

MICHAEL KEARNEY BMH WS 1418, 21

Con Meany, OC Seventh Battalion, Second Cork Brigade, gives a list of over a dozen bridges destroyed by the IRA to impede the progress of Crown troop movements.

CON MEANY BMH WS 787, 14

Early January 1921 saw the formation of a flying column in the Donoughmore Battalion area; its OC was Jackie O'Leary.

MICHAEL MULLANE BMH WS 1689, 7

Jeremiah McCarthy, OC Schull Company, was arrested by an NCO in the British Marines. Following this incident, a failed plan was made to shoot the arresting officer at Byrne's public house at Crookhaven.

SEÁN O'DRISCOLL BMH WS 1518, 13

A failed attempt was made to capture Passage West RIC barracks.

HENRY O'MAHONY BMH WS 1506, 5

The Second Cork Brigade held a training camp at Nadd in the Kanturk Battalion area, the object being to train a flying column OC for each battalion in north Cork.

WILLIAM C REGAN BMH WS 1069, 6

A raid was carried out on the Ford's factory in Cork; pig-iron, scrap iron and moulding sand were taken to an IRA bomb-making factory in Knockraha.

MICHAEL WALSH BMH WS 1521, 14

The end of January 1921 saw the flying column of Mallow Battalion take up positions at Mourneabbey in the unrealised expectation of meeting an enemy patrol.

JOHN O'SULLIVAN BMH WS 1376, 9

Castletownroche Battalion flying column moved into Castletownroche to attack Crown posts in late January of 1921, but the element of surprise was given away by the accidental discharge of a shotgun. The IRA's lack of familiarity with the handling of fire arms is evident from such incidents.

WILLIAM C REGAN BMH WS 1069, 8

The Ninth Battalion of the First Cork Brigade were instructed by Seán Hegarty, brigade OC, to place a levy for arms on all 'well-to-do' people in the battalion area. It yielded £200.

EDWARD SISK BMH WS 1505, 4

Kanturk Battalion formed a flying column in late January of 1921, with Denis Murphy as its OC.

JOHN WINTERS BMH WS 948, 4

February 1921

1 February 1921

Captain Cornelius Murphy, OC Rathduane Company, Seventh Battalion, of Ballydaly, Millstreet, was arrested and found to be in possession of a firearm on 4 January 1921. He was sentenced to death. A Sinn Féin member of Millstreet Rural District Council, he was executed by firing squad in Victoria barracks in Cork, the first of such executions under martial law.[127]

DANIEL BROWNE BMH WS 785, 2

Dan O'Driscoll, OC Drimoleague Company, Bantry Battalion, relates that a group drawn from the battalion took positions behind a wall at the main street at Drimoleague, close to the RIC barracks. There they lay in wait for four RIC men to leave Beamish's public house. Shortly after, fire was opened on the four men, with Constable Patrick O'Connor being killed and Constable Griffin wounded. The IRA retired to a billet in the Castledonovan area. Parties of British military from Bantry and Auxiliaries from Dunmanway converged on the village, with O'Driscoll describing a 'show-down' between the two forces.[128] There were, inevitably, examples of tension between the 'new' police and their more disciplined counterparts in the British Army.

DANIEL O'DRISCOLL BMH WS 1352, 9; TED O'SULLIVAN BMH WS 1478, 30

---

[127] Keane, p175.
[128] Kingston, p131; Keane, p175; Abbott, p191.

Mick Bowler, Fermoy Company OC, was arrested on this date, his replacement was Jack Herlihy. Herlihy, in turn, was arrested within a week, and was replaced by James Hackett who became OC Fermoy Company.

JAMES HACKETT BMH WS 1080, 4

The IRA called to the house of Thomas Bradfield, a cousin of Thomas J Bradfield (see 23 January 1921). He was under suspicion of supplying information to the Essex Regiment. Bradfield was tricked into believing that the men before him, led by Tom Barry, were of the Crown forces. He willingly gave information that ultimately led to his capture,, trial and execution.[129]

JAMES 'SPUD' MURPHY BMH WS 1684, 12; DENIS LORDAN BMH WS 470, 14; DENIS CROWLEY AND OTHERS BMH WS 560; MICHAEL J CROWLEY BMH WS 1603

Tom Barry's flying column occupied Burgatia House, a mile from Rosscarbery, charging its owner Thomas Kingston with supplying information to the Crown forces. He was ordered to leave the country. The following morning the postman, who had seen the column members about the house, was questioned by the IRA; he swore not to disclose the flying column's presence for twenty-four hours. However, in the afternoon armed Black and Tans were seen advancing on the house, and a gun battle ensued. Section Leader James 'Spud' Murphy and a party of eight men was ordered by Barry to outflank the Crown forces; they were successful in this, firing at the Black and Tans' rear and thus

---

[129] Keane, p176.

allowing the main guard to exit the house, taking Volunteer Bob Brennan, who was wounded, with them. Murphy's section withdrew to Reenascreena, the rest of the flying column to Kilbree. Burgatia House was later burned.

MICHAEL COLEMAN BMH WS 1254, 11; JAMES MURPHY BMH WS 1684, 13; DENIS COLLINS BMH WS 827, 11; JACK HENNESSY BMH WS 1234, 10; DENIS LORDAN BMH WS 470, 16; WILLIAM McCARTHY BMH WS 1255, 3; TIMOTHY WARREN BMH WS 1275, 11; DENIS KEOHANE BMH WS 1255, 3

Mallow battalion flying column under its OC, Jack Cunningham, opened fire at Mallow railway station on a group of Black and Tans, inadvertently killing Alice King, wife of the local RIC inspector. In the following minutes, three railway workers were shot dead by the RIC, and another died of wounds sustained by being thrown down the steps of the signal box. Those who died were:

Mrs Alice King

Volunteer Denis Bennett, Mourneabbey Company

Patrick Devitt

Daniel Mullane

Joseph Greensmyth[130]

JEREMIAH DALY BMH WS 1015, 5; JOHN BOLSTER/ RICHARD WILLIS BMH WS 808, 11; LEO CALLAGHAN BMH

---

[130] Keane, p55.

978, 13; JOHN MOLONEY BMH WS 1036, 8; JOSEPH MORGAN BMH WS 1097, 11

2 February 1921

Members of Fermoy Battalion took up positions at Keam, Glenville, in anticipation of a British convoy passing by. It failed to show.

WILLIAM BUCKLEY BMH WS 1009, 15

3 February 1921

Ballinhassig Company, in command of its OC Michael Walsh, ambushed a patrol of Black and Tans near the village of Ballinhassig. Two policemen were killed and one wounded, with the remainder of the patrol managing to flee the scene. Raids and indiscriminate shooting by Crown forces from several parts of the county was the inevitable response to this ambush. The casualties were:

Constable Edward Carter

Constable William Taylor[131]

EDWARD SISK BMH WS 1505, 4

4 February 1921

Volunteer Bob Brennan, who had been wounded in the leg at Burgatia House on the night of 1 February, was in hiding in the Drinagh area. He was transferred by horse and side-car to the Kilcrohane Company district on the 4 February.

---

[131] Keane, p177; Abbott, p198.

DANIEL O'DRISCOLL BMH WS 1352, 10

Captain Mary O'Neill (later Walsh), an officer in Cumann na mBan, gives an account of a raid by the Essex Regiment at Clogagh, near Timoleague. Two O'Neill sisters placed themselves in the firing line to prevent the Essex, led by Major Percival, from shooting at retreating volunteers. The body of Lieutenant Patrick Crowley was found some distance away. He was buried at Clogagh; Charlie Hurley, OC Third Cork Brigade, spoke at his graveside.[132]

MARY WALSH BMH WS 556, 5; MICHAEL J CROWLEY BMH WS 1603, 21; JAMES O'MAHONY AND OTHERS BMH WS 560; DENIS COLLINS BMH WS 827, 14; CHARLES O'DONOGHUE BMH WS 1607, 9

James 'Spud' Murphy, a section leader in Barry's flying column, and Jim Hurley, OC Clonakilty Battalion, sought to execute the postman who had given information to Crown forces regarding IRA deployment at Burgatia House on 2 February. They discovered that he had fled to England.

JAMES MURPHY BMH WS 1684, 15

Denny Mullane, OC Freemount/Tullylease Company, Newmarket Battalion, managed to escape a British military raid during mass at Freemount. Two RIC men, McDermott and Reilly, acted as 'spotters'.

DENNY MULLANE BMH WS 789, 18

---

[132] Keane, p178.

5 February 1921

Alfred Kidney, who had been shot by the IRA at Youghal on 3 February 1921, died in the workhouse hospital. He had been under suspicion of giving information to the police.[133]

6 February 1921

Conway's house, Island, Burnfort, was the location of a Mallow Battalion council meeting. Plans were made to ambush a convoy of British army lorries on the 8 February, a plan that never went ahead.

TIMOTHY (TADHG) LOONEY BMH WS 1196, 9

Dunmanway Battalion council held a meeting at O'Donoghue's of Ballinavard on the 6 February 1921.

HENRY O'MAHONY BMH WS 1506, 5

The home of Paddy O'Brien of Girlough, an officer in Dunmanway Battalion, Third Cork Brigade, was burned to the ground by K Company Auxiliary Division of the RIC; his father, aged sixty-five, was dragged from his bed and shot in the face, losing an eye. Farm animals, fowl and farm equipment were stolen.

PATRICK O'BRIEN BMH WS 812, 27

Daniel Maloney, a farmer in his seventies, was shot dead by the Essex Regiment while they were conducting raids in Barryroe. He was from Lislevane, Courtmacsherry.[134]

---

[133] Keane, p179.
[134] Keane, p179.

DENIS COLLINS BMH WS 827, 14; MICHAEL J CROWLEY BMH WS 1603, 15

Volunteer Michael John Kelleher, aged seventeen, was killed when the British Army opened fire on a group of hurlers; two other boys were injured. The incident took place at Knocknagree.[135]

SEÁN MOYLAN BMH WS 838, 186.

7 February 1921

Volunteers Denis Collins and David Manning were arrested in a round up by Major Percival's Essex Regiment; Manning was threatened with execution by Percival when he refused to give information. The two men were brought to Charles Fort in Kinsale, where a sergeant in the Essex treated them kindly. Volunteer Collins gives a fascinating account of life as a prisoner in Victoria barracks in Cork, to where they were removed.

DENIS COLLINS BMH WS 827, 15

Frank Neville, an officer in Knockavilla Company, travelled from his home to Kilcoe with a cartful of rifles, ammunition and other material. It was in Kilcoe that Barry's flying column were billeted. Shortly afterwards, Neville was hospitalised with rheumatic fever.

FRANK NEVILLE BMH WS 443, 11

---

[135] Keane, p179.

Clondrohid Company, Macroom Battalion, First Cork Brigade IRA demolished Clondrohid bridge. 'We claim it was the first bridge in Ireland to be broken by the IRA.'

TIM BUCKLEY BMH WS 1641, 14

Patrick O'Sullivan, a civilian aged aged seventeen, was shot by two men in civilian clothes, probably policemen, at Scott Lane, off Patrick's Quay. Peter Shea, a civilian from the Cork suburb of Blackpool, was seriously wounded.[136]

8 February 1921

Henry O'Mahony, OC Passage West Company, was arrested by the Cameron Highlanders at Monkstown. He was interned at Spike Island, from where he escaped in November of 1921.

HENRY O'MAHONY BMH WS 1506, 5

A section of Barry's flying column marched from Reenascreena to Kilcoe, leaving at eight in the evening. As they slept that night, Vice OC Skibbereen Battalion Patrick O'Driscoll of Mohanna Company, Third Cork Brigade, was accidentally shot dead. Thinking it unsafe to stay, Barry's men marched a further eight miles before resting in broad daylight. That night Barry's flying column made its attack on Skibbereen.[137]

PATRICK O'SULLIVAN BMH WS 1481, 8; FRANK NEVILLE BMH WS 443, 11; DENIS LORDAN BMH WS 470, 17; WILLIAM

---

[136] Keane, p180.
[137] Keane, p181.

NORRIS BMH WS 595, 7; TIMOTHY WARREN BMH WS 1275, 12; DENIS COLLINS BMH WS 827, 13

About the 8 February Mallow Battalion flying column, in command of its OC Jack Cunningham, gathered at Gleanndine, Ahadillane; they moved on to Gleannavigue in the Mourneabbey area, staying at the houses of Sullivan and Connell for a number of days.

LEO CALLAGHAN BMH WS 978, 14; JOSEPH P MORGAN BMH WS 1097, 12

William Johnston, a Protestant who intended to join the RIC, was shot and killed at Kilbrittain by the IRA.[138]

9 February 1921

According to Jack Hennessy, an officer in Ballineen Company, the King's Liverpool Regimemt and about eighty Black and Tans were stationed in Skibbereen. About a dozen men of the Third Cork Brigade flying column with their commander, Tom Barry, entered the town and proceeded to fire on the barracks, but the Crown forces were not inclined to return fire. The greater portion of the column were situated east of the town, on the approach from Clonakilty.

JACK HENNESSY BMH WS 1234, 11; JAMES MURPHY BMH WS 1684, 15; JAMES DOYLE BMH WS 1640, 14

According to William Barry, OC D Company, Second Battalion of the First Cork Brigade, an organisation drawn from members of the Freemasons and from the Young Men's Christian

---

[138] Keane, p181.

Assosiation devoted to supplying the Crown forces with information on IRA activity had been formed in Cork city. He wrote that their paymaster was Reilly, manager of Thompson's bakery. Barry received instructions to have him killed. Reilly's body was left by the gate of his house in Rochestown with the words 'Spies and Informers Beware' attached to it.[139]

WILLIAM BARRY BMH WS 1708, 7; MICHAEL MURPHY BMH WS 1547, 36

10 February 1921

Some soldiers of the King's Liverpool Regiment were captured the night Barry's flying column entered Skibbereen. They were treated well by the Irish soldiers, being given much alcohol; 'they returned to Skibbereen next day in "singing" form'. This incident might serve to show how different regiments of the British Army were viewed by the IRA. Tom Barry's view of the Essex Regiment would be in stark contrast to the event described here.

JAMES MURPHY BMH WS 1684, 16

A meeting of Bantry Battalion council held at Colomane wood saw the unannounced arrival of Liam Deasy, Brigade adjutant, and Tom Barry, OC Third Cork Brigade flying column. Barry asked for a detailed description of Drimoleague RIC barracks, as well as a member of Cumann na mBan to drive him in a horse and trap to reconnoitre the village. The barracks was attacked the following night.

---

[139] Keane, p181.

DENIS KEOHANE BMH WS 1426, 10; DAN O'DRISCOLL BMH WS 1354, 10

11 February 1921

Two nights after the flying column of the Third Cork Brigade entered Skibbereen, they travelled to Drimoleague. A mine placed at the RIC barracks exploded, but failed to breach the wall. After a short period of firing the column withdrew, billeting in Castledonovan that night.

WILLIAN MCCARTHY BMH WS 1255, 5; JACK HENNESSY BMH WS 1234, 11; JAMES MURPHY BMH WS 1684, 16; DENIS KEOHANE BMH WS 1426, 10

Black and Tans from Macroom fired wildly and indiscriminately at Clondrohid, shooting dead Daniel O'Mahony, a boy of fifteen, for not providing information on the destruction of Clondrohid bridge the previous day; elderly people were seized and brought to Macroom Castle for interrogation.[140]

TIM BUCKLEY BMH WS 1641, 14; CHARLES BROWNE BMH WS 873, 33

A site near Glebe Bridge, close to Rathcoole Railway station on the Mallow to Killarney line, was selected by members of Millstreet flying column for an attack on Crown forces. The train driver was forced at gunpoint to stop the train at a pre-arranged spot; fire was opened on the train by the IRA and returned by the Royal Fusiliers, and after twenty minutes they surrendered. Sergeant Frederick Boxold died at the scene and

---

[140] Keane, p183.

Private John Holyome died two days later of his wounds, and other injuries were sustained by the Fusiliers. More than a dozen rifles and hundreds of rounds of ammunition were captured.[141]

DAN COAKLEY BMH WS 1406, 5; MATTHEW KELLEHER BMH WS 1319, 7; JOHN O'KEEFFE BMH WS 1291, 2; CORNELIUS HEALY BMH WS 1416, 13; CON MEANY BMH WS 787, 14; SÉAMUS HICKEY BMH WS 1218, 8; WILLIAM REARDEN BMH WS 1185, 7; GEORGE POWER BMH WS 451, 16

12 February 1921

Members of Charleville Battalion flying column made an attack on Churchtown RIC barracks, during which a policeman was killed. He was Constable Patrick J Walsh, aged twenty-four, and he came from Rosmuc in Co Galway. He had been in the RIC for four years.[142]

THOMAS CULHANE BMH WS 831, 7; MICHAEL GEARY/ RICHARD SMITH BMH WS 754, 20.

Robert Eady of Clonakilty was accused by the local IRA of supplying the RIC with information, he having been seen several times entering Clonakilty barracks. He was abducted from his home and shot dead.[143]

TED HAYES BMH WS 1575, 8

---

[141] Keane, p182.
[142] Keane, p183; Abbott, p198.
[143] Keane, p184.

13 February 1921

Tim Buckley, OC Clondrohid Company, was the officer in charge of an abortive ambush on the approach to Macroom, the intended target being Macroom Auxiliaries. Four other volunteers were present: David Burke, Mick Murphy, Murt Kelleher, Denis O'Shea.

TIM BUCKLEY BMH WS 1641, 14

14 February 1921

Kelleher's of Crowhill was the destination of eight rifles stored in the Newcestown Company area. John O'Callaghan, an officer in the company, was in charge of their delivery.

DANIEL CANTY BMH WS 1619, 26

John O'Leary, a civilian employee in Victoria barracks in Cork, was 'known to be bringing information' to Captain Kelly, intelligence officer in the barracks. O'Leary was shot in Nicholas Street; he died in the North Infirmary the following day.[144]

MICHAEL MURPHY BMH WS 1547, 36

William O'Sullivan, an employee of Cork Corporation, was observed leaving the RIC headquarters at Empress Place after curfew. Despite being warned, he continued giving information. He was eventually located at a public house in Sullivan's Quay, taken to the Curragh Road, and shot dead by members of the Second Battalion, First Cork Brigade.[145]

---

[144] Keane, p186.
[145] Keane, p185.

JEROME COUGHLAN BMH WS 1568, 9; ROBERT AHERN BMH WS 1676, 8; LM NEVILLE BMH WS 1639, 8; MICHAEL MURPHY BMH WS 1547, 37; WILLIAM BARRY BMH WS 1708, 7

Volunteers James and Timothy Coffey were executed in Breaghna, Desertserges, Enniskeane by persons unknown. It is thought that an 'Anti-Sinn Féin' organisation, organised by local loyalists, was in existence in the area at the time, and a note found on the bodies alludes to this; it read, 'Convicted Vide Bradfield – Anti Sinn Fein – of murder'. It is probable their deaths were in revenge for the killing of Thomas Bradfield a fortnight earlier (see 1 February).[146]

DENIS COLLINS BMH WS 827, 14

15 February 1921

Leary's Rock near Mourneabbey, in the Mallow Battalion area, was the scene of a planned ambush against a convoy of British military, in which it was expected that General Cumming, OC Buttevant military barracks, was travelling. While laying in wait, the IRA saw enemy troops in extended order coming in their direction, and fire was opened on the Burnfort Company from its rear. Knowing that this was an encirclement, the Mallow Battalion flying column OC Jack Cunningham withdrew his troops under heavy rifle and machine gun fire. They suffered no injuries and marched to Laharn Cross, where they were billeted in five different homes. The Burnfort company, however, had been almost surrounded by the enemy, and three volunteers were

---

[146] Keane, p186.

shot dead, with another dying later of his injuries. Volunteers Patrick Ronayne and Thomas Mulcahy were captured and subsequently executed in Cork. A member of Kanturk Company, Shiels – an ex-British soldier – was suspected of informing the British military. Much effort was made to track him, but to no avail. Those who died were:

Volunteer Patrick Flynn

Volunteer Patrick Dorgan

Volunteer Éamon Creedon

Volunteer Michael Looney (subsequently died of his wounds)[147]

TIMOTHY SEXTON BMH WS 1565, 6; LEO CALLAGHAN BMH WS 978, 14; JOSEPH MORGAN BMH WS 1097, 12; RICHARD WILLIS/JOHN BOLSTER BMH WS 808, 12; JEROME BUCKLEY BMH WS 1063, 9; JEREMIAH DALY BMH WS 1015, 6; JOHN O'SULLIVAN BMH WS 1376, 9; JOHN RONAYNE BMH WS 1269, 7; TADHG McCARTHY BMH WS 965, 9; JACK LOONEY BMH WS 1169, 8; TIMOTHY LOONEY BMH WS 1196, 9; JOHN MOLONEY BMH WS 1036, 9

Ten volunteers from Knockavilla Company, along with officers from staff of the Third Cork Brigade, lay in wait at Upton train station for what they believed would be a small detachment of British military. The IRA commenced firing, eliciting a quick response from the Crown forces; Volunteers Seán Phelan and Batt Falvey were killed almost immediately. Charlie Hurley, OC Third Cork Brigade, now with a bad head wound, sounded

---

[147] Keane, p187.

the whistle to retreat, and but for the covering fire of Commandant Tom Kelleher both he and the other IRA men might not have got away. Volunteer Dan O'Mahony was wounded in the hip and died some years later of his injuries. Ten civilians, between passengers and railway workers, were killed at the station. Volunteer John Hartnett, shot through the lung, recovered. Volunteer Pat O'Sullivan was shot in the stomach and despite being admitted to a hospital in Cork, he subsequently died. Brigadier Charlie Hurley recovered of his wounds but was shot dead in a British raid on the morning of the battle of Crossbarry, 19 March 1921. Those who died at, or as a result of the Upton ambush are as follows:

Richard Arthur

James Byrne

William Donoghue

William Finn

Mary Hall

Seán Hegarty

William Penrose Johnston

Thomas Perrott

John Sisk

John Spiers

Volunteer Section Commander Batt Falvey

Lieutenant Patrick O'Sullivan

Lieutenant Seán Phelan[148]

FRANK NEVILLE BMH WS 443, 11; PATRICK CRONIN BMH WS 710, 2; MICHAEL RIORDAN BMH WS 1638, 21; CHARLES O'DONOGHUE BMH WS 1607, 10

The house of Michael O'Keeffe in Bweeing was the location of a meeting of officers of the three Cork Brigades. An idea was discussed whereby men would be selected to conduct assassinations of politicians at the British House of Commons. Those at the meeting came to the conclusion that the Cork Volunteers had enough to do at home.

MICHAEL O'CONNELL BMH WS 1428, 12

A bridge and a section of road on the way from Kilbrittain to Bandon was demolished with a view to stopping enemy supply lorries reaching Kilbrittain RIC barracks.

JAMES O'MAHONY AND OTHERS BMH WS 560, 18

16 February 1921

Charles Beale of College Road, Cork city, described as 'a YMCA [Young Men's Christian Association] senior secret service agent', was shot dead as a spy; his body was found near the African Missions church in Wilton. He is buried in Douglas.[149]

MICHAEL MURPHY BMH WS 1547, 37; JEREMIAH KEATING BMH WS 1657, 8; PATRICK COLLINS BMH WS 1707, 8

---

[148] Keane, 188.
[149] Keane, p59.

Two privates in the British Army based at Buttevant barracks and posing as deserters were captured by the IRA on the Freemount-Kanturk road. They were subsequently released.

DENNY MULLANE BMH WS 789, 18

Captain Mary O'Neill, OC Kilbrittain Squad of Cumann na mBan, writes that four volunteers from the Kilbrittain Company were surprised by a patrol of the Essex Regiment and shot while trenching a road at Crois na Leanbh. The bodies were waked at the house of a Mr M Crowley, and Major Percival, OC Essex Regiment in Bandon, called during the following day 'but took no action'. They were buried temporarily, receiving a permanent burial after the Truce in Kilbrittain church yard. Lieutenant Denis Collins is convinced that the position of the Kilbrittain men was relayed to the British by a named officer of the Ballinspittle Company, whom Collins named as John Madden The four volunteers of Kilbrittain Company, Bandon Battalion, Third Cork Brigade who lost their lives were:

Volunteer Timothy Connolly

Volunteer Jeremiah O'Neill

Volunteer Cornelius McCarthy

Volunteer John McGrath[150]

MARY WALSH BMH WS 556, 5; DENIS COLLINS BMH WS 827, 27; JAMES O'MAHONY AND OTHERS BMH WS 560, 18; RICHARD RUSSELL BMH WS 1591, 18; MICHAEL J CROWLEY BMH WS 1603, 14; CHARLES O'DONOGHUE BMH WS 1607, 9

---

[150] Keane, p189.

First Lieutenant Michael Riordan of Kilpatrick Company, Bandon Battalion, managed to get the services of Dr O'Sullivan of Cloughduv to tend the head wound of Charlie Hurley, OC Third Cork Brigade. Hurley had been wounded at Upton railway station the day before, being brought to Tim Sullivan's house in Cloughduv by Riordan and Commandant Tom Kelleher in a horse and trap, with Volunteers Jeremiah Donovan of Quarries Cross and Charlie Kenny of Kilpatrick scouting the way.

MICHAEL RIORDAN BMH WS 1638, 21

17 February 1921

Lieutenant Denis Collins of Ballinspittle Company was transferred with several others from custody in Charles Fort in Kinsale to Victoria barracks in Cork. It was at this time that the trial of the IRA men captured at Dripsey commenced.

DENIS COLLINS BMH WS 827, 18

18 February 1921

Two members of C Company Macroom Auxiliaries were believed to have been wounded at the town hall in Macroom when volunteers from Macroom A and A Companies attacked the building with grenade and gunfire.

DANIEL McSWEENEY BMH WS 1651, 8; CHARLES BROWNE BMH WS 873, 38

Michael Walsh, suspected on information captured in the mails of being a spy, was taken from the Cork Union Workhouse – now St Finbarr's Hospital – and shot dead.[151]

EDWARD HORGAN BMH WS 1644, 10; MICHAEL MURPHY BMH WS 1547, 37; PJ MURPHY BMH WS 869, 9; SEÁN HEALY BMH WS 1643, 22

19 February 1921

A large section of Fermoy Battalion flying column moved into Tallow in Co Waterford to engage the Black and Tans, moving on to Kilcronat and Payfield when they failed to show.

WILLIAM BUCKLEY BMH WS 1009, 18

Two Protestants from Mohana near Skibbereen, William Connell and Mathew Sweetman, were approached by the IRA who demanded a levy from them. They refused, identifying the IRA men to a military tribunal. They were both shot by members of Lisheen Company on 19 February 1921. Three houses were burned by Crown forces in reprisal.[152]

PATRICK O'SULLIVAN BMH WS 1481, 8; WILLIAM CROWLEY BMH WS 1502, 9

George Tilson, from Blackrock in Cork, was found close to death on a train near London. He had travelled from Cork, convinced that the IRA were determined to kill him for

---

[151] Keane, p189.
[152] Keane, p190.

informing on them. He had cut his own throat, and he died that afternoon.[153]

20 February 1921

Finbarr O'Sullivan, who lived in the D Company, Second Battalion area of Cork's southside, was suspected of spying on the IRA. He was an ex-British soldier. He is described variously as a tailor, as being unemployed, and as a member of the Black and Tans. He was shot dead by revolver fire on the banks of the Douglas river.[154]

ROBERT AHERN BMH WS 1676, 8; WILLIAM BARRY BMH WS 1708, 8; LM NEVILLE BMH WS 1638, 8; JEROME COUGHLAN BMH WS 1568, 10; MICHAEL MURPHY BMH WS 1547, 37.

The Cork city IRA reported one Mullaly killed as a spy. This was surely William Mohally, upon whose life an unsuccessful attempt was made. While he was recovering in hospital, IRA men entered the ward, ordered staff to carry him out on a stretcher, and shot him dead.[155]

MICHAEL MURPHY BMH WS 1547, 37

The greatest losses the IRA incurred in Co Cork during the Irish War of Independence happened on 20 February 1921, when twelve members of the East Cork flying column were shot dead in a combined attack by the Hampshire Regiment and the Black and Tans; two volunteers were subsequently executed at Cork.

---

[153] Keane, p60.
[154] Keane, p191.
[155] Keane, p191.

According to one witness, the men had been billeted at an empty thatched cottage for five weeks. On the day in question, their OC Diarmuid Hurley left on a reconnaissance trip to Cobh Junction, leaving Captain John P O'Connell in charge. Around three o' clock in the afternoon, two volunteers left the house to get water; firing by the Crown forces commenced. A sortie was attempted by the volunteers, in which three were killed, O'Connell managing to escape. The remaining volunteers fought on until ammunition became scarce, and with the roof now aflame their senior officer, Patrick J Higgins, surrendered. The survivors were lined up, and according to the statement of Higgins and that of Diarmuid O'Leary, seven were shot dead by the Black and Tans before a British Army officer intervened. Higgins himself had a revolver 'put to my mouth and fired. I felt as if I was falling through a bottomless pit. Then I thought I heard a voice saying, "This fellow is not dead, we will finish him off". Only for the military officer coming along, I, too, would be gone'. Several of the Crown forces claimed that the IRA had continued firing from within the house after some of their comrades had exited the house with their hands up (see appendix after witness statement of Patrick J Higgins). Two Cobh Company men, Volunteer Paddy O'Sullivan and Volunteer Maurice Moore, were executed at Victoria barracks, Cork, on 28 April 1921. Captain Diarmuid O'Leary, OC Killeagh Company, was aquitted. Patrick J Higgins was freed under the terms of the Truce. The British suffered no casualties at Clonmult. One witness mentions Volunteers Harty, Terry, Walsh and Garde as having been released by the British, possibly because of their age and not being members of the East Cork flying column. Those who died at Clonmult were:

Volunteer Michael Hallahan

Volunteer Richard Hegarty

Captain James Aherne, OC A Company, Fourth Battalion

Volunteer David Desmond

Volunteer Michael Desmond

Volunteer Christopher O'Sullivan

Volunteer Dónal Dennehy

Volunteer Joseph Morrissey

Volunteer John-Joe Joyce

Volunteer Liam Aherne

Volunteer James Galvin

Volunteer Jeremiah Aherne[156]

PATRICK J HIGGINS BMH WS 1467, 3; JOHN P O'CONNELL BMH WS 1444, 7; DIARMUID O'LEARY BMH WS 1589, 5; PATRICK J WHELAN BMH WS 1449, 49; MICHAEL KEARNEY BMH WS 1418, 21; JOHN KELLEHER BMH WS 1456, 23; DANIEL CASHMAN BMH WS 1523, 9.

20 February 1921

Mrs Mary Lindsay, 'a British loyalist who was alleged to have informed the British of the preparations for the Dripsey ambush', and her chauffer James Clarke were kidnapped by the IRA and held in various houses in the Donoughmore and

---

[156] Keane, 62, 192.

Rylane areas (see 28 January 1921; 28 February 1921). Their abduction was thought to be an insurance against the five IRA captured at Dripsey being hanged. But the death penalty was applied to them, and James Clarke and Mary Lindsey were executed soon after.[157]

JOHN MANNING BMH WS 1720, 24

21 February 1921

Members of Fermoy Battalion, Second Cork Brigade, gathered for an attack on the RIC barracks at Castletownroche, but the accidental discharge of a shot by an IRA man necessitated its calling-off.

DAVID O'CALLAGHAN BMH WS 950, 10

22 February 1921

Volunteer Michael Noonan of Freemount Company, Newmarket Battalion, was arrested on this day, and was released in December 1921.

DENNY MULLANE BMH WS 789, 30

Intelligence was received that Colonel Hope of Buttevant barracks was about to join the Duhallow Hunt on this date. His groom spotted members of Newmarket Battalion near a fox-covert; he made contact with Hope, warning him to stay away.

DENNY MULLANE BMH WS 789, 19

---

[157] Keane, p65.

Walshestownmore, between Midleton and Clonmult, was the location of a planned attack by Fermoy Battalion flying column and Midleton Battalion. No enemy showed.

WILLIAM BUCKLEY BMH WS 1009, 18

22 February 1921

Constable Joseph Prendergast, stationed at Union Quay RIC barracks, was checking his rifle when an accidental shot was loosed, mortally wounding George Fletcher, a messenger boy aged seventeen. Fletcher lived at Kyle Street.[158]

23 February 1921

D McDonald, known as 'Monkey Mac', was well known as a 'spotter' for the RIC and military. He was eventually shot in the Evergreen area of the southside of the city by volunteers from D Company, Second Battalion. The IRA learned subsequently that he had only been wounded. He emigrated to England after the Truce.

ROBERT AHERN BMH WS 1676, 8; WILLIAM BARRY BMH WS 1708, 7; JEROME COUGHLAN BMH WS 1568, 10; LM NEVILLE BMH WS 1638, 8; MICHAEL MURPHY BMH WS 1547, 37

Members of the Third Cork Brigade flying column, in command of Tom Barry, column OC, entered the town of Bandon after curfew; they split up into three groups, one of which hoped to engage a curfew patrol at the bridge. Fire was opened on a group of Black and Tans at North Main Street, Tom Barry pursuing one

---

[158] Keane, p192.

of them into a nearby house where he shot him dead. Another group under John Lordan arrested two soldiers of the Essex Regiment, both of whom were shot dead, and one naval radio operator, who was released.

The fatalities that night in Bandon were:

Private James Knight, Essex Regiment

Lance Corporal Herbert Stubbs, Essex Regiment

Constable Frederick Perrier[159]

JACK HENNESSY BMH WS 1234, 12; JAMES MURPHY BMH WS 1633, 16; JAMES DOYLE BMH WS 1640, 16; WILLIAM McCARTHY BMH WS 1255, 7; CON FLYNN BMH WS 1621, 19; DANIEL CANTY BMH WS 1619, 25; SEÁN MURPHY BMH WS 1445, 12; MICHAEL J MURPHY BMH WS 1603, 15

25 February 1921

Volunteers from the Seventh and Eighth Battalions, First Cork Brigade, engaged the Crown forces at Coolavookig. In a four-hour battle, the Macroom-based Auxiliaries were pinned down, seeking refuge in two roadside cottages, their OC, Major Seafield Grant, sustained mortal injuries. The IRA scouts reported that reinforcements were seen leaving Macroom, and altogether several hundred Crown forces were dispatched from the surrounding towns. The Irish, under the command of Seán O'Hegarty, OC First Cork Brigade, disengaged, many heading in a north-westerly direction, where a second battle took place at Coomnaclohy, where the British were beaten off. Following

---

[159] Kingston, p73; Keane, p192; Abbott, p202.

the battle, many of the Irish believed they had inflicted heavy casualties on the British, but only three are recorded:

Major James Seafield Grant, MC

Constable William Cane

Auxiliary Cadet Clevel L Soady (died of wounds on 1 March 1921)[160]

SEÁN LUCEY BMH WS 1579, 9; JAMES MURPHY BMH WS 1633, 11; EDWARD NEVILLE BMH WS 1665, 5; DANIEL HARRINGTON BMH WS 1532, 12; TIM BUCKLEY BMH WS 1641, 16; DANIEL McSWEENEY BMH WS 1651, 9; WILLIAM POWELL BMH WS 1699, 14; PATRICK J LYNCH BMH WS 1543, 16; MICHAEL O'SULLIVAN BMH WS 793, 12; PATRICK O'SULLIVAN BMH WS 794, 15; CHARLES BROWNE BMH WS 873, 33; DAN CORKERY BMH WS 1719, 16

27 February 1921

Cornelius O'Sullivan, OC Innishannon Company, was arrested by a party of Essex soldiers at the home of Richard Russell, a fellow officer. He afterwards went on hunger strike on Spike Island, being transferred to Maryborough (Portlaoise) prison. He was released in December 1921.

CORNELIUS O'SULLIVAN BMH WS 1740, 16; RICHARD RUSSELL BMH WS 1591, 18

Alfred Cotter of Ballineen, who despite warnings from the IRA continued to supply the Essex Regiment with bread from his

---

[160] Keane, p194; Abbott, p203.

bakery, was accused of spying for the Crown forces. He was executed on orders of the Third Cork Brigade on 27 February 1921.[161]

JACK HENNESSY BMH WS 1234, 12; TIMOTHY WARREN BMH WS 1275, 1

28 February 1921

The flying column of Macroom Battalion occupied a disused house at Laharn, Rusheen, where the following week was spent training.

CHARLES BROWNE BMH WS 873, 39

According to Seán Healy, OC A Company, First Battalion, First Cork Brigade, six IRA prisoners were executed in Victoria barracks in Cork. Five had taken part in the failed Dripsey ambush; the sixth was a volunteer from Tipperary. That day, a general order to shoot all personnel of the Crown forces, armed or unarmed, was issued by the IRA, two being killed by A Company in Hayes' Lane near the barracks, with four more fatalities happening in other parts of the city, as well as five injuries.

The list of fatalities that day reads:

Captain Seán Allen, OC A Company, Fourth Battalion, Third Tipperary Brigade

Volunteer Daniel O'Callaghan

Volunteer Thomas O'Brien

---

[161] Keane, p194.

Volunteer John Lyons

Volunteer Timothy McCarthy

Volunteer Patrick O'Mahony

Private Alfred Whitear

Private George Bowden

Private Thomas Wise

Private William Gill

Lance Corporal John Beattie

Lance Corporal Leonard Hodnett[162]

SEÁN HEALY BMH WS 1479, 60; DENIS COLLINS BMH WS 827, 18; MICHAEL J CROWLEY BMH WS 1603, 17; JAMES HACKETT BMH WS 1080, 5; STEPHEN FOLEY BMH WS 1669, 9

Clashgarrive, near Macroom, was the scene of an intended ambush by members of the local battalion on the district inspector of police, Macroom, who was expected to pass by. Instead, a convoy of five lorries made their way past.

CHARLES BROWNE BMH WS 873, 39

Volunteer Charles Daly, G Company, Second Battalion, was taken from the main railway station in Cork, his place of work, by Auxiliaries from nearby Empress Place. His body was found at the entrance to the railway tunnel; he had been shot.[163]

---

[162] Keane, p195.
[163] Keane, p196.

PATRICK CROWE BMH WS 775, 4; SEÁN HEALY BMH WS, 15

Volunteer Michael John O'Mahony of B Company, Ninth Battalion, aged eighteen, died at his home in Railway Street, Passage West. He worked in the local dockyard and passed off a leg injury he had sustained as being work-related. He had, in fact, been injured during a gunfight with British military.[164]

---

[164] Keane, p 195.

February 1921 (no date available)

Fermoy Battalion volunteers under its OC Con Leddy took up positions at Glenville to await an enemy patrol. The IRA, aware of a spotter plane overhead, withdrew when a volunteer accidentally discharged his shotgun.

WILLIAM BUCKLEY BMH WS 1009, 16

A large-scale roundup by Crown forces at Barryroe resulted in the arrest of several volunteers. It was the second such sweep in several weeks, the first leading to the death of Volunteer Patrick Donovan on the 16 January. Following the latest raid, the Third Cork Brigade ordered the widespread trenching of roads and destruction of bridges.

MICHAEL COLEMAN BMH WS 1254, 10

Patrick O'Leary, OC Knockavilla Company, and five others were arrested at this time by Crown forces. Several of them, including O'Leary, were not recognised and were released after a few weeks.

FRANK NEVILLE BMH WS 443, 13

Three members of Mallow flying column waited in vain for the arrival of the OC of Mallow military barracks at the house of K B Williams, Navigation Road.

JACK MOLONEY BMH WS 1036, 12

Mallow and Kanturk flying columns went on a joint course of training, their headquarters being Paddy McCarthy's house in Nadd. Foot drill, care and use of arms, outpost duty and scouting were taught.

JACK MOLONEY BMH WS 1036, 12

A large roundup operation by British military was in operation in the Lombardstown area, making it difficult for the volunteers to deliver arms to Liam Lynch, OC Second Cork Brigade.

JACK O'CONNELL BMH WS 1211, 8

A man dressed in civilian clothing was seen loitering near the IRA prisoner compound at Victoria barracks in Cork. According to Volunteer Denis Collins of Ballinspittle Company and the Third Cork Brigade flying column, he was Jimmy Donovan from Ballinspittle, and Collins says he was shot dead as a spy in 1922.

DENIS COLLINS BMH WS 827, 21

Seán O'Driscoll, OC Schull Battalion and a member of the Third Cork Brigade flying column, along with Tom Barry column OC and Seán Lehane, fired at an RIC man as he entered the door of Rosscarbery barracks. It is believed that two policemen were injured in the incident.

SEÁN O'DRISCOLL BMH WS 1518, 13

A Black and Tan stationed at Ballyporeen frequently came to Mitchelstown. He was fired on by two members of Mitchelstown Company. He survived, however, and was often brought to the local barracks to identify new IRA prisoners.

LEO SKINNER BMH WS 940, 4

A consignment of 'Belfast boycotted goods' arrived at Charleville railway station, where they were seized by the local company and destroyed. Seed potatoes and machinery were among the items taken.

MICHAEL GEARY/RICHARD SMITH BMH WS 754, 21

Glounalougha, on the Newmarket-Ballydesmond road, was the scene where the Kiskeam and Kingwilliamstown (Ballydesmond) Volunteers waited in vain for an expected convoy.

DANIEL GUINEY BMH WS 1347, 12

Grave reservations were expressed by Millstreet Battalion flying column regarding one of their their members, an ex-British soldier named Shiels, whom they suspected of being a spy.

CORNELIUS HEALY BMH WS 1416, 14

Members of Innishannon Company, Bandon Battalion opened fire on an RIC patrol at Innishannon bridge. The patrol returned safely to barracks, although one policeman was wounded.

RICHARD RUSSELL BMH WS 1591, 17; CORNELIUS O'SULLIVAN BMH WS 1740, 14

A trap mine, consisting of two unpinned Mills bombs, in a timber box, was placed by British Army personnel under the command of Major Percival at the Crooked Bridge, between Skibbereen and Ballydehob. Volunteers from Skehanore Company, on discovering the trap, replaced the pins with makeshift ones and posted the grenades to Percival, enclosing a note of thanks.

EDWARD O'SULLIVAN BMH WS 1501, 5

In early February 1921, Castletownroche flying column assembled at Scargannon, on the Doneraile to Kildorrery road. Two military policemen were fired on in an attempt to draw out a patrol from Ballyvonare army camp. Finally two lorries, one armoured, arrived. Firing commenced, several grenades proved useless, and the lorries got through. Machine guns were then fired in the IRA's direction, with no effect. The IRA claimed four British injuries. It was shortly after this that Thomas Barry, the battalion OC, was arrested, and was replaced by William C Regan.

WILLIAM C REGAN BMH WS 1069, 9; GEORGE POWER BMH WS 451, 17

March 1921

1 March 1921

Jim Hurley, Clonakilty Battalion OC, and two others opened fire at a party of Black and Tans at about 9 pm on the 28 February in Rosscarbery. Constable Alfred Brock, aged thirty-one and from London, was shot in the stomach. Constable Brock, who had been in the RIC for seven months, died of his wounds on the 1 March 1921.[165]

JAMES 'SPUD' MURPHY BMH WS 1684, 18

Members of D Company, Second Battalion of the First Cork Brigade claimed to have killed the driver of Sir Peter Strickland on the Douglas Road in Cork city. This may be Private Albert (or Alfred) Whitear of the Hampshire Regiment, who died on the 28 February or 1 March 1921.[166]

WILLIAM BARRY BMH WS 1708, 10; JEROME COUGHLAN BMH WS 1568, 11

An attack was made on a group of Black and Tans as they left Cork prison on College Road. The Tans retreated indoors, firing as they went. First lieutenant Edward Horgan of H Company, First Battalion says that a policeman died of his wounds in this incident, though no record can be found to show this. Volunteer Augustine O'Shea of H Company was wounded, though not seriously.

---

[165] Kingston, p97; Keane, p197; Abbott, p204.
[166] Keane, p195.

EDWARD HORGAN BMH WS 1644, 11

Kiskeam and Kingwilliamstown Companies were situated at Meenagorman awaiting an enemy patrol. Word came through that hostages had been taken on board the patrol at Newmarket, a development that was to feature in the last months of the War of Independence. The IRA retired.

JAMES CASHMAN BMH WS 1270, 10

A patrol of RIC was fired on by the local IRA battalion at Charleville, with no casualties recorded. That night a patrol of Black and Tans fired shots through the front door of the house of Seán O'Brien, chairman of the local UDC and president of the Gaelic League branch; he was killed instantly.[167]

MICHAEL GEARY/RICHARD SMITH BMH WS 754, 21; PATRICK O'BRIEN BMH WS 764, 36; MICHAEL SHEEHY BMH WS 989, 7

Lieutenant Hammond, an intelligence officer based at Victoria barracks, was in hot pursuit of a group of IRA men in Cork city centre. They hid in a house in Caroline Street. Hammond fired through a window, killing Daniel Casey, a civilian aged thirty.[168]

Thomas Cotter of Curraclough, near Kilmurry, was shot dead by the IRA outside his home, a note saying 'Convicted Spy, IRA' pinned to his clothing. He had been involved for many years in a land dispute with a next-door neighbour. Cotter, a

---

[167] Keane, p198.
[168] Keane, p 199.

member of the Church of Ireland, had been boycotted several times.[169]

WILLIAM DESMOND BMH WS 832, 36

2 March 1921

Members from Charleville Battalion flying column and a flying column from Kerry under Tom McEllistrim lay in ambush at the Bower, west of Rathmore. Members of the American Relief Committee, together with some journalists, passed by on their way to Killarney. Fearing that their position was compromised, the IRA retired, choosing Clonbanin Cross as an ambush site instead.

JOHN JONES BMH WS 759, 9; DENNY MULLANE BMH WS 789, 20; PATRICK O'BRIEN BMH WS 764, 36

Denis O'Brien, a civilian aged seventy, was shot dead by a British Army patrol in Castle Street, Cork. It was during curfew time.[170]

3 March 1921

Members of the Second Cork Brigade fired at a Black and Tan patrol at Mocollop, on the Fermoy to Ballyduff road. One policeman was killed and several wounded. The IRA were aware of an aeroplane tracking their movements as they made their way towards the Kilworth mountains, where they sought cover in a wood. The RIC man killed was Constable Joseph

---

[169] Keane, p199.
[170] Keane, p 200.

Duddy, from Armagh, who had been in the force for three months.[171]

RICHARD WILLIS/JOHN BOLSTER BMH WS 808, 28; WILLIAM BUCKLEY BMH WS 1009, 18

Volunteers Daniel and Michael Daly of Rathcormac Company, Fermoy Battalion, Second Cork Brigade were arrested at their home on the 2 January 1921. Michael was interned at Ballykinlar. Daniel was sent to Fermoy military barracks, being used as a hostage on lorry patrols in the locality. He was charged with 'the murder of Gunner Cambridge at Deerpark on 10th December, 1920'. On the 3 March he made an attempt, along with his cellmate Volunteer Paddy Condon, to escape, dislodging an iron bar in his cell and going out over the perimeter wall. Assuming Volunteer Condon had not escaped, he made for open country, and after a while he got to Araglen, where to his surprise he was reunited with his cellmate. Unbeknownst to Volunteer Daly, General Strickland, GOC British Army Munster, had ordered a 'Drumhead Courtmartial' for the day after his escape.

DANIEL DALY BMH WS 743, 9

4 March 1921

Lieutenant James McCarthy of Eyeries Company, Castletownbere Battalion was arrested during a British military roundup at Furious Pier. He was imprisoned at Bere Island, Spike Island and finally Maryborough (Portlaoise), being released after the Treaty was signed.

---

[171] Abbott, p205.

JAMES McCARTHY BMH WS 1567, 20

Bridget Noble of Ardgroom in the Beara peninsula was accused by the IRA of giving information to the RIC. She disappeared on this date; no body was found.[172]

5 March 1921

Captain Jeremiah O'Mahony, OC Coppeen Company, was killed by an accidental shot fired by a fellow volunteer. Folllowing his death, Volunteer Philip Chambers was made OC. Canon O'Connell of Enniskeane administered the last rites. Captain O'Mahony was buried temporarily on his own farm, then to his final resting place beside the three volunteers shot at Kilmichael.[173]

PHILIP CHAMBERS BMH WS 738, 6

Clonbanin Cross, on the Killarney to Mallow road, was the location of a gun battle between the IRA and the East Lancashire Regiment. Under orders from Seán Moylan, Newmarket Battalion flying column and Charleville Battalion Column (under Commandant Paddy O'Brien) were deployed north of the road; Second Kerry Brigade column (Tom McEllistrim) and Millstreet Battalion column (Con J Meany) were on the southern side. Shortly after 10 am a convoy of three lorries, a touring car and an armoured car came from the west. Land mines laid by the IRA failed to explode, a common occurrence. Fire was commenced, the driver of the touring car crashing his vehicle. Brigadier

---

[172] Keane, p200.
[173] Keane, p201.

General Cummings was killed almost immediately by gunfire. The armoured car played a central role in keeping the British casualties down, spraying the IRA positions for almost two hours. Eventually, probably due to lack of ammunition, the IRA retired. The British losses at Clonbanin were:

Brigadier General Hanway Cumming

Lieutenant Harold Maligny

Private Harold Turner

Private William Walker[174]

WILLIAM REARDEN BMH WS 1185, 9; JAMES CASHMAN BMH WS 1270, 11; DAN COAKLEY BMH WS 1406, 8; JOHN JONES BMH WS 759, 8; SÉAMUS HICKEY BMH WS 1218, 11; MATT MURPHY BMH WS 1375, 12; JOHN O'KEEFFE BMH WS 1291, 4; MICHAEL O'CONNELL BMH WS 1428, 15; GEORGE POWER BMH WS 451, 17; THOMAS ROCHE BMH WS 1222, 15; CORNELIUS BARRETT BMH WS 1405, 6; CORNELIUS HEALY BMH WS 1416, 16; DANIEL BROWNE BMH WS 785, 9; CON MEANY BMH WS 787, 16; HUMPHREY O'DONOGHUE BMH WS 1351, 8; THOMAS CULHANE BMH WS 831, 9; PATRICK O'BRIEN BMH WS 764, 37; JAMES J RIORDAN BMH WS 1172, 10; JAMES CASHMAN BMH WS 1270, 12

6 March 1921

Volunteer Cornelius Foley of J Company, Macroom Batallion was wounded in a raid by C Company Auxiliary Division RIC at Toames. He was taken to the Auxiliary headquarters at

---

[174] Keane, p201.

Macroom Castle, where he died. His body was taken to Macroom workhouse, after which it was claimed by the family. About twenty arrests were made that day.[175]

CHARLES BROWNE BMH WS 873, 40; MOLLIE CUNNINGHAM BMH WS 1681, 4; DANIEL McSWEENEY BMH WS 1651, 11; NORA CUNNINGHAM BMH WS 1690, 4; DANIEL CORKERY BMH WS 1719, 19

8 March 1921

Members of Kanturk Battalion flying column opened fire on an RIC patrol at Fr Murphy's Bridge, Shronbeha, Banteer. Constable Nicholas Somers, from Wexford, was killed, and Constable McCarthy wounded. Several revolvers and rifles were captured.[176]

 DENIS MULCHINOCK AND OTHERS BMH WS 744, 13; JEREMIAH DALY BMH WS 1015, 9; JAMES O'CONNELL BMH WS 949, 8; JOHN MOLONEY BMH WS 1036, 12; JOSEPH P MORGAN BMH WS 1097, 14; JOHN WINTERS BMH WS 948, 5

A raid on the mails at Millstreet railway station was made on this day, Con Meany, OC Millstreet Battalion, in command. No useful information was obtained.

CORNELIUS HEALY BMH WS 1416, 17

---

[175] Keane, p 202.
[176] Keane, p 203; Abbott, p 206.

9 March 1921

The house of Cornelius Connolly, OC Skibbereen Battalion and a member of the Third Cork Brigade flying column, was burned down on this date by a force of Black and Tans and Auxiliaries.

CORNELIUS CONNOLLY BMH WS 602, 2

10 March 1921

Jeremiah Daly, an officer in Mallow Battalion, along with men from Kanturk flying column, burned down Dromagh Castle.

JEREMIAH DALY BMH WS 1015, 9

John Good of Timoleague, described as a spy, was shot dead by the IRA. His cattle were taken and distributed to volunteers in Kilbrittain and Barryroe.[177]

JOHN O'DRISCOLL BMH WS 1250, 8

The house of David Herlihy at Nadd, known as 'The Barracks', was the scene of a raid by British military on 10 March 1921. The house was an unofficial headquarters for members of the Second Cork Brigade. The British gained entry silently and arrested several volunteers within. A British firing party was assembled at the gable end of the house and the IRA men lined up. Volunteer Tim Kiely, playing for time, asked the officer in charge some delaying questions. Two survivors claim that the Irish soldiers were given a chance to make a dash for safety, quoting the officer: 'When I say run – run'. Volunteers Morgan and Moloney got away, though both were wounded. Volunteers

---

[177] Keane, p204.

Tim Kiely, Ned Waters and David Herlihy were shot dead at the scene, and Volunteer Edward Twomey was killed earlier that day at nearby Lacka Bridge. A Boherbue native, William Shiels, a member of Kanturk Battalion flying column and an ex-British soldier, was suspected of supplying the information that led to the shootings at Nadd.

Volunteer Edward Waters

Volunteer Michael Kiely

Volunteer David Herlihy

Volunteer Edward Twomey[178]

SEÁN MOYLAN BMH WS 838, 209; JOSEPH P MORGAN BMH WS 1097, 14; JOHN MOLONEY BMH WS 1036, 11; LEO CALLAGHAN BMH WS 978, 21; MICHAEL O'CONNELL BMH WS 1428, 14; DENIS MULCHINOCK AND OTHERS BMH WS 744, 14; TIMOTHY LOONEY BMH WS 1196, 13; JOHN WINTERS BMH WS 948, 5; TADHG McCARTHY BMH WS 965, 12; GEORGE POWER BMH WS 451, 18

11 March 1921

John Good was shot dead in Tower Street. Good, who worked in Cork Labour Exchange, was described as a spy.

MICHAEL MURPHY BMH WS 1547, 38

Daniel Canty, OC Newcestown Company, Bandon Battalion, was given orders to move all arms in the company area –

---

[178] Keane, p203.

seventy-four in total – to Castletown Kenneigh for distribution to the brigade flying column.

DANIEL CANTY BMH WS 1619, 26

12 March 1921

William Foley, an officer in the Third Cork Brigade, was sent to Donoughmore by his brigade OC Charlie Hurley to oversee the setting up of a bomb-making factory.

WILLIAM FOLEY BMH WS 1560, 7

The Third Cork Brigade flying column mobilised at Castletown Kenneigh on this date, a week before the battle of Crossbarry.

PATRICK O'BRIEN BMH WS 812, 25

13 March 1921

Liam Deasy (brigade adjutant) and Tom Barry (brigade column OC) inspected suitable ambush sites on the Innishannon to Kinsale road at Shippool.

RICHARD RUSSELL BMH WS 1591, 19

Philip Chambers, OC Coppeen Company, witnessed the shooting of Tim Hourihane, an unarmed civilian, by a group of Auxiliaries. They remained in the Coppeen locality until nightfall.[179]

PHILIP CHAMBERS BMH WS 738, 7

---

[179] Keane, p205.

14 March 1921

Volunteer Richard Newman of Allihies died of gunshot wounds having been shot by a British soldier near his village. The usual excuse of shot while trying to escape was given.[180]

Thomas Hennessy, a widower and civilian aged forty-nine, was shot dead by a party of crown forces at Crosshaven.[181]

13 – 17 March 1921

The flying column of the Third Cork Brigade, in the days prior to the battle of Crossbarry, moved around constantly, staying at Balteenbrack, Castletown Kenneigh, Newcestown, Quarries Cross, Crosspound, arriving at Shippool at 6.30am on 17 March.

DANIEL CANTY BMH WS 1619, 26

15 March 1921

A dispensary doctor who refused to treat Charlie Hurley, Third Brigade OC, was tried by the IRA and given a day to leave the country. Several other people who were willing to act as 'civil guards' for the British in the Ballineen-Enniskeane area were arrested by the IRA.

WILLIAM DESMOND BMH WS 832, 36 & 38

Michael Murray, a civilian, was shot dead by a British soldier in the vicinity of Victoria barracks. Murray apparently had

---

[180] Keane, p206.
[181] Keane, p206.

been molesting a local woman on the side of the street near his home.[182]

John Brennan, QM Freemount Company, Newmarket Battalion, was released from prison on this date. He had been charged with taking part in the Ballydrochane ambush, in which Sergeant Jackson died.

DENNY MULLANE BMH WS 789, 30

Volunteer Charles O'Reilly of Newmarket Company was challenged to stop while travelling with some volunteer comrades near Newmarket. He ran, was hit twice, but managed to get away. He died of his wounds the next day.[183]

17 March 1921

Ted O'Sullivan, a member of the Third Brigade flying column, travelled to Cork to secure two thousand rounds of Lee-Enfield ammunition.

TED O'SULLIVAN BMH WS 1478, 33

The flying column of the Third Cork Brigade, about one hundred in number, took up positions in the early hours of Saint Patrick's Day at Shippool, about a mile from Innishannon on the road to Kinsale. The IRA was spread out over three hundred yards, and two land mines were positioned. There they waited in vain for an expected convoy from the Kinsale direction, and billets were arranged in the locality that night and all the next day.

---

[182] Keane, p206.
[183] Keane, p207.

DANIEL DONOVAN BMH WS 1608, 11; CON FLYNN BMH WS 1621, 20; TIM KEOHANE BMH WS 1295, 9; CHRISTOPHER O'CONNELL BMH WS 1530, 17; CORNELIUS CALNAN BMH WS 1317, 6; DENIS MURPHY BMH WS 1318, 7; WILLIAM DESMOND BMH WS 832, 37

18 March 1921

An RIC patrol was fired on at Castletownroche by members of the local flying column, resulting in the injury of two policemen, one of whom died the following day. He was Constable William Elton from Middlesex, a Black and Tan who had been in the RIC for three months.[184]

SÉAMUS O'MAHONY BMH WS 730, 13; WILLIAM C REGAN BMH WS 1069, 9; DAVID O'CALLAGHAN BMH WS 950, 11

Nellie Carey, a civilian from Fermoy, was in the company of her fiancé Private Price of the Royal Field Artillery when she was hit by a burst of gunfire from the IRA. She died the following day.[185]

WILLIAM BUCKLEY BMH WS 1009, 19; WILLIAM C REGAN BMH WS 1069, 9

19 March 1921

In the early hours of the morning of the 19 March, after Tom Barry (flying column OC) had deployed his men for the coming battle at Crossbarry, Captain William Desmond of Newcestown

---

[184] Keane, p208; Abbott, p210.
[185] Keane, p207.

Company was ordered to Humphrey Forde's house to check on Commandant Charlie Hurley, OC Third Cork Brigade, who had been wounded at the Upton ambush on 15 February. Desmond was arrested as he approached the house and was later taken away to Essex headquarters in Bandon in the same lorry as the four Irish that were killed that day. Volunteer Flor Begley, who played the warpipes during the battle, gives an account of how Commandant Hurley was killed. Major Hallinan knocked on the front door of Forde's house; Commandant Hurley, having rushed down the stairs, shot and wounded him by firing through the door, but was in turn shot dead by a sentry as he attempted to run out the back door.[186]

WILLIAM DESMOND BMH WS 832, 37; FLORENCE BEGLEY BMH WS 1771, 5; JIM AHERN BMH WS 810, 24

Diarmuid O'Leary, OC Killeagh Company and a member of the East Cork flying column, who had been captured after taking part in the battle at Clonmult on 20 February, was sentenced to death by British military court in Victoria barracks. However, the advent of the Truce on 11 July 1921 saved him from execution.

DIARMUID O'LEARY BMH WS 1589, 10

The Third Cork Brigade flying column, under its OC Tom Barry, left the Innishannon area under cover of darkness, reaching Crossbarry at one o'clock next morning, 19 March. The men, one hundred and four in number, were roused from their billets at 3 am and ordered to 'stand to'. The distant rumble of vehicles of the

---

[186] Keane, p69.

Crown forces was detected by both the local company and by the column scouts. Barry had decided to divide the column into seven sections, each to be deployed north of the road and just west of the village of Crossbarry. Shortly after 8am, fire was opened on the first lorry. The battle raged for some time, heavy losses being incurred by the British military. Sections 1, 2 and 3, two of which had occupied Beasley's and Harold's farmhouses, were now ordered away from the road. It was noticed that a party of Black and Tans was in hot pursuit. Barry ordered a volley which resulted in two of them being hit, one fatally. While the battle continued, a section under Tom Kelleher held a covering position to the north. The column now made their way to Gurranreagh, sixteen miles distant, where they billeted until after dark on 21 March. During the battle Volunteer Flor Begley – 'the Piper of Crossbarry' – played the warpipes in the yard of Harold's farm. Four Irish soldiers were killed that day, and two wounded. Commandant Charlie Hurley, OC Third Cork Brigade, was shot dead at nearby Ballymurphy during a British military sweep on the morning of the battle. During the battle three were killed: Volunteer Peter Monaghan, a Scots deserter from the Cameron Highlanders Regiment; Volunteer Jeremiah O'Leary, from Leap; and Volunteer Con Daly, from Ballinascarthy. Those fighting on the Irish side that day firmly believed they had inflicted greater casualties in the British, Captain William Desmond of Newcestown Company counting eighteen bodies at Harold's farmyard in Crossbarry and the same number of coffins at the Essex Regiment headquarters in Bandon.

The following is a list of those who died on 19 March 1921, or who died of wounds afterwards:

Lieutenant Geoffery Hotblack, Essex Regiment

Lieutenant Towers, Essex Regiment

Sergeant Edward Watts, Essex Regiment

Private Stanley Stewart, Essex Regiment

Private William Wilkins, Essex Regiment

Private Joseph Crafer, Essex Regiment

Private Sidney Cawley, Essex Regiment

Driver Cyril Martin, Royal Army Service Corps

Driver Alfred Gray, Royal Army Service Corps

Driver Harold Baker, Royal Army Service Corps

Constable Arthur Kenward

Commandant Charlie Hurley

Volunteer Peter Monaghan

Volunteer Jeremiah O'Leary

Volunteer Con Daly[187]

DANIEL CANTY BMH WS 1619, 28; MICHAEL COLEMAN BMH WS 1254, 13; DANIEL DONOVAN BMH WS 1608, 11; PETER KEARNEY BMH WS 444, 6; JAMES MURPHY BMH WS 1633, 18; DENIS O'BRIEN BMH WS 1306, 9; DENIS O'BRIEN BMH WS 1353, 11; CHRISTOPHER O'CONNELL BMH WS 1530, 17; JAMES DOYLE BMH WS 1640, 17; DANIEL HOLLAND BMH WS 1341, 9; TIMOTHY KEOHANE BMH WS 1295, 10; WILLIAM McCARTHY

---

[187] Keane, pp69, 208; Abbott, p210.

BMH WS 1255, 8; JOHN O'DRISCOLL BMH WS 1250, 9; TIMOTHY WARREN BMH WS 1275, 14; DENIS LORDAN BMH WS 1619, 27; FLORENCE BEGLEY BMH WS 1771, 1; MICHAEL O'REGAN BMH WS 1524, 6; WILLIAM NORRIS BMH WS 595, 9; MICHAEL J CROWLEY BMH WS 1603, 18

Cornelius Sheehan, described as an informer, was shot dead by the IRA as he tried to flee from his house in Blarney Street.[188]

PJ MURPHY BMH WS 869, 24; CHARLES O'CONNELL BMH WS 566, 3

20 March 1921

David Nagle, a postman from Waterfall near Ballincollig, was arrested by the IRA as a spy; he was tried and executed.[189]

TIM HERLIHY AND OTHERS BMH WS 810, 31; MICHAEL O'REGAN BMH WS 1524, 5; PATRICK CRONIN BMH WS 710, 2

A spy, unnamed in the witness statement, was found guilty of giving information to Crown forces and killed by members of Kanturk Battalion. He was, in fact, John Sheehan, a local man, and his body was found in a field at Droumalour, Kanturk, with a notice warning spies, traitors and informers to beware.[190]

MICHAEL COURTNEY BMH WS 744, 14; DENIS MULCHINOCK BMH WS 744, 14

---

[188] Keane, p209.
[189] Keane, p209.
[190] Keane, pp210, 215.

The flying column of the Third Cork Brigade, having billeted in Gurranreigh, parish of Kilmichael, since the battle of Crossbarry on 19 March, left their billet on this night, moving to Ahiohill and then to Mounteen in the Timoleague area.

DANIEL DONOVAN BMH WS 1608, 14

Jeremiah Mullane, a civilian ex-soldier, was shot and killed after curfew hour by British military in North Main Street, Cork.[191]

22 March 1921

A large sweep by British military took place at Ballynoe and Kilcronat areas. Volunteer Arthur Mulcahy, who came from Currabeha in Conna, was killed, apparently 'attempting to escape' – a common euphemism meaning shot out of hand.[192]

WILLIAM BUCKLEY BMH WS 1009, 19

Volunteer James Barrett, who was wounded and captured by the Manchester Regiment at the abortive ambush at Dripsey (see 28 January 1921), died of his wounds while in British military custody on 22 March 1921.[193]

DENIS DWYER BMH WS 713, 5; DANIEL McCARTHY BMH WS 1457, 6; JOHN MANNING BMH WS 1721, 6; DAN McCARTHY BMH WS 1697, 13; DIARMUID O'LEARY BMH WS 1589, 9; MICHAEL MULLANE BMH WS 1689, 8

---

[191] Keane, p210.
[192] Keane, p210.
[193] Keane, p65.

22/23 March 1921

Captain Mary O'Neill (later Walsh) of Kilbrittain Cumann na mBan kept vigil with the Volunteers at Clogagh church as the funeral service for Third Cork Brigade OC Charlie Hurley, killed on the morning of the battle of Crossbarry, took place. Volunteer Flor Begley played *Wrap the Green Flag Round me Boys* as the Volunteers and Cumann na mBan walked from the church to Clogagh graveyard, where Hurley was buried at 4 am, with shots being fired over the grave.

DANIEL DONOVAN BMH WS 1608, 15; MARY WALSH BMH WS 556, 6; DANIEL CANTY BMH WS 1619, 30; JAMES MURPHY BMH WS 1684, 21

23 March 1921

Six volunteers from C Company, 1 Battalion, were surprised by the RIC/Black and Tans at Ballycannon, Clogheen, as they lay asleep in an outhouse of the farm of Cornelius O'Keeffe. The six were lined up and ordered to run for their lives, whereupon they were all shot in the back, their bodies being mutilated after death. Several witnesses to this event made sworn depositions to a Cork legal firm. The six IRA men, all from the northside of Cork city, were:

Volunteer Daniel Crowley

Volunteer William Deasy

Volunteer Thomas Dennehy

Volunteer Jeremiah O'Mullane

Volunteer Daniel Murphy

Volunteer Michael O'Sullivan[194]

SÉAMUS FITZGERALD BMH WS 1737, 28 (PLUS VARIOUS APPENDIXES THAT GIVE SWORN STATEMENTS FROM OTHER WITNESSES); DANIEL HEALY BMH WS 1656, 13; WILLIAM DESMOND BMH WS 832, 15; MICHAEL MURPHY BMH WS 1547, 39; PJ MURPHY BMH WS 869, 27; FELIX O'DOHERTY BMH WS 739, 48

24 March 1921

The manager of the Provincial Bank in Schull was robbed of £500 by a masked gang. A Sinn Féin court convicted the raiders and sentenced them to deportation.

WILLIAM LANNIN BMH WS 1520, 6; EDWARD O'SULLIVAN BMH WS 1501, 8; RICHARD COLLINS BMH WS 1542, 7; CHARLIE COTTER BMH WS 1519, 8

25 March 1921

Father Sheehan, parish priest of Aghinagh, said mass for Macroom Battalion flying column on Good Friday (sic), with breakfast served to the entire column in the priest's house afterwards.

CHARLES BROWNE BMH WS 873, 40

John Cathcart, regarded as a spy by the IRA, was shot dead by them at Pearse's Square in Youghal.[195]

---

[194] Keane, p211.
[195] Keane, p212.

26 March 1921

A daring plan was made by Second Battalion Cork city to free some prisoners from Cork prison. With the help of the prison chaplin Canon Duggan from Kinsale, daggers, handguns and a mallet were smuggled into the prison, but the prisoner who had the job of knocking out Warder Griffin with the mallet could not bring himself to do it, and the plan failed.

MICHAEL MURPHY BMH WS 1547, 38; PATRICK COLLINS BMH WS 1707, 10; SEÁN CULHANE BMH WS 746, 16

At Clubhouse, near Dunmanway, the Second lieutenant of the local company was court-martialled for refusing to report for duty the following day, saying he intended to go to Holy Communion. He was sent to work in the Newcestown area for one month as punishment. This type of punishment, where an IRA man who refused to follow orders was forced to work on the farm of another republican, was quite common.

PETER KEARNEY BMH WS 444, 10

27 March 1921

Volunteer Timothy Whooley of Clonakilty Company was killed in an accidental shooting at Shannonvale, just north of the town, when his 'Peter the Painter' machine gun was manhandled by a comrade.[196]

TED HAYES BMH WS 1575, 9

---

[196] Keane, p213.

28 March 1921

Commandant Michael Leahy entered Italy via the Swiss border on this date. His orders were to secure an arms shipment to Ireland, a plan that ultimately failed.

MICHAEL LEAHY BMH WS 555, 2

William Good, an ex-British Army captain, was returning to the Timoleague area to settle the estate of his father John, who had been killed by the IRA a fortnight previously. William Good was struck on the head and killed by the IRA.[197]

30 March 1921

Frederick C Stenning and Lieutenant Colonel Peacocke, described as 'two enemy agents', were sought out by James 'Spud' Murphy and others at Innishannon. When Stenning opened the door to Bandon Battalion vice OC John Lordan, he fired harmlessly in the direction of his assailants, who shot him dead in the hallway. Luckily for Peacocke, he was not at home when they went to his house.[198]

JAMES MURPHY BMH WS 1684, 21; RICHARD RUSSELL BMH WS 1591, 21

The flying column of the Third Cork Brigade rested at Benduff, west of Rosscarbery. At 9pm they were paraded and informed they were going to attack Rosscarbery RIC barracks that night.

CHRISTOPHER O'CONNELL BMH WS 1530, 22

---

[197] Keane, p213.
[198] Keane, p214.

Denis Donovan of Watergate Street in Bandon, an ex-Royal Navy man, was regarded as a spy by the IRA. He was shot dead at his doorstep.[199]

31 March 1921

Members of the local Donoughmore Company raided the offices of the clerk of petty sessions in Coachford and Donoughmore, taking away books and ledgers. A sweep by British troops followed almost immediately, though the volunteers got away. Airplanes assisted the British efforts.

MAURICE BREW BMH WS 1695, 22.

The early hours of the last day of March 1921 saw the flying column of the Third Cork Brigade attack Rosscarbery RIC barracks. A bomb was carried in silence to the door of the building and a huge explosion followed, damaging both the barracks and the house across the street. A cry of 'We surrender' was heard, followed by a cry of 'We hold the barracks'. In the hail of bullets and grenades, the garrison was forced upstairs. The building was now aflame. The four-hour battle came to an end when the garrison within, numbering about twenty, decided to surrender, first throwing their weapons into the flames. Three witness statements (Con Flynn BMH WS 1621, 20; Daniel Canty BMH WS 1619, 32 and John O'Driscoll BMH WS 1250, 11) allude to a false surrender by the RIC. The next day, as the rubble of the destroyed barracks was being searched by the RIC, a grenade found in the ruins was thrown away in panic by

---

[199] Keane, p214.

Constable Doyle, causing the deaths of three civilians, one of them a boy of four. The list of fatalities is as follows:

Sergeant Ambrose Shea

Constable Charles Bowles

Patrick Collins

George Wilson

Frank Fitzpatrick[200]

DANIEL CANTY BMH WS 1619, 31; CON FLYNN BMH WS 1621, 20; MICHAEL COLEMAN BMH WS 1254, 16; PETER KEARNEY BMH WS 444, 10; WILLIAM McCARTHY BMH WS 1255, 11; DENIS O'BRIEN BMH WS 1353, 15; MICHAEL O'DRISCOLL BMH WS 1297, 8; CHRISTOPHER O'CONNELL BMH WS 1530, 22; TED O'SULLIVAN BMH WS 1478, 35; TIMOTHY WARREN BMH WS 1275, 15; EDWARD YOUNG BMH WS 1402, 19; JOHN O'DRISCOLL BMH WS 1250, 11; JAMES DOYLE BMH WS 1640, 21

---

[200] Keane, p76; Abbott, p216.

March 1921 (no date available)

Members of Timoleague and Barryroe Companies took part in the burning of Courtmacsherry Hotel, which had been earmarked as a base for the Auxiliary Division of the RIC. The burning of Poole's of Mayfield and Longfield's of Kilcoleman took place around this time.

WILLIAM FOLEY BMH WS 1560, 7; MICHAEL COLEMAN BMH WS 1254, 18

As the war progressed, the Crown forces resorted to taking hostages with them on patrols, thus ensuring that they would not be fired on. Meenagorman, on the Newmarket to Rockchapel road, was an example of this strategy, when the flying column of the Newmarket Battalion were forced to retire.

DANIEL GUINEY BMH WS 1347, 12

Clonakilty courthouse was burned around this time.

TED HAYES BMH WS 1575, 9

A cache of arms belonging to the National Volunteers and consisting of eight rifles and five hundred rounds of ammunition was taken by Fermoy Company; it was moved to Araglin.

JAMES HACKETT BMH WS 1080, 4

A flying column was formed in the Third Battalion area of the First Cork Brigade, Leo Murphy being appointed OC.

JAMES AHERN BMH WS 810, 21

Adrigole Company held up some British officers on board the ship *Lady Elsie* at Adrigole, relieving them of their revolvers.

EUGENE DUNNE BMH WS 1537, 7

Passage West and Rochestown Companies attacked a party of RIC and Black and Tans on the Rochestown Road, one RIC man being reported killed. There are no records of RIC deaths in that part of Co Cork in March1921.

JOHN BARRETT BMH WS 1538, 3

The RIC barracks at Victoria Cross in Cork was vacated by the garrison; it was burned down the following day by G Company, First Battalion.

EDWARD HORGAN BMH WS 1644, 12

In the middle of March 1921, the South Tipperary Brigade flying column under Seán Hogan found themselves surrounded by an enemy encirclement at Ballygiblin. A local scout, Jim O'Donoghue, of his own volition walked into the enemy patrol, thus distracting them and allowing Hogan and his men to get away. O'Donoghue (called Sheehy by one witness) was released shortly after.

PATRICK LUDDY BMH WS 1151, 18; SÉAMUS O'MAHONY BMH WS 730, 15; LEO SKINNER BMH WS 940, 7

Sheskin railway bridge was damaged and shots fired at the British military barracks at Bantry, with no reply from the garrison.

DENIS KEOHANE BMH WS 1426, 12

John Jones, an officer in Kingwilliamstown (Ballydesmond) Volunteers, was accidentally shot by a comrade cleaning a .32 pistol. He spent three weeks recovering.

JOHN JONES BMH WS 759, 10

A meeting of the brigade council of the Third Cork Brigade took place at Curraghdrinagh, at which Charlie Hurley (brigade OC) stressed that future engagements with the enemy would be on a bigger scale. (CharlieHurley was recovering from wounds incurred at Upton station; it is possible that the council meeting took place before this time.)

SEÁN MURPHY BMH WS 1445, 3

Daniel O'Keeffe, captain Mitchelstown Company, Galtee Battalion, was arrested by the Lincolnshire Regiment at Ballyarthur and threatened with dire consequences because of what had happened to Crown forces at Glencurrane.

DANIEL O'KEEFFE BMH WS 1587, 25; SÉAMUS O'MAHONY BMH WS 730, 14

Some flying column members of the Third Cork Brigade were demobbed after Crossbarry, replacements being installed; the column strength was now about sixty. This column assembled at Ahiohill at the end of March.

TED O'SULLIVAN BMH WS 1478, 34

The marine station at Schull was fired on by the local battalion, some of whom were setting fire to Schull workhouse.

SEÁN O'DRISCOLL BMH WS 1518, 14

Small patrols by the crown forces were now a thing of the past in mid-Cork, due to the risk of attack by the IRA. Several hundred British military, with a mule column and armoured cars, camped at Aherla in March of 1921, arresting several members of Aherla Company.

MICHAEL O'REGAN BMH WS 1524, 8

Raiding was discontinued around this time by British military and the RIC in north Cork, large sweeps and roundups now proving more effective against the IRA.

PATRICK O'BRIEN BMH WS 764, 35

An 'enemy spy' was arrested by Knockavilla Company, in the Third Brigade area. He was handed over to the First Cork Brigade to be shot.

FRANK NEVILLE BMH WS 443, 13

April 1921

1 April 1921

Volunteer John D Crimmins and two other volunteers were arrested when his home was surrounded by British military. He was taken to Ballyvonare camp, ending up in Bere Island camp until after the Treaty.

JOHN D CRIMMINS BMH WS 1039, 9; MAURICE NOONAN BMH WS 1098, 8

Macroom Auxiliaries burned the houses of Daniel Corkery, Macroom Battalion OC, and Captain C Kelleher, OC K Company; these were official reprisals. Later that day Charles Browne, an officer in Macroom Battalion, evaded capture at an Auxiliary checkpoint at Coppeen by giving a false name.

CHARLES BROWNE BMH WS 873, 41

James Foley, captain of D Company (Aherla), Third Battalion, died following the accidental discharge by a comrade of a rifle. His post as company captain was taken by Patrick Cronin.[201]

PATRICK CRONIN BMH WS 710, 5; TIM HERLIHY AND OTHERS BMH WS 810, 28; MICHAEL O'REGAN BMH WS 1524, 7; MICHAEL FOLEY BMH WS 1534, 1, 6

Having successfully attacked Rosscarbery RIC barracks the previous day, the flying column of the Third Cork Brigade made its way to the Newcestown area.

JAMES DOYLE BMH WS 1640, 23

---

[201] Keane, p198.

7 April 1921

Shanachrane, a townland north of Dunmanway, was the venue for a meeting to discuss the importation of arms from Italy to Ireland. The First and Third Cork Brigades were represented, along with the Second Kerry Brigade. Liam Lynch, OC Second Cork Brigade, was the senior officer.

FLORENCE O'DONOGHUE BMH WS 554, 3

8 April 1921

An attack was made on a Black and Tan patrol at Mashanaglass, Macroom, by F Company, Macroom Battalion, in command of Lieutenant John Powell. One was killed; he was Constable Frederick Lord, from London, who had been a policeman for six months.[202]

CHARLES BROWNE BMH WS 873, 43

Volunteer Liam Hoare was shot dead by Crown forces in Ballymacoda; having failed to halt his bicycle when challenged, he made a run for freedom, when he was struck by gunfire. Kevin Murphy, in his witness statement, gives a different story as to how Volunteer Hoare was killed; he maintained that members of the Cameron Highlanders Regiment had tied Hoare to a lorry and killed him by dragging him along the road.[203]

KEVIN MURPHY BMH WS 1629, 8

---

[202] Keane, p215; Abbott, p219.
[203] Keane, p216.

9 April 1921

Denis 'Din Din' Donovan was shot dead as a spy in Ballygarvan, a 'spies and informers beware' sign affixed to his body.[204]

LEO BUCKLEY BMH WS 1714, 7 & 12; GEORGE HURLEY BMH WS 1630, 4; SEÁN O'CONNELL BMH WS 1706, 3

10 April 1921

Members of Kildorrery Company in north Cork ambushed two Black and Tans, killing both, near the village. It was discovered after the attack that they were unarmed (William C Regan). They were Constable Joseph Boynes from Northumberland, who had been in the force for five months, and Constable George Woodward from Surrey, who had ten months' service.[205]

WILLIAM C REGAN BMH WS 1069, 11; GEORGE POWER BMH WS 451, 19

Shell cases discarded by the British military at Fort Camden and Fort Carlisle were used to make landmines at Ballinacurra, Midleton. One was used to blow up a convoy of Cameron Highlanders at Ballyedkin, Churchtown. The first lorry took the brunt of the explosion, and the soldiers in the remaining vehicles acted swiftly, taking to the fields and firing at their enemy. There were no fatalities that day.

DANIEL CASHMAN BMH WS 1523, 11; JOHN P O'CONNELL BMH WS 1444, 16; MICHAEL KEARNEY BMH WS 1418, 24;

---

[204] Keane, p217.
[205] Keane, p218; Abbott, p220.

JOHN KELLEHER BMH WS 1456, 24; PATRICK J WHELAN BMH WS 1449, 60

11 April 1921

Private Michael O'Brien, an ex-British Army soldier, was found guilty 'on a charge of espionage' and executed by the IRA.[206]

12 April 1921

The IRA fired bombs into a British military lorry in Washington Street in Cork. A witness statement says they failed to explode, but William Kenefick, a civilian from Blarney Street, died from shrapnel wounds the next day.[207]

PATRICK A MURRAY BMH WS 1584, 22

Macroom Battalion flying column were billeted in Liscarrigane, north-west of the town, for a week.

CHARLES BROWNE BMH WS 873, 43

13 April 1921

As a reprisal for the deaths of two Black and Tans by the IRA in Kildorrery on 10 April, Captain Stafford of the British garrison in Fermoy ordered the houses of the following to be burned in reprisal: Jeremiah Magner, David Daly, Seán Creed, Seán Noonan, Seán Cronin, William Shinnick. The IRA then burned Lord Listowel's house at Ballyhooley and Penrose Welstead's at Shanballymore.

---

[206] Keane, p218.
[207] Keane, 205.

DAVID O'CALLAGHAN BMH WS 950, 11; SÉAMUS O'MAHONY BMH WS 730, 17

14 April 1921

Captain Denny Mullane, OC Freemount Company, was caught in arms by Crown forces on this date.

DENNY MULLANE BMH WS 789, 21

16 April 1921

Spain and Spellman, two Black and Tans who shot dead Seán O'Brien, an innocent civilian, at Charleville the previous month, were traced to an incoming train at the town's railway station. Several IRA men awaited their arrival, but at the critical time a British military lorry arrived to take supplies away. Shots were exchanged, but Spain and Spellman got away.

MICHAEL GEARY/RICHARD SMITH BMH WS 754, 23

17 April 1921

Constable MacDonald, a member of the Black and Tans and 'a particularly obnoxious individual', was shot and injured in Cove Street by city IRA men. He died five days later, on 22 April. John Cyril MacDonald, aged twenty-eight and from London, had been in the RIC for four months.[208]

MICHAEL MURPHY BMH WS 1547, 41

20 April 1921

---

[208] Keane, p219; Abbott, p222.

Members of Macroom Battalion attacked an Auxiliary patrol at the Glen Gates, on the western side of the town. Charles Browne, an officer in the battalion, writes that one auxiliary was killed, though no records of a casualty exist. An enemy lorry was fired on at Coolcower the same night.

CHARLES BROWNE BMH WS 873, 43

Company Captain Tadhg O'Sullivan was held up by two British intelligence officers in Douglas Street. He dashed to a nearby house, getting access to the roof of an adjoining building, but he was shot dead by his pursuers.[209]

MICHAEL MURPHY BMH WS 1547, 41; ROBERT C AHERN BMH WS 1676, 12; L M NEVILLE BMH WS 1639, 12; MICHAEL O'SULLIVAN BMH WS 793, 17; GEORGE HURLEY BMH WS 1630, 1

21 April 1921

Patrick Goggin, a boy aged seven, was shot and wounded by Crown forces at his parents' farm at Carrigthomas, Ballinagree. He died of his wounds a week later in Macroom hospital.[210]

22 April 1921

Bicycles were banned by the British authorities in east Cork.

FRANCIS HEALY BMH WS 1694, 14

---

[209] Keane, p218.
[210] Keane, p219.

23 April 1921

Volunteers Patrick Clifford and Michael O'Sullivan of Mitchelstown Company were caught in arms at Ballygiblin Bridge by a party of British military. They were sentenced to death, but were released after the Truce.

PATRICK CLIFFORD BMH WS 946, 6; WILLIAM ROCHE BMH WS 1362, 4; LEO SKINNER BMH WS 940, 4

26 April 1921

Private Norman Fielding of the East Lancs Regiment based at Buttevant, posing as a deserter, was shot as a spy in the Charleville Battalion area.[211]

DENNY MULLANE BMH WS 789, 26; PATRICK O'BRIEN BMH WS 764, 40

27 April 1921

At a meeting at Kippagh, near Millstreet, it was decided to rename all brigades in Cork, Kerry, West Limerick and West Waterford as the First Southern Division.

TED O'SULLIVAN BMH WS 1478, 38; GEORGE POWER BMH WS 451, 19; MATTHEW KELLEHER BMH WS 1319, 9; JJ BRENNOCK BMH WS 1113, 15; WILLIAM BUCKLEY BMH WS 1009, 20

---

[211] Keane, p220.

28 April 1921

Private Jack Butler and Private Harry Honeywell of the British Army testified against Newmarket Battalion QM Bill Dwyer, who was arrested on this date. Dwyer received a sentence of seven years' penal servitude, but was released after the Treaty. Volunteer Michael Larkin was also arrested on this day, being released around the same time.

DENNY MULLANE BMH WS 789, 19

Four IRA Volunteers were executed in Cork on this day, two who had been captured at the battle of Mourneabbey on 15 April 1921, and two at the battle of Clonmult on 20 February 1921. They were:

Volunteer Patrick Roynane (Mourneabbey)

Volunteer Thomas Mulcahy (Mourneabbey)

Volunteer Patrick Sullivan (Clonmult)

Volunteer Maurice Moore (Clonmult)[212]

MICHAEL KEARNEY BMH WS 1418, 23; PATRICK J HIGGINS BMH WS 1467, 7

Constable John Bunce was engaged with other members of the RIC in filling in a trenched road at Castlelack, Bandon. Shortly after while doing sentry duty, he caused a rifle to fire accidentally, wounding him in both legs.[213] He died on the 29 May 1921.

---

[212] Keane, p220.
[213] Keane, p211; Abbott, p315.

30 April 1921

Lieutenant Denis O'Brien of Barryroe Company was arrested in a round up. He was taken to Bandon military barracks and eventually to Maryborough (Portlaoise) prison, from where he was released after the signing of the Treaty. O'Brien was a member of the flying column of the Third Cork Brigade and had fought at Crossbarry the month before his arrest.

DENIS O'BRIEN BMH WS 1306, 11

Michael O'Keeffe of Main Street, Carrigtwohill, was shot as a spy by members of the Fourth Battalion, First Cork Brigade. O'Keeffe, who was an ex-British soldier, had 'Spies and informers beware, IRA' pinned to his body.[214]

FRANCIS HEALY BMH WS 1694, 17; MICHAEL J BURKE BMH WS 1424, 28

Stephen O'Callaghan, an ex-British soldier, was shot at Anderson's Quay in Cork. Despite being brought to hospital, he died shortly afterwards.[215]

An RIC man was wounded when a police patrol was fired at in Skibbereen.

PADDY O'BRIEN BMH WS 764, 41

Constable Arthur Harrison was kidnapped at Coachford station by the IRA and subsequently shot. He had resigned

---

[214] Keane, p223.
[215] Keane, p369.

from the force the day of his abduction, having joined up in September 1920.[216]

Major Geoffery Compton Smith of the Royal Welch Fusiliers, DSO, Legion d'Honneur, was British IO for Munster. He was arrested by Frank Busteed, Donoughmore Battalion vice OC, and held in the Donoughmore Company area. His life depended on whether four IRA men under sentence of death were released (two captured at Mourneabbey and two at Clonmult). The men were executed on the 28 April 1921, and Compton Smith was subsequently shot. He was buried near Blarney, and his body exhumed in 1926, when it was sent to Collins barracks (formerly Victoria barracks) in Cork. His widow, who had remarried and was now living in Italy, for some reason did not take possession of it, and he was buried under Irish Free State military honours at Fort Carlisle, near Crosshaven.[217]

FELIX O'DOHERTY BMH WS 737, 50; MAURICE BREW BMH WS 1695, 23

---

[216] Keane, p223; Abbott, p312.
[217] Keane, p222.

April 1920 (no date available)

Liam Deasy (OC Third Brigade) and Tom Barry (column OC) were in the Maultrehane area of west Cork in mid-April. They were making arrangements for the landing of a shipment of arms to Union Hall from Italy.

PATRICK O'SULLIVAN BMH WS 1481, 9

Members of Newmarket Battalion flying column moved to Abbeyfeale in west Limerick to take part in what proved to be an abortive raid on an RIC patrol near the town.

JAMES J RIORDAN BMH WS 1172, 13

Two British Army deserters from Tralee barracks were arrested in Knocknagree. They were questioned separately by Seán Moylan, battalion OC, and they described how a man named Sullivan, a travelling man and collector and singer of songs, called to Tralee barrack weekly. The IRA identified the man, and Sullivan was arrested, and both he and the deserters were handed over to the Kerry Brigade.

JAMES J RIORDAN BMH WS 1172, 13

Dick Barrett, QM Third Cork Brigade, was arrested in early April 1921, his post being filled by Tadhg O'Sullivan. Barrett, along with two other volunteers, was sent to Spike Island.

RICHARD RUSSELL BMH WS 1591, 20; FRANK NEVILLE BMH WS 443, 15

The flying column of the Third Cork Brigade was divided into two sections. The men from the Fifth (Bantry), Sixth (Castletownbere) and Seventh (Schull) Battalions returned to their own area. Those from the First (Bandon), Second (Clonakilty), Third (Dunmanway) and Fourth (Skibbereen) under Seán Hales (OC Bandon Battalion) moved to Inchy Bridge, between Timoleague and Ballinascarthy, where an expected troop train was derailed, although no troops travelled that day.

RICHARD RUSSELL BMH WS 1591, 21; TIMOTHY WARREN BMH WS 1275, 16

A permanent IRA scouting post was established at Drumkeen, Innishannon, to give an advance warning to IRA men on the run in the Balinadee area.

RICHARD RUSSELL BMH WS 1591, 22

A party of British military from Ballyvonare barracks went by the fields to Ballyhea, arresting Volunteer Brassil and wounding Volunteer Dillon.

MICHAEL GEARY/ RICHARD SMITH BMH WS 754, 24

Members of the Cork city IRA held up a lorry of supplies with seven British Army personnel on board; the lorry's contents were captured and the seven released.

WILLIAM BARRY BMH WS 1708, 10

An elaborate dugout measuring twenty-two feet by eighteen feet was dug out of a mountain at Barrafohona, in the Fermoy Battalion area. Built to be used by IRA men on the run, its design included corrugated iron, sheeting boards and sods.

JJ BRENNOCK BMH WS 1113, 15; WILLIAM BUCKLEY BMH WS 1009, 20

A daring rescue from Spike Island was made by Seán Mac Swiney (brother of the martyred Lord Mayor) and two IRA men, Seán Forde of East Limerick and Seán Twomey of Cork. Captain Michael J Burke, OC Cobh Company, secured a motor launch and waited offshore while the three, who were on work detail, chose their moment to knock out the sentries. Mac Swiney, Forde and Twomey boarded the boat and got ashore at Ringaskiddy.

MICHAEL J BURKE BMH WS 1424, 21

The First Cork Brigade HQ was now in the Ballingeary area. The local company were on alert and on duty round the clock; they were guarding, at various times, Seán O'Hegarty (First Brigade OC) and staff, Liam Lynch (First Southern Division OC) and staff, as well as the Third Cork Brigade flying column and its commander, Tom Barry.

CORNELIUS CRONIN BMH WS 1726, 9

An ambush of British military lorries took place at Aultagh wood, near Dunmanway, by the flying column of the Third Cork Brigade. No casualties were reported for either side.

DENIS CROWLEY BMH WS 560, 19

Around this time the income tax office and the RIC barracks at the Lower Road in Cork city were burned by members of the First Battalion of the First Brigade.

SEÁN HEALY BMH WS 1479, 35

A member of the Black and Tans was believed to be seriously wounded by gunfire while standing outside Kilbrittain RIC barracks, and died while being taken to Bandon by lorry. There is no record of any RIC personnel being killed at Kilbrittain at that time.

DENIS CROWLEY BMH WS 560, 19

According to Seán Murphy, OC Aultagh Company and QM Dunmanway Battalion, Crown forces began to use bloodhounds to track down the IRA for the first time in the Dunmanway area.

SEÁN MURPHY BMH WS 1445, 13

An unsuccessful attempt was made by members of the First Battalion, First Cork Brigade to kill Captain Kelly, chief IO in the British garrison at Victoria barracks in Cork.

SEÁN HEALY BMH WS 1479, 35

Official British reprisals in the Crossbarry and Knockavilla areas began, with the following houses burned: Kelleher's of Crowhill, O'Mahoney's and Delaney's of Belrose, O'Leary's of Ballyhandle and Hartnett's of Killeens. Harold's and Beasley's, which had featured so prominently in the battle of Crossbarry, were, in turn, burned by the IRA.

FRANK NEVILLE BMH WS 443, 15

Christopher O'Connell, vice OC Castletownbere Battalion, was arrested in a round up by the King's Own Scottish Borderers and detained at a local commandeered house. He escaped later that day.

CHRISTOPHER O'CONNELL BMH WS 1530, 25

A raid on the mails took place at Burrane, Timoleague. A letter from a local woman was intercepted by the local company. 'She informed the British that she was a member of Cumann na mBan and was in a position to give them valuable information.' Following her trial, she was ordered to leave the country.

JOHN O'DRISCOLL BMH WS 1250, 13

Lord Bandon was kidnapped at around this time and for several weeks was detained by the local company at Barryroe. He was released at the time of the Truce.

DENIS MURPHY BMH WS 1308, 11

Early April 1921 saw the formation of an active service unit in Cork city. Several IRA men in the city had been arrested, and those city men who had gone to the Ballyvourney area now returned home. Six men were chosen from the First Battalion (Danny Healy, Stephen MacSwiney, Jim Barrett, Liam O'Callaghan, Seán Twomey, Pa Murray) and seven from the Second Battalion (Florrie O'Donoghue, Jim Counihan, Ned Fitzgibbon, George Burke, Jim Fitzgerald, Peter Donovan and one more).

SEÁN HEALY BMH WS 1479, 35

May 1921

1 May 1921

A group of IRA men whom Crown forces claim had been trenching a section of road near Churchtown were fired on in the early hours of the morning. Joseph Coughlan, described as being a Volunteer aged fourteen, was shot dead. He was, most probably, a member of Na Fianna.[218]

PATRICK O'BRIEN BMH WS 764, 41

William Desmond, lieutenant and later captain of Newcestown Company, was transferred with about forty others to Spike Island in Cork Harbour, from where two IRA men had escaped that morning. He gives a lengthy account of day-to-day life in the prison.

WILLIAM DESMOND 832, 51

Four off-duty RIC men were fired at near Castlemartyr House in east Cork. The two ensuing fatalities were Black and Tans: Constable William Smith, from Lancashire, and Constable John Webb, from London (he died the following day).[219]

3 May 1921

Volunteers Tom Lane, Jim Lane and James 'Spud' Murphy, all of Clonakilty Company, threw a bomb into Kingston's pub on Barrack Hill (now MacCurtain Hill) in the town. Murphy believed that one Black and Tan had been killed and another

---

[218] Keane, p225.
[219] Keane, p225; Abbott, p227.

wounded. Having sustained a wound to the buttock as a result of the explosion, Murphy spent several weeks recovering in Daly's of Froe. Two RIC members, in fact, died as a result of this incident. Constable James Cullen, a Black and Tan, had been in the force for three months; he was from Wiltshire. Constable Martin Fallon, from Roscommon, had eleven years' service.[220]

JAMES MURPHY BMH WS 1684, 22

Colonel Cameron of the Sixteenth Infantry Brigade in Fermoy ordered the houses of the following burned: Michael Walsh, Farrehy; James Burke, Rockmills; M Magner, Shanballymore; Ned Creed, Meadestown, Kildorrery; Linehan's public house, The Bridge, Ballyhooley.

SÉAMUS O'MAHONY BMH WS 730, 17

A travelling singer and collector of songs named Sullivan, accused of giving information to the British military at Tralee, was shot dead by the IRA, his body dumped on the roadside near Rathmore village in Co Kerry. When members of the Black and Tans and 'old' RIC came to claim the body, the IRA from the Second Cork Brigade and Second Kerry Brigade opened fire; five policemen were killed outright and three more died in the following days. They were:

Sergeant Thomas McCormack

Constable Walter Brown

Constable William Clapp

---

[220] Keane, p231.

Constable Robert Dyne

Constable Alfred Hilyer

Constable James Phelan

Constable Samuel Watkins

Constable Hedley Woodcock[221]

PATRICK O'BRIEN BMH WS 764, 48; DANIEL BROWNE BMH WS 785, 9; JOHN JONES BMH WS 759, 11; JAMES J RIORDAN BMH WS 1172, 15; THOMAS ROCHE BMH WS 1222, 16

4 May 1921

Members of Charleville Battalion flying column were billeted in safe houses at Knocktoosh, two miles west of Tullylease. In the morning a British military party from Buttevant barracks converged on the area, shooting two scouts – Volunteer John Stokes, who was killed, and injuring John Roche; battalion OC Seán Moylan narrowly escaped capture, as did Captain Paddy O'Brien.[222]

PATRICK O'BRIEN BMH WS 764, 42

5 May 1921

A large convoy of RIC from Macroom negotiated their way through the Gearagh, a flooded woody area near Macroom. Some members of Kilmichael Company, Seventh Battalion, sought refuge on Deshure Hill, one of them, Company OC

---

[221] Abbott, p230.
[222] Keane, p225.

Cornelius Kelleher, discovering that his house had been set aflame.

CORNELIUS KELLEHER BMH WS 1654, 12

James Lynch, a civilian, had been accused by the IRA of giving information to Crown forces, a charge he denied. He was shot dead within yards of his house in Whitegate, near Midleton.[223]

7 May 1921

A civilian named Purcell, originally from Tipperary, was suspected of spying against the IRA. He was taken from his lodgings in Cork city centre and shot dead at Tory Top Lane.[224]

MICHAEL MURPHY BMH WS 1547, 42

Thomas Collins, an ex-British soldier who had served in the Cheshire Regiment, was shot and wounded by the IRA at Youghal. He associated closely with the British military in the town, and his funeral was attended by a party of the Cameron Highlanders.[225]

8 May 1921

Volunteers Seán Noonan, Paddy McCarthy and Pad Murphy of Freemount Company, Newmarket Battalion were arrested on this day. To prevent any more arrests, scouts were placed night and day near the local RIC barracks. The ringing of the

---

[223] Keane, p226.
[224] Keane, p227.
[225] Keane, p226.

church bell and the blowing of tin horns were effective ways of warning any volunteers on the run of the approach of the RIC.

DENNY MULLANE BMH WS 789, 22

Volunteer William Bransfield of D Company, Fourth Battalion and a flying column commander of the Midleton Battalion of the First Cork Brigade, 'was taken out of bed and shot on the roadside by British forces' (the Cameron Highlanders) on this date.[226]

FRANCIS HEALY BMH WS 1694, 18

Commandant Michael Murphy, OC Second Battalion, and two fellow volunteers had several drinks with Sterland, a British intelligence officer. Afterwards Sterland was shot dead at the door of the Rob Roy Hotel in Cook Street in the city. Constable Frederick Sterland, aged twenty-three, from Birmingham, had been a member of the RIC for three months.[227]

MICHAEL MURPHY BMH WS 1547, 41; ROBERT AHERNE BMH WS 1676, 9; WILLIAM BARRY BMH WS 1708, 8; LAWRENCE NEVILLE BMH WS 1639, 10; JEROME COUGHLAN BMH WS 1568, 10; JOHN M MCCARTHY BMH WS 883, APPENDIX, 11; JEREMIAH KEATING BMH WS 1657, 9

John Hodnett, a civilian, was shot dead by British soldiers while going to mass at Courtmacsherry. They claimed he failed

---

[226] Keane, p229.
[227] Keane, p227; Abbott, p233.

to stop when challenged, a recurring feature of British military excuse during the War of Independence.[228]

9 May 1921

Constable James Cullen and Constable Martin Fallon died in hospital on this day. Both men had been seriously wounded when the IRA threw a bomb into the bar in which the policemen had been drinking at Barrack Hill, Clonakilty on 3 May 1921.

JAMES 'SPUD' MURPHY BMH WS 1684, 22

Captain Frank Hurley, OC Farnivane Company, Bandon Battalion, was captured along with Volunteers O'Leary and O'Donovan. They ran in to a patrol of the Essex Regiment at Scott's farmyard at Carhoo, west of Bandon. Charles O'Donoghue, an officer in Bandon Battalion, says Hurley tried to escape while being led through the Park outside Bandon and was shot dead. He was buried in Kilbrogan graveyard on 13 May 1921, with a British military cordon surrounding the burial site, according to Captain Mary O'Neill (later Walsh), an officer in Cumann na mBan.[229]

CHARLES O'DONOGHUE BMH WS 1607, 7; MARY WALSH BMH WS 556, 7; ANNA HURLEY-O'MAHONY BMH WS 540, 3; JOHN M MCCARTHY BMH WS 883, APPENDIX, 11 7

Captain Mary O'Neill (later Walsh), an officer in Cumann na mBan, gives an account of how the Essex Regiment raided her

---

[228] Keane, p228.
[229] Keane, p231.

parents' house. The O'Neill family, particularly the women, were severely manhandled and terrorised, the mother being beaten unconscious by rifle butts. Captain O'Neill's testimony was quoted in The Catholic Herald of 21 June 1921.

MARY WALSH BMH WS 556, 8

Volunteer Godfrey Canty was trying to avoid a sweep by British military at Murragh when he was shot and fatally wounded. A roadside monument was placed some distance from where he fell.[230]

CHARLES O'DONOGHUE BMH WS 1607, 10

10 May 1921

Volunteer Michael Burke was arrested at Cobh by the Cameron Highlanders. After much questioning at Belmont Huts, to his astonishment he was released. This was probably a procedural error by the Camerons, for they surrounded his house later the same day. He managed to get away.

MICHAEL BURKE BMH WS 1424, 26

Daniel Donovan, OC Clogagh Company, was arrested at Burrane, Clonakilty by a party of Major Percival's Essex Regiment. He was released from Bere Island after the signing of the Treaty.

DANIEL DONOVAN BMH WS 1608, 15

The O'Donnell house at Aughrim, Milford was the scene of a gun battle and a daring attempted escape by three IRA men.

---

[230] Keane, p231.

Commandant Patrick O'Brien and his brother Dan, along with battalion QM John O'Regan, were alerted by a loud knock at the door. All three dashed from the house, Patrick O'Brien, armed with a Colt handgun, keeping his pursuers at bay. He got safely away, but O'Regan, by now severely wounded, was taken prisoner, as was Volunteer Daniel O'Brien of Liscarrol Company; he was tried by British military court martial and executed on 16 May 1921.

PATRICK O'BRIEN BMH WS 764, 45; MICHAEL O'DONNELL BMH WS 1145, 8

11 May 1921

Cloundireen, Kilbrittain was the location of a roundup by British soldiers of the Essex Regiment under Major Percival. Volunteer David O'Sullivan and Captain Con Murphy were pursued by the Essex, and Murphy was shot and killed. An old man living nearby was pressed into service to bring his body to Bandon in a pony and cart. Silver, based in Courtmacsherry, was the British officer in charge. Captain Con Murphy was buried in Clogagh graveyard with full military honours.[231]

JOHN O'DRISCOLL BMH WS 1250, 14; MICHAEL COLEMAN BMH WS 1254, 18; MARY WALSH BMH WS 556, 6; CHARLES O'DONOGHUE BMH WS 1607, 9; JOHN M MCCARTHY BMH WS 883, APPENDIX, 11; MICHAEL COLEMAN BMH WS 1254, 18

---

[231] Keane, p232.

12 May 1921

The house of James Dunlea at Garlands, Castletown Kenneigh was the location of a meeting of Commandant Tom Barry and other Third Cork Brigade officers. They planned a daylight attack on Bandon. An insight into Barry's attitude to insubordination is revealed in this witness statement. A volunteer who had refused to carry out an order given by an officer was ordered by the commandant to work on the farm of a volunteer who was in prison or on the run.

PHILIP CHAMBERS BMH WS 738, 9

13 May 1921

Twenty members of Newcestown Company were mobilised on this date, a time of enemy raiding parties and reprisals. Tom Barry, Third Cork Brigade flying column OC, chose three men, though for what purpose it is unclear.

DANIEL CANTY BMH WS 1619, 33

14 May 1921

A huge operation against the Auxiliaries involving over a hundred men from three battalions of the First Cork Brigade at Macroom was cancelled at the last minute, to the bafflement of Charles Browne, an officer in the Seventh Battalion of that brigade.

CHARLES BROWNE BMH WS 873, 44; DANIEL MCSWEENEY BMH WS 1651, 11; TIM BUCKLEY BMH WS 1641, 18; MORTIMER CURTIN BMH WS 1679, 10

As a result of IRA men being executed on 28 April 1921, a general order was given to all IRA battalions in the city and county of Cork to shoot on sight all Crown forces personnel, armed or unarmed. Acting on these orders, Volunteers Daniel Cashman and Phil Hyde, members of the east Cork flying column, shot two British marines at Ramhill, Ballinacurra. The two marines were members of the Royal Marine Artillery. They were Gunner Bernard Francis, aged 22, from Sussex; and Gunner William Parker, 24, from Manchester.[232]

DANIEL CASHMAN BMH WS 1523, 12; JOHN KELLEHER BMH WS 1456, 26; JOHN M MCCARTHY BMH WS 883, APPENDIX, 11

Michael Coleman, OC Barryroe Company, and other local volunteers entered Courtmacsherry village. They opened fire on a group of British soldiers, killing one and wounding two. The fatality was Lance Corporal Roland Madell, aged 30, from Guernsey. He belonged to the First Battalion Essex Regiment.[233]

MICHAEL COLEMAN BMH WS 1254, 19; JOHN O'DRISCOLL BMH WS 1250, 14; WILLIAM MCCARTHY BMH WS 1255, 11; LAWRENCE SEXTON BMH WS 1290, 8; SEÁN MOYLAN BMH WS 838, 347

At Dunmanway at 2 pm, around fifty IRA men entered the town and split into three groups. Several horse-and-carts were brought into the market place, the horses shot, thus blocking access and exit to several roads. The RIC barracks was fired on

---

[232] Keane, p234.
[233] Keane, p231.

by the IRA, but neither the police nor the Auxiliaries based outside the town ventured out to give battle.

TED O'SULLIVAN BMH WS 1478, 38; EDWARD YOUNG BMH WS 1402, 20; RICHARD RUSSELL BMH WS 1591, 23; PADDY O'BRIEN BMH WS 812, 25

Three members of the King's Own Scottish Borderers were shot dead near Furious Pier by volunteers from Rossmacowen Company, Castletownbere Battalion area. Several reprisals in the form of house burnings took place in the following days. The soldiers killed were:

Private John Hunter, aged 20, from Glasgow

Private Donald Chalmers, 21, from London

Private Robert McMillan, 19, from Rutherglen[234]

LIAM O'DWYER BMH WS 1527, 17; EUGENE DUNNE BMH WS 1537, 8; CHRISTOPHER O'CONNELL BMH WS 1530, 26; TED O'SULLIVAN BMH WS 1478, 38; JOHN M MC CARTHY BMH WS 883, APPENDIX, 11

Tom Barry, OC Third Cork Brigade flying column, and four other officers from the brigade drove into Bandon from the Dunmanway direction, a Lewis machine gun mounted at the windscreen. Some soldiers of the Essex Regiment, surrounded by armed sentries, were playing soccer on the Grammar School pitch. Fire was opened by the IRA, and a gun battle ensued, during which an Essex soldier was killed. The dead soldier was named as Private Francis Shepherd of the First Battalion Essex

---

[234] Keane, p236.

Regiment. Later that day, in a separate incident, two civilians, Cornelius Looney and Patrick Walsh, were struck by bullets, Looney dying that night.[235]

PETER KEARNEY BMH WS 444, 13; MICHAEL J CROWLEY BMH WS 1603, 23

Members of Bandon Battalion, Third Cork Brigade ambushed an RIC patrol at Innishannon, during which a policeman was killed. Constable John Kenna, aged 24 and from Co Tipperary, had three years' police service.[236]

CON FLYNN BMH WS 1621, 24; RICHARD RUSSELL BMH WS 1591, 24; TED O'SULLIVAN BMH WS 1478, 38; JOHN M MCCARTHY BMH WS 883, APPENDIX, 11

Members of the east Cork flying column shot Sergeant Coleman, RIC, in a Midleton public house. Later in the day, two policemen were shot dead in the street. Sergeant Joseph Coleman was from London and aged 39; Constable Thomas Cormyn, aged 35, was from Co Cavan; Constable Harold Thompson, 28, was from Australia.[237]

JOHN KELLEHER BMH WS 1456, 26; JOHN M MCCARTHY BMH WS 883, APPENDIX, 11

A party of RIC were attacked in an IRA grenade attack at Watercourse Road in the Cork suburb of Blackpool. Constable Peter Carolan (or Coughlan), from Co Cavan, died that day.

---

[235] Keane, p236
[236] Keane, p237; Abbot, p237.
[237] Keane, p233; Abbott, p238

Constable John Ryle, from Kerry, died on the 15 May, and Constable Patrick Hayes, a Corkman, died on 31 May.[238]

PATRICK A MURRAY BMH WS 1584, 24; CHARLES O'CONNELL BMH WS 566, 3; JOHN M MCCARTHY BMH WS 883, APPENDIX, 11

The witness statement of Lieutenant John Kelleher of Midleton Company differs somewhat from that of Francis Healy (BMH WS 1694, 20). Kelleher says the Cameron Highlanders shot and killed a volunteer named McNamara at the local golf links, then later killed Volunteer Richard Barry at his home a mile outside Midleton. They then went to find and presumably kill Jackeen Ahern, a volunteer, at his house; not finding him, they took away his brother Michael, whose body was found next day. Volunteer John Ryan of Woodstock was taken from his house and shot dead by the Cameron Highlanders. An elderly civilian, Richard Hayes, was also killed.[239]

JOHN KELLEHER BMH WS 1456, 28; FRANCIS HEALY BMH WS 1694, 20

Two members of the RIC were hurt when Kilbrittain RIC barracks was attacked by the local IRA.

DENIS O'BRIEN BMH WS 1353, 16

---

[238] Keane, p235; Abbott, 238.
[239] Keane, p238.

15 May 1921

British military conducted a sweep in north Cork on this date; Seán Moylan, a senior officer in the Second Cork Brigade and a newly-elected TD, was arrested, as was Daniel Flynn, an officer in Kiskeam Company.

DANIEL FLYNN BMH WS 1240, 11; JAMES J RIORDAN BMH WS 1172, 17; THOMAS ROCHE BMH WS 1222, 17

Fr James O'Callaghan, a Catholic priest staying in the home of Alderman Liam de Róiste at Upper Janemount in the Cork suburb of Sunday's Well, was set upon and shot dead by members of the Royal Irish Constabulary in the early hours of the morning. He died in hospital at six o'clock that evening.[240]

P J MURPHY BMH WS 869, 28

Constable Hugh McLean, from Moray in Scotland, a member of the Black and Tans, was ambushed and mortally wounded by members of Skibbereen Battalion some distance from the town. He died that evening.[241]

CORNELIUS CONNOLLY BMH WS 1602, 2

Patrick Sheehan, a civilian and a native of Templmartin, was shot dead by unknown men, but most probably members of the RIC, at his lodgings in Lankford Row, Cork. Married just two weeks, his wife witnessed the killing.[242]

---

[240] Keane, p240.
[241] Keane, p239; Abbott, p241.
[242] Keane, p239.

16 May 1921

Volunteer Daniel O'Brien, Liscarrol Company, Charleville Battalion, was executed 'following a Drumhead Courtmartial'. He had been caught in arms by a British military raiding party at the O'Donnell house at Aughrim, Milford, along with Newmarket Battalion QM John O'Keeffe. (See 10 May 1921.)[243]

PATRICK O'BRIEN BMH WS 764, 48 SEÁN MOYLAN BMH WS 838, 243

Lieutenant John Kelleher of Midleton Company was in Midleton the day the funerals of the three RIC men who were killed on 14 May took place. He was taken away to the Belmont hutments by the Cameron Highlanders Regiment and interrogated.

JOHN KELLEHER BMH WS 1456, 28

Members of Glenville Company arrested David Walsh of Shanagarry on suspicion of giving information to Crown forces which led to the massacre of the East Cork flying column at Clonmult (see 20 February 1921). Walsh was tried, and executed at Doon, Glenville.[244]

JAMES COSS BMH WS 1065, 11; WILIAM BUCKLEY BMH WS 1009, 21; PATRICK J HIGGINS BMH WS 1467, 7; JOHN P O'CONNELL BMH WS 1444, 13

---

[243] Keane, p241.
[244] Keane, p241.

18 May 1921

Lance Corporal Arthur Hill, believed by the IRA to be an intelligence officer, was shot dead by them in the Tivoli area of Cork city. There does not appear to be any reference to Hill in the witness statements of the Bureau of Military History.[245]

The house at Coppingerstown of John Kelleher, an officer in Midleton Company, was blown up by the Cameron Highlanders.

JOHN KELLEHER BMH WS 1456, 28

19 May 1921

A large roundup by the Essex Regiment under Major Percival took place at Ballinagree, Clondrohid and Ballyvourney. Members of the Seventh Battalion flying column engaged a section of the Essex at Ballinagree, with no casualties being reported on either side.

CHARLES BROWNE BMH WS 873, 45

20 May 1921

Three spies were shot and wounded by the IRA at the quarry at Asylum Road, Cork. Edward Hawkins, an ex-soldier employed by the British military, died later that day.[246]

MATTHEW O'CALLAGHAN BMH WS 561, 2

---

[245] Keane, p243.
[246] Keane, p242.

Francis Leo McMahon, described as a civilian spy, an employee of the War Pensions Office in Cork, was abducted and shot by members of the city active service unit.[247]

DANIEL HEALY BMH WS 1656, 14; MATTHEW O'CALLAGHAN BMH WS 561, 2

21 May 1921

The trial of John C Murphy, IO Mallow Company, took place at Cork Military Detention Barracks, Victoria Barrcks, Cork on this date. He had been arrested at Mallow the previous October. He was charged, along with five others, with the murder of Sergeant Gibbs of the Seventeenth Lancers on 28 September 1920, the day Mallow barracks was captured by the IRA. He was found guilty and sentenced to death along with Volunteers Harold, Barter, McCarthy and Buckley. Apparently Murphy was aware that peace talks were going ahead at this time. The Truce intervened, and thirty prisoners who had incurred the death sentence were released from Cork Male Prison in January 1922.

JOHN C MURPHY BMH WS 1217, 7

Volunteer William Burke of Castletownroche Battalion was shot dead by British military for supposedly failing to halt when challenged.[248]

THOMAS BARRY BMH WS 430, 26

---

[247] Keane, p243.
[248] Keane, p243.

23 May 1921

Volunteer Stephen Dorman, E Company, Second Battalion, was killed by a bomb blast in the Douglas Street area of Cork. He does not appear to be mentioned in the witness statements of the Bureau of Military History.[249]

Two British soldiers of the Machine Gun Corps were arrested near Charleville by the IRA. 'At their trial they admitted they were on intelligence duties. They were executed and died very bravely.' Their names are not known, but they may have been Private Patrick Cagney and Private Walter Musgrove. Their makeshift graves were disturbed accidentally by a local farmer in 1953; they are now buried under a Commonwealth War Graves Commission headstone in Charleville.[250]

MICHAEL GEARY BMH WS 754, 25

The flying column (or active service unit, as it was called in an urban setting) of the First Battalion, First Cork Brigade made an attempt on the life of Captain Kelly, an Irishman who was IO British forces based in Victoria Barracks in Cork. Kelly had been responsible for the interrogation under torture of many IRA men, including Tom Hales, OC Third Cork Brigade, and Pat Harte, its QM. Two bombs were thrown at Kelly's car, one landing in the vehicle but failing to explode, the other bouncing away harmlessly. Shots were exchanged, and Kelly got away.

PATRICK A MURRAY BMH WS 1584, 24

---

[249] See Keane, p244.
[250] Keane, p244.

William McCarthy, a civilian from Mallow, went missing from his home on 23 May 1921. Some time later, his wife received a letter from the IRA stating that her husband had been shot as a spy.[251]

24 May 1921

Members of Watergrasshill Company arrested a man in their area. He was Lieutenant Seymour Vincent, an IO based in Fermoy barracks, and he was captured while carrying out intelligence work. He was tried, sentenced to death and executed.[252]

CON LEDDY BMH WS 756, 14; WILIAM BUCKLEY BMH WS 1009, 21; GEORGE POWER BMH WS 451, 15; JAMES HACKETT BMH WS 1080, 6

Patrick Hickey, a civilian, was cutting turf at Laravoulta, Enniskeane, when he was fired on by a patrol of the Essex Regiment. It is possible he may not have heard a challenge to halt.[253]

25 May 1921

The house of Liam O'Dwyer, Castletownbere Battalion OC, and Volunteer Jeremiah O'Connor in Ardgroom were burned by Crown forces on this date. The following day, the house of Mícheál O' Sullivan, OC Rossmacowen Company, and Volunteer Tim Spillane were burned. These burnings were probably in reprisal for the shooting dead of three members of the King's

---

[251] Keane, p244.
[252] Keane, p245.
[253] Keane, p245.

Own Scottish Borderers near Furious Pier on 14 May 1921. Dunboy Castle, on the Beara peninsula, was burned by the IRA around this time.

LIAM O'DWYER BMH WS 1527, 18; CHRISTOPHER O'CONNELL BMH WS 1530, 27

Patrick Keating, a civilian, was shot and wounded when fired on after curfew hour by a British Army patrol on Shandon Street.He died three days later, on 25 May 1921.[254]

27 May 1921

Christopher O'Sullivan, a civilian spy who lived in Blarney Street in Cork's northside, was shot by Cork city active service unit at Model Farm Road. Knowing that RIC Sergeant Hollywood, badly wanted by the IRA, was going to attend the funeral, several ASU men attended, following Hollywood back to the city and and intending to kill him. However, the site chosen was beside the house of Seán O'Hegarty, OC First Cork Brigade, and the plan was cancelled at the last moment. It was believed that Hollywood was one of the two RIC men that killed Captain Tadhg O'Sullivan in Douglas Street on 19 April 1921.[255]

L AURENCE NEVILLE BMH WS 1639, 12

---

[254] Keane, p246.
[255] Keane, p247.

28 May 1921

Two attacks were planned by the Third Cork Brigade flying column on this day. The first was at Drimoleague, where an RIC man was wounded. At Gloundaw, a party of men under Seán Murphy, Dunmanway Battalion OC, waited in the vain expectation that K Company Auxiliaries based at Dunmanway would travel west to relieve their colleagues at Drimoleague.

DAN O'DRISCOLL BMH WS 1352, 15; JOHN J O'SULLIVAN BMH WS 1578, 21; PETER KEARNEY BMH WS 444, 14

Macroom Union workhouse was burned by B Company, Seventh (Macroom) Battalion.

CHARLES BROWNE BMH WS 873, 45

Daniel McCarthy, a native of Bantry, aroused the IRA's suspicions when he was seen to mingle with republican prisoners at Ballincollig military barracks. He was subsequently captured in Cork city; his body was discovered next to Ovens post office. He was buried at Carr's hill, on Cork's southside.[256]

TIM HERLIHY BMH WS 810, 32

Lieutenant Denis Collins of Ballinspittle Company was one of thirty republicans transferred from Spike Island to Bere Island by sea. There were now 150 prisoners on the island, and Collins in his statement gives an account of a tunnel breakout.

DENIS COLLINS BMH WS 827, 22

---

[256] Keane, p247.

Diarmuid Hurley, OC Midleton Battalion and the east Cork flying column, was walking from Carrigtwohill to Midleton when he came across a foot patrol of Black and Tans and 'old' RIC. He ran for his life, but he was killed by a bullet in the back. The Crown forces left his body where it fell, and he was buried temporarily at Churchtown, and after the Truce in the Republican Plot at Midleton, in the same place as those who fell at Clonmult.[257]

MICHAEL KEARNEY BMH WS 1418, 25; DANIEL CASHMAN BMH WS 1523, 12; CON LEDDY BMH WS 756, 15; JOHN P O'CONELL BMH WS 1444, 18; PATRICK J WHELAN BMH WS 1449, 9 & 63; SÉAMUS FITZGERALD BMH WS 1737, 35

Two civilians, Thomas and Henry Fitzgerald, were taken from their home between Mallow and Killavullen. The two brothers were both shot dead a small distance away by the IRA.[258]

THOMAS BARRY BMH WS 430, 27, 33

29 May 1921

An attack on Skibbereen was planned by Tom Barry's Third Cork Brigade flying column, despite Barry's knowledge of a huge concentration of Major Percival's Essex Regiment in the Leap area. When intelligence came through that a big roundup was planned for Skibbereen, the flying column went in the direction of Guagán Barra.

WILLIAM CROWLEY BMH WS 1502, 10

---

[257] Keane, p248.
[258] Keane, p249.

John Sullivan Lynch, an employee of the Great Southern and Western Railway, was observed entering Ballincollig military barracks on several occasions. He was arrested by H Company and shot as a spy.[259]

TIM O'KEEFFE BMH WS 810, 32

John O'Connell, a civilian in his sixties, was stopped by the Cameron Highlanders while out walking in Cobh. O'Connell was the owner of a quarry near the town. A party of Camerons had been challenged and disarmed the previous year by members of Cobh Company (see 25 August 1920). Although he had played no part in that incident, he was shot dead by Gordon Duff, a captain in the regiment.[260]

MICHAEL LEAHY BMH WS 1492, 28; MICHAEL J BURKE BMH WS 1424, 19

31 May 1921

Members of Fourth Battalion, First Cork Brigade electrically exploded a mine near Youghal. A passing patrol of the Hampshire Regiment was en route to a firing range outside the town. The IRA believed several had been killed and wounded. Those of the Hampshire Regiment who died were:

Corporal Whichlow

Bandsman Francis Burke

Lance Corporal Reginald McCall

---

[259] Keane, p250.
[260] Keane, p250.

Private Frederick Washington

Boy Frederick Evans

Boy George Simmons

Boy Frederick Hesterman[261]

PATRICK J WHELAN BMH WS 1449, 59

John Kenure, a civilian, was driving a Father Roche when he was challenged to halt in the town of Youghal. It was early morning, less than half an hour after a huge explosion had caused several deaths of the Hampshire Regiment. The British military fired, killing Kenure almost instantly and injuring the priest.[262]

Volunteer Patrick White of Meelick, Co Clare, a prisoner in Spike Island, was playing hurling with his comrades when the ball went out of bounds. Attempting to retrieve it, he was shot dead by a British Army sentry.[263]

---

[261] Keane, p252.
[262] Keane, p253.
[263] Keane, p251.

May 1921 (no date available)

The houses of loyalists called Dobbin and Pike were burned, along with the premises of Douglas golf club, 'a regular den of imperialists'.

MICHAEL MURPHY BMH WS 1547, 42; EDWARD HORGAN BMH WS 1644, 12

Men in the flying columns were now 'attacked by another insidious enemy...Practically every man in the column became affected by itch'. This was probably an attack of scabies, and it was treated with sulphur ointment.

MICHAEL MURPHY BMH WS 1547, 43

Volunteers Michael O'Sullivan and Paddy Clifford were court-martialled at this time. They had been caught in arms by a British Army patrol on their way to Ballygiblin Bridge, near Mitchelstown. Initally sentenced to death, they hired the services of Sir John Simon – 'leading light of the English Bar' – at £300 per day. The money was collected all over the Mitchelstown Battalion area, and the Truce intervened at the end.

WILLIAM ROCHE BMH WS 1362, 5

A spy, James Saunders, was tried and executed by the IRA. He confessed to providing information to the Crown forces regarding the Mourne Abbey ambush, in which four IRA men fell in combat and two more were captured and later hanged (see 15 February 1921 and 28 April 1921).[264]

---

[264] Keane, p254.

TIMOTHY SEXTON BMH WS 1565, 6; RICHARD WILLIS AND JOHN BOLSTER BMH WS 808, 5

Michael Sheehy, newly-appointed Charleville vice-commandant, was sent to Dublin to arrange a trip south for Éamon de Valera, President of the Executive Council. Sheehy met Michael Collins and Richard Mulcahy while in Dublin.

MICHAEL SHEEHY BMH WS 989, 9

Michael Walsh was arrested and interrogated by Sergeant Kelly, as well as by other intelligence officers – Henderson, Hendy and Hammond – at Victoria Barracks. He was beaten and tortured and ended up in Spike Island, when the Truce intervened.

MICHAEL WALSH BMH WS 1521, 15

First Cork Brigade organised a signalling camp at Kealkill around this time. The men were taught semaphore, Morse and lamp signalling for a period of a week.

RICHARD RUSSELL BMH WS 1591, 25

The movements of Crown forces in the Charleville area were signalled by the lighting of paraffin torches and by the use of bugles. A rota of men was organised to be deployed on high ground.

MICHAEL GEARY, RICHARD SMITH BMH WS 754, 24

Eccles Hotel having been used as a barracks for the Auxiliaries, it was feared by the IRA that the same fate would befall Vickery's Hotel in Glengarriff. It was burned by members of Bantry Battalion.

JAMES O'SULLIVAN BMH WS 1455, 11

Millstreet Battalion HQ, situated at Clydagh Mountain, was in danger of being encircled by British military in May of 1921. The battalion staff escaped arrest due to sniping by Millstreet Battalion flying column.

CORNELIUS BARRETT BMH WS 1405, 6; MATTHEW KELLEHER BMH WS 1319, 9

Following the execution of Volunteer Daniel O'Brien on 16 May 1921, volleys of shots were fired at Crown forces in Fermoy, Moore Park and Kilworth camps. There were no fatalities.

RICHARD WILLIS/JOHN BOLSTER BMH WS 808, 29

Three British sloops were boarded by Cobh Company IRA at Carrigaloe; all the vessels were scuttled.

MICHAEL BURKE BMH WS 1424, 24

The Cameron Highlanders raided the home of Volunteer Maurice Moore, who had been executed for his part in the Clonmult battle on 20 February 1921. Moore's brother Michael was seized and after a struggle managed to get away. He died two years later of a blow to the stomach incurred that night. Several nights later a bomb was thrown into the house; no casualties were caused.

MICHAEL BURKE BMH WS 1424, 28

Dan 'Sandow' Donovan and Seán Culhane, both members of the active service unit of First Battalion, First Cork Brigade, were caught in a British military cordon in Evergreen Street in the city. Culhane, who had killed Divisional Commander

Smyth RIC at the Cork and County Club and Swanzy, the organiser of Lord Mayor Mac Curtain's death, feared the worst when he saw the words "Awaiting Courtmartial' on his cell door. However, he was interned instead on Spike Island, from where he escaped three months after the Truce.

SEÁN CULHANE BMH WS 746, 20

Two volunteers from Cobh Company set a delayed explosion on a British destroyer at Haulbowline dockyard, causing it to be badly damaged. Volunteer Dónal Collins of Cobh, one of the two volunteers who set off the explosion, was chosen to show a British admiral the damage the next day.

MICHAEL BURKE BMH WS 1424, 25

Members of Dooneen Company burned down the workhouse at Millstreet.

CORNELIUS HEALY BMH WS 1416, 20

Members of the flying column of First Battalion, Second Cork Brigade opened fire on an RIC-Black and Tan patrol near the village of Ballyduff in west Waterford. The witness statement reports one policeman killed and one wounded. No record exists for a fatality in west Waterford in May 1921.

CON LEDDY BMH WS 756, 14

Members of Cork city active service unit were waiting at High Street to shoot Sergeant Cook, RIC Blackrock barracks, when news of an imminent raid by Crown forces came through. The shooting was called off.

L NEVILLE BMH WS 1634, 11

The middle of May 1921 saw Mount Leader House taken over by a detachment of the Auxiliary Division RIC. Mount Leader House, unoccupied until then, was situated close to Millstreet.

CON MEANY BMH WS 787, 20

Local volunteers attempted in vain to shoot Bob Ruddock, described as a spy, at Courtmacsherry. They were not aware that Ruddock had a military escort.

JOHN O'DRISCOLL BMH WS 1250, 46

An area between Durrus and Ballydehob was used by the IRA as a holding-place for men accused of robbing the bank at Schull some time previously. Some of the captors 'were observed by a lady member of a Protestant family named Daly'. The area was raided by British military from Bantry that day, the IRA group having previously moved out, and the Daly house at Lisheencreagh was burned as a reprisal. Shortly after, the Black and Tans burned the house of Mrs O'Sullivan of Coolagh.

SEÁN O'DRISCOLL BMH WS 1518, 15

John Lehane, Millstreet Battalion QM, and Volunteer John O'Keeffe of Rathcoole Company were arrested in a military sweep. O'Keeffe, who had served in the British Army during the First World War in France, Greece and the Dardanelles, subsequently gave his captors the slip.

JOHN O'KEEFFE BMH WS 1291, 6

About the end of May of 1921, the Essex Regiment column were camped at the town park at Skibbereen.

STEPHEN O'BRIEN BMH WS 603, 2

Liscarroll Castle was briefly reoccupied by British military, they having vacated the site a year previously. Liscarroll Company IRA opened fire on them, causing them to leave the next day.

PATRICK O'BRIEN BMH WS 764, 40

Volunteer Con Lehane, Timoleague Company, Bandon Battalion, had been arrested by a patrol of the Essex Regiment. After a struggle, he overpowered the soldier guarding him, taking his rifle, and had his wounds dressed at the O'Neill household at Maryboro near Timoleague by Captain Mary O'Neill (later Walsh), an officer in Cumann na mBan.

MARY WALSH BMH WS 556, 7

A party of Auxiliaries from Macroom were billeted in Rosscarbery after the barracks had been burned by the IRA (31 March 1921). The flying column of the Third Cork Brigade engaged with them in an exchange of gunfire until darkness intervened.

DENIS LORDAN BMH WS 470, 29

An internal report on British intelligence in Cork city was captured by the IRA. 'It stated that the last of their officers in the city had been executed and that they were now without civilian intelligence in the city.'

PATRICK A MURRAY BMH WS 1584, 23

The RIC were aware that a consignment of arms for the IRA was likely to land on the coast of west Cork. Seán O'Driscoll, OC Schull Battalion, was ordered to Dublin to tell Michael Collins of this. On his way back, O'Driscoll had a close encounter with a party of Auxiliaries at Crookstown railway station and got off at Dooniskey to walk to O'Sullivan's of Gurranreagh, a well-known republican safe house. Approaching Gurranreagh, he was warned by a local woman that Major Percival's Essex Regiment were billeted there. He travelled back to Schull by foot, a journey that took three days.

SEÁN O'DRISCOLL BMH WS 1518, 15

June 1921

1 June 1921

Members of First Battalion, Second Cork Brigade travelled to Kilworth to ambush an RIC man. The policeman was out walking with his girlfriend; he sustained several wounds which proved fatal. Constable Joseph Holman, aged twenty-one, was from Sussex. He had been in the police service for eight months.[265]

CON LEDDY BMH WS 756, 15

Lieutenant Colonel Warren Peacocke, according to a Bureau of Military History witness statement, 'had been operating in the [Innishannon] area as an intelligence agent and had guided raiding parties of military'. Peacocke, who normally stayed at the military barracks in Bandon, was shot dead at his home at Innishannon by Tom Kelleher, OC Knockavilla Company, and Volunteer Jim Ryan. Shots were exchanged with Peacocke's police guard.[266]

RICHARD RUSSELL BMH WS 1591, 25; FRANK NEVILLE BMH WS 443, 15

Two employees in Macroom post office deciphered codes relating to a British military sweep of Seventh and Eight (Macroom and Ballyvourney) Battalion area. This information, confirmed by Temporary Cadet Paddy Carroll, a Galwayman and member of

---

[265] Keane, p255; Abbott, p247.
[266] Keane, p254.

the Auxiliaries based at their headquarters in Macroom Castle, was conveyed to the IRA, who took evasive action.

CHARLES BROWNE BMH WS 873, 46

2 June 1921

Daniel O'Driscoll, OC Drimoleague Company, and two fellow volunteers were surrounded and arrested by Auxiliaries of K Company, Dunmanway. They were taken to Dunmanway workhouse, their headquarters. O'Driscoll was eventually released from Waterford prison in January of 1922.

DANIEL O'DRISCOLL BMH WS 1352, 17

3 June 1921

Millstreet workhouse was burned by two companies of the local battalion.

CON MEANY BMH WS 787, 20

5 June 1921

A large camp of bell-shaped tents signified a huge British Army presence in Ballyvourney. From there they went in all directions hoping to trap the flying columns.

MICHAEL O'SULLIVAN BMH WS 793, 25; PATRICK O'SULLIVAN BMH WS 794, 12

Newmarket Battalion flying column, under its OC Michael O'Sullivan, made a foray into Abbeyfeale in Co Limerick, where fire was opened on RIC-Black and Tan patrol, resulting in one casualty and two woundings. Constable Robert W Jolly, aged thirty-seven, from Kent, had seven months' service in the RIC.[267]

JAMES CASHMAN BMH WS 1270, 13; JOHN JONES BMH WS 759, 12; THOMAS ROCHE BMH WS 1222, 16; JAMES CASHMAN BMH WS 1270, 14; PATRICK O'BRIEN BMH WS 764, 51

Phil Singleton, OC Lombardstown Company, Mallow Battalion, Second Cork Brigade, was arrested in a roundup by Crown forces, John O'Connell becoming acting OC.

JOHN O'CONNELL BMH WS 1211, 10

Three bandsmen of the Manchester Regiment based at Ballincollig were arrested at Kilcrea Abbey after a chase from Ovens. They were shot as suspected spies and buried near a house southeast of Aherla. The remains of all three were repatriated to England after the Civil War. They were:

Bandsman Matthew Carson

Bandsman Charles Chapman

Bandsman John Cooper[268]

TIM HERLIHY AND OTHERS BMH WS 810, 18; PATRICK CRONIN BMH WS 710, 1

A civilian, Daniel O'Riordan, described by locals as an 'innocent', was shot dead at Carrigaphooca by the Cameron Highlanders Regiment. It would appear that there is no reference to Daniel

---

[267] Abbott, p253.
[268] Keane, p256.

O'Riordan's death in the witness statements of the Bureau of Military History.[269]

TIMOTHY BUCKLEY BMH WS 19

Eugene Swanton, a civilian and ex-British soldier, was taken, most probably by the IRA, from his home near Midleton on this date. His body was never recovered.[270]

6 June 1921

Captured British Army stores were seized at Dooniskey railway station by members of Kilmurry Company. The material was moved to Gurranreagh.

JOHN O'MAHONEY BMH WS 1662, 15

8 June 1921

Volunteer Daniel Crowley of Aultagh Company, Dunmanway Battalion, was shot dead at his home at Behigullane by members of O Company of the Auxiliaries stationed in Dunmanway.[271]

SEÁN MURPHY BMH WS 1445, 15

Seán O'Hegarty, OC First Cork Brigade, set up HQ at Delaney's of Toames on the 4 June. Major Percival's Essex Regiment was passing through the area by the 8 June, having come from Ballyvourney; they fired on Volunteer Daniel (Sonny) Buckley of J Company, Macroom Battalion, killing him.[272]

---

[269] Keane, p256.
[270] Keane, p255.
[271] Keane, p258.
[272] Keane, p257.

CHARLES BROWNE BMH WS 873, 48; JAMES MURPHY BMH WS 1633, 13; MICHAEL O'SULLIVAN BMH WS 793, 27; JEREMIAH MURPHY BMH WS 772, 9; DENIS MURPHY BMH WS 1318, 7

Members of Castlelyons Company sniped at Rathcormac RIC barracks, injuring a Black and Tan called Faulkener.

WILLIAM BUCKLEY BMH WS 1009, 22

A civilian, Seán Kelleher, was shot and wounded by the Cameron Highlanders Regiment at Ballyvourney. He was aged sixty-five and came from Shanacloon, a nearby townland. He died of his wounds in the Mercy Hospital in Cork on the 8 June 1921.[273]

9 June 1921

A note bearing the words 'Spies beware' and signed 'IRA' was found on the body of David Fitzgibbon at Killinane, Liscarroll.[274]

Thomas O'Keeffe of Corporation Buildings, in the Cork suburb of Blackpool, a civilian, was sitting on grass with a friend near Victoria barracks. They were ordered to go; as he was leaving, a shot was fired at him. He died on the spot. No inquiry was held.[275]

A large number of Black and Tans and Auxiliaries from Millstreet raided the Cullen area. The next morning saw a big British Army presence at Cullen, and five IRA men were arrested: Lieutenant

---

[273] Keane, p256.
[274] Keane, p258.
[275] Keane, p259.

Humphrey O'Donoghue, and Volunteers Seán O'Leary, Roger Kiely, Daniel O'Riordan and Martin Dennehy.

MATTHEW MURPHY BMH WS 1375, 14; HUMPHREY O'DONOGHUE BMH WS 1351, 9

10 June 1921

As the flying column of Major Percival's Essex Regiment advanced from Ballyvourney to Toames to Gurranreagh and on to Quarries Cross, they shot dead Volunteer Matthew Donovan, a member of the local company, two hundred yards from his home.[276]

MAURICE DONOVAN BMH WS 1736, 7; CHARLES BROWNE BMH WS 873, 48; CHARLES O'DONOGHUE BMH WS 1607, 10

11 June 1921

The following houses were destroyed by fire on, or near this date: Corr Castle, Peacocke's, Dennehy's, Stenning's and Caulfield's. All were in the Innishannon area. The local RIC barracks was fired on in order to keep the occupants from patrolling out.

CON FLYNN BMH WS 1621, 24; FRANK NEVILLE BMH WS 443, 15; RICHARD RUSSELL BMH WS 1591, 27

John Lucey, an unarmed civilian, was shot dead after curfew hour by a British patrol in Cork city.[277]

---

[276] Keane, p260; Crowley, p280.
[277] Keane, p259.

13 June 1921

Michael Murphy, Commandant Second Battalion, First Cork Brigade and OC of its ASU, who had spent a number of weeks in the Eight Battalion area in mid Cork, returned to the city on 13 June 1921. He was arrested in Mrs Stenson's public house on Douglas Street on the morning of his return, two of his comrades being wounded in the arrest. Murphy was taken to Victoria barracks, but he was not recognised, and was finally released from Spike Island in November of 1921. Other ASU volunteers that day included Frank Mahony, Jerry O'Brien, C Cogan, Jim Fitzgerald.

MICHAEL MURPHY BMH WS 1547, 44; P J MURPHY BMH WS 869, 28

The body of Michael Driscoll, a civilian 'who had spent two years in a lunatic asylum', was found propped against a hedge across from the gates of Charles Fort in Kinsale. He had been shot by the Essex Regiment. There appears to be no reference to this event in the Bureau of Military History.[278]

14 June 1921

Members of Bantry Battalion opened fire on a small British military convoy at Ballylickey. Two men in the convoy were injured, according to John J O'Sullivan, an officer in the battalion.

JOHN J O'SULLIVAN BMH WS 1578, 21

Seán Healy, Captain of A Company, First Battalion, First Cork Brigade, was arrested at his place of work at Cork railway

---

[278] Keane, p260.

station by men in plain clothes and taken to Empress Place, headquarters of the Auxiliary Division of the RIC. He claimed to be a nephew of Tim Healy QC, a lie which probably saved him from torture.

SEÁN HEALY BMH WS 1479, 61

Leo Corby, a civilian, was shot and killed by the IRA when he failed to stop his motorcycle in the Mitchelstown area. British Army documents were found in his possession. He is not mentioned in the BMH statements.[279]

15 June 1921

The body of a British soldier was found some years after the War of Independence. He was Private F Roughley of the Manchester Regiment, stationed in Ballincollig. It is not clear if he is mentioned in the BMH. It is probable he was killed around 15 June 1921.[280]

16 June 1921

A stretch of 1200 yards between Drishanebeg and Rathcoole, two and a half miles east of Millstreet on the Banteer road, was the battleground when men from Charleville, Kanturk, Millstreet, Mallow and Newmarket battalions engaged a force of Auxiliaries stationed in Millstreet. Six mines had been laid on the roadway at dawn, and the IRA waited in Rathcoole wood for most of the day. At 5 pm a convoy of four lorries entered the battle zone. Fire was concentrated on the last lorry,

---

[279] Keane, p261.
[280] Keane, p262.

and three of the mines having been exploded ensured that the Auxiliaries were not capable of driving out of the ambush. However, the operation of Lewis guns in the second and third lorries kept the IRA from pressing home an outright victory, and they withdrew after an hour's firing.

Towards the end of the war, the western end of the Second Cork Brigade area became known as Fourth Cork Brigade, and Patrick O'Brien of Liscaroll became its OC. O'Brien, who was in command of the Irish forces at Rathcoole, and several others on the Irish side believed that extensive losses were inflicted on the Auxiliaries. There were, in fact, two deaths and four injuries. Those who died were:

Cadet William Boyd, aged twenty-one, from Sussex

Cadet Frederick Shorter, same age, from Middlesex[281]

PATRICK O'BRIEN BMH WS 764, 52; CON MEANY BMH WS 787, 21; THOMAS CULHANE BMH WS 831, 14; MATTHEW KELLEHER BMH WS 1319, 10; CORNELIUS BARRETT BMH WS 1405, 7; LEO CALLAGHAN BMH WS 978, 23; JAMES CASHMAN BMH WS 1270, 14; JAMES O'CONNELL BMH WS 949, 9; DANIEL COAKLEY BMH WS 1406, 10; JOHN JONES BMH WS 759, 12; JEREMIAH DALY BMH WS 1015, 11; CORNELIUS HEALY BMH WS 1416, 18; SEÁN HEALY BMH WS 1339, 15; GEORGE POWER BMH WS 451, 20; WILLIAM REARDEN BMH WS 1185, 11; JAMES J RIORDAN BMH WS 1172, 18; JOHN WINTERS BMH WS 948, 9; MATTHEW MURPHY BMH WS 1375, 15; TADHG MCCARTHY BMH WS 965, 16

---

[281] Keane, p262; Abbott, p256.

According to John O'Mahoney, QM Kilmurry Company, Macroom Battalion, word went round the locality that Warrenscourt House was to be occupied by the Crown forces. In order to prevent this, the house was burnt down by volunteers from Crookstown and Kilmurry. Crookstown House was destroyed the following week.

JOHN O'MAHONEY BMH WS 1662, 16

18 June 1921

An attack by Cork city ASU was launched on Tuckey Street RIC barracks, during which some Black and Tans were injured. A woman named Josie Scannell was shot dead by Auxiliary gunfire. Several others innocent people were injured, some of them chidren.[282]

PATRICK MURRAY BMH WS 1584, 25

A number of IRA men from Schull Battalion sailed from Cape Clear to the Fastnet Rock, where they surprised the three lightkeepers and made away with seventeen boxes of guncotton. They landed their cargo at Leamcon, near Schull harbour.

CHARLIE COTTER BMH WS 1519, 10; WILLIAM LANNIN BMH WS 1520, 7; SEÁN O'DRISCOLL BMH WS 1518, 18; RICHARD COLLINS BMH WS 1542, 9

---

[282] Keane, p263.

21 June 1921

Daniel O'Callaghan, aged thirty, was shot dead as a spy at Carrigtwohill by the local IRA. The Crown forces described him as 'loyal'.[283]

Captain Patrick J Higgins, OC Aghada Company, who had been shot in the roof of the mouth following his surrender at the battle of Clonmult, started his trial by military court in Cork. John A Costello, later Taoiseach, was in his legal team. Higgins was sentenced to death, but an attack of appendicitis delayed the carrying out of the court order, and his life was saved by the coming of the Truce on 11 July 1921.

PATRICK J HIGGINS BMH WS 1467, 7

Following the arrest of Dan Holland, QM Bandon Battalion, Third Cork Brigade, his position was taken by Charles O'Donoghue of Farnivane Company.

CHARLES O'DONOGHUE BMH WS 1607, 8

Six IRA men from Castletownroche Company fired on a three-lorry convoy of British military at Pall, on the Castletownroche-Mallow road. The attackers believed that six soldiers were injured.

DAVID O'CALLAGHAN BMH WS 950, 11

Volunteer William Daly of Shannonvale, Clonakilty was captured in the act of demolishing Jones's Bridge near Ballinascarthy. While awaiting trial at Victoria Barracks in Cork, several leading loyalists were kidnapped by the IRA – the Earl of Bandon (whose

---

[283] Keane, p264.

house was burned the same night) and three justices of the peace: Charles Sealy King, J Fitzpatrick and St Leger Gillman. The Truce intervened in the case of Volunteer Daly (and two comrades, Volunteers Con Minehane and Jack O'Driscoll), and so the rest were released. Lord Bandon was held at three different houses in the Barryroe area.

JAMES MOLONEY BMH WS 1310, 7; DENIS LORDAN BMH WS 470, 29; TED O'SULLIVAN BMH WS 1478, 42; DANIEL CANTY BMH WS 1619, 33; JOHN O'DRISCOLL BMH WS 1250, 35

22 June 1921

Volunteer John Murphy, aged twenty-two, who worked on the Hales farm at Ballinadee, was surprised there by a British military patrol. He was bayoneted to death.[284]

CHARLES O'DONOGHUE BMH WS 1607, 9

Howes Strand coastguard station was destroyed by fire on this date. William Foley, an officer in the Bandon Battalion, incurred severe burns on the face and hands; he was put in the care of Dr Dorothy Stopford.

WILLIAM FOLEY BMH WS 1560, 8

It was believed by the IRA in Skibbereen that the local workhouse was to be occupied by Major Percival's Essex Regiment. It was destroyed by fire on this date by the local company. The Third Cork Brigade OC, Liam Deasy, was in command. On the same

---

[284] Keane, p264.

night, a group in command of Commandant Tom Barry burned the workhouse at Bandon.

DANIEL KELLY BMH WS 1590, 8; PATRICK O'SULLIVAN BMH WS 1481, 10; TED O'SULLIVAN BMH WS 1478, 41

23 June 1921

Cadet George Duckham, a member of the Auxiliaries based at Millstreet, was arrested and shot dead by the IRA near Macroom, his arms captured. According to Tim Buckley, OC Clondrohid Company, he had a list in his possession of IRA men to be shot on sight.[285]

CHARLES BROWNE BMH WS 873, 50; TIM BUCKLEY BMH WS 1641, 19; DANIEL CORKERY BMH WS 1719, 25

Schull Battalion flying column, hearing that British military were planning to raid the Mizen peninsula, sailed northwards from Dunmanus Pier to Muintir Bháire peninsula. 'We remained across the bay all day and watched the enemy searching for us', according to Richard Collins, a signals officer in Schull Battalion.

RICHARD COLLINS BMH WS 1542, 10

24 June 1921

There were several attacks launched by the IRA on this date in Cork city, one of them at Douglas RIC barracks; there were no casualties.

JEROME COUGHLAN BMH WS 1568, 14; ROBERT AHERN BMH WS 1676, 12

---

[285] Keane, p265.

The home of Volunteer Michael Dineen of Kilcorney Company, Millstreet was raided by Auxiliaries. He was accused of IRA membership and of having been involved in the Rathcoole ambush (see 16 June 1921). He was beaten and shot dead. Crown forces cordoned off the Kilcorney area that day, but several senior IRA officers were led by scouts to safety. [286]

MATTHEW KELLEHER BMH WS 1319, 12; CON MEANY BMH WS 787, 26

26 June 1921

Seán Twomey, OC Cork city ASU, and Seán Lucey, OC B Company, First Battalion, were arrested on this date, Twomey receiving serious wounds as he attempted to escape; a woman was killed in the crossfire. She was Mary Parnell, aged thirty, a war widow. Both men were released following the Truce.[287]

MARK WICKHAM AND OTHERS BMH WS 558, 4

Constable Thomas Shanley and Sergeant Ryan of the RIC were returning from mass at Kildorrery when they came under fire from the IRA; Constable Shanley, from Leitrim, was shot dead.[288]

SEUMAS O'MAHONY BMH WS 730, 16; MARK WICKHAM AND OTHERS BMH WS 558, 4

---

[286] Keane, p266.
[287] Keane, p266.
[288] Keane, p266; Abbott, p259.

27 June 1921

Private Frederick Crowther and Private Spooner, while out walking in Cork city, were picked up by the IRA. Both were shot, Crowther fatally. A third soldier managed to escape. Private Crowther came from Staffordshire.[289]

Schull workhouse was burned, and the local marine station fired on, by members of Schull and Glaun Companies.

WILLIAM LANNIN BMH WS 1520, 7; CHARLIE COTTER BMH WS 1519, 10; RICHARD COLLINS BMH WS 1542, 10; FRANK NEVILLE BMH WS 443, 16; DANIEL KELLY BMH WS 1590, 8

Four men in civilian clothes surrounded Mrs Donovan's public house in Waterfall in search of Leo Murphy, Commandant of Third (Ovens) Battalion, First Cork Brigade. In a bid to escape, Murphy was shot dead by Major Evans of the Manchester Regiment based at Ballincollig, or Captain Vining, IO at the same barracks, or perhaps both. He was buried in the Republican plot in Saint Finbarr's Cemetry. Many volunteers and civilians were arrested by the British Army that evening in Waterfall.[290]

MICHAEL O'REGAN BMH WS 1524, 8; JIM AHERN AND OTHERS BMH WS 810, 14 & 28

28 June 1921

Charles James Daly, Captain D Company, Second Battalion, was arrested at Waterfall on the evening Commandant Leo Murphy was shot dead (see 27 June 1921). Lieutenant Hammond, MC, of the Dorset Regiment, says that Daly was shot while attempting

---

[289] Keane, p267.
[290] Keane, p267.

to escape after showing the British military an alleged arms dump at Vernon Mount, Douglas, at the highly improbable hour of midnight. In all probability, Daly was shot out of hand at close quarters, the doctor's opinion being that it was 'fairly close range'.[291]

JEROME COUGHLAN BMH WS 1568, 3; TIM HERLIHY AND OTHERS BMH WS 810, 14; MICHAEL MURPHY BMH WS 1547, 38

William Horgan, a civilian, was shot dead outside the Opera House in Cork. According to Lieutenant d'Ydewalle of the South Staffordshire Regiment, Horgan tried to wrest his revolver from him, and in the struggle he was shot dead.[292]

William O'Regan, a native of Kilcor near Skibbereen, and a member of the IRA in Cork city, died around this time; the cause of death is not given. He was buried at Skibbereen Abbey, shots being fired over his grave by Seán O'Driscoll, OC Schull Battalion.

SEÁN O'DRISCOLL BMH WS 1518, 21

Ballydehob Company, in command of Seán O'Driscoll, burned the houses of 'two British loyalists', one Daly of Lisheencreagh and R J Wood of Fort View, Ballydehob. Another house of Daly's had been burned some time previously.

SEÁN O'DRISCOLL BMH WS 1518, 15 & 21

Members of Fermoy Battalion flying column waited across the street from Rathcormac RIC barracks to ambush a policeman

---

[291] Keane, p268.
[292] Keane, p269.

who had recently fired on a local civilian. Despite waiting for ten hours, there were no signs of movement from the barracks.

JAMES BRENNOCK BMH WS 1113, 18

29 June 1921

Patrick J Sheehan and John O'Sullivan were observed several times visiting the RIC barracks at Charleville. They were eventually arrested, tried and executed by the IRA.[293]

MICHAEL GEARY/RICHARD SMITH BMH WS 754, 26; JOHN D CRIMMINS BMH WS 1039, 10; MAURICE NOONAN BMH WS 1098, 8; TIMOTHY D CRIMMINS BMH WS 1051, 10

Timothy (Patrick) Murphy, a civilian, was out walking near his home late at night; a curfew patrol of the South Staffordshire Regiment shot him dead. The British Army claimed he was attempting to flee the scene. Murphy had served with the South Irish Horse under an assumed name during the Frist World War.[294]

Clohina, in the Kilnamartra area, was the location of a gunbattle on 29 June 1921, when the local company opened fire on a convoy of seven British military lorries. The British swiftly replied with machine gun and rifle fire and got away unscathed.

TIMOTHY DINNEEN BMH WS 1585, 9

A party of IRA men from Aultagh Company, armed with revolvers, entered Dunmanway seeking out an RIC patrol. Two policemen were located, but one of them was a constable who

---

[293] Keane, p269.
[294] Keane, p271.

frequently warned the IRA of impending raids by Crown forces. This, most probably, was Constable Cahill (see Patrick O'Brien BMH WS 812, 18; 13 December 1920). The attack was cancelled. There were four such raids during the month of June.

SEÁN MURPHY BMH WS 1445, 16

30 June 1921

Charles Browne of Macroom, an officer in the Seventh Battalion, was released from custody from Victoria barracks in Cork on this date. He had been arrested in a British sweep at Gurranreagh earlier in the month.

CHARLES BROWNE BMH WS 873, 49

According to James 'Spud' Murphy, he went with Jim Hurley and Tim Donoghue, two senior officers in Clonakilty Battalion, to Rosscarbery to execute a spy named Frank O'Donoghue, accused of informing Crown forces of the presence of the IRA Third Cork Brigade flying column at Burgatia House. It was, in fact, Frank Sullivan who was executed.[295]

JAMES MURPHY BMH WS 1684, 24

Volunteer Bernard Moynihan, aged nineteen, from Shankill, Kilcorney, was fired on and killed by a patrol of Auxiliaries as he worked in a hayfield.[296]

---

[295] Keane, p290.
[296] Keane, p272.

June 1921 (no date available)

An unnamed civilian was arrested by the IRA in the Cork suburb of Douglas on the grounds that he gave information to the enemy in connection with the Mourne Abbey ambush. He said he got his information from a friend, one Sanders. He was shot on instructions from the First Cork Brigade and buried in the Douglas area.

WILLIAM BARRY BMH WS 1708, 11

A detatchment of Major Percival's flying column secreted themselves in Kilpatrick national school, north of Bandon, the rest of them withdrawing to that town. It was an unsuccessful ruse which was intended to catch the IRA unawares.

JAMES DOYLE BMH WS 1640, 24

Early June of 1921 saw the arrest by Crown forces of Daniel Holland, an officer in Bandon Battalion, Third Cork Brigade; he was convicted of giving a false name and address. He spent the first three weeks of his incarceration in a hospital ward, the result of his ill-treatment during interrogation at Clonakilty.

DANIEL HOLLAND BMH WS 1341, 15

Goggin's Corner in Skibbereen was the scene of an exchange of gunfire between the local IRA company and a group of RIC. No one was injured.

PATRICK FEHILLY BMH WS 604, 1 & 3

Two men were punished for a misdemeanour at the house of Canon Haynes, Protestant rector of Kenneigh. The punishment decreed by the IRA was to have the men chained to the railings of Enniskeane church the following Sunday. Philip Chambers, OC Coppeen Company, who was ordered to enforce the punishment, regarded this action with disgust, considering it degrading.

PHILIP CHAMBERS BMH WS 738, 9

IRA soldiers from Mallow and Fermoy Battalions, armed with a Hotchkiss machine gun, made a night-time attack on Fermoy aerodrome, spraying the hangars, searchlights and wooden huts with a sustained fire. As the War of Independence progressed, aerial reconnaissance became a feature of British operations.

RICHARD WILLIS/JOHN BOLSTER BMH WS 808, 30

Members of the First Battalion flying column, Second Cork Brigade, fired on a group of Black and Tans swimming in a river near Tallow; 'they ran for their lives along the opposite bank leaving their clothes behind them'.

RICHARD WILLIS/JOHN BOLSTER BMH WS 808, 31

Volunteers Dick Browne, Con O'Leary and Denis O'Connell, all members of the Seventh (Macroom) Battalion flying column, were arrested by Black and Tans at a house in Carrigaphooka, two miles west of Macroom.

TIMOTHY BUCKLEY BMH WS 1641, 19

Many IRA members from the Cullen Company were arrested when the British Army converged on the area in early June of 1921.

TIMOTHY CONDON BMH WS 1374, 5

Rathcormac RIC barracks was fired on by members of Second Cork Brigade. There were no injuries on either side.

RICHARD WILLIS/JOHN BOLSTER BMH WS 808, 32

A suspected spy named Willie Ginn was arrested at Castlelyons on suspicion of giving information to the Crown forces. He was ordered to be deported.

RICHARD WILLIS/JOHN BOLSTER BMH WS 808, 32; JJ BRENNOCK BMH WS 1113, 17

The newly-formed First Southern Division of the IRA met at Ballydesmond, with Liam Lynch presiding as OC.

JOHN JONES BMH WS 759, 11

Three British marines were taken prisoner at Castletownsend by members of Skibbereen Battalion. They were detained near Leap for two weeks, eventually making a successful escape.

DANIEL KELLY BMH WS 1590, 8

Timothy Keohane, Second Lieutenant of Timoleague Company, was arrested during a British military sweep of the Timoleague area. He was imprisoned at Spike Island and Maryborough (now Portlaoise), eventually being released after the signing of the Treaty in December of 1921.

TIMOTHY KEOHANE BMH WS 1285, 11

The end of June and the early days of July 1921 saw British military and Black and Tan posts in Mallow fired on several times. There were no casualties.

TADHG MCCARTHY BMH WS 965, 18

Five volunteers of Timoleague Company were surprised while making a dugout at Castleview. Volunteer Con Lehane replied to enemy fire, thus enabling his comrades to escape. He managed to get away some miles distant, only to be arrested by another patrol. He disarmed the soldier tasked with guarding him, escaping with his rifle.

JOHN O'DRISCOLL BMH WS 1250, 34

Late June and early July of 1921 saw the almost almost complete withdrawal of police and British military patrols in Cork city and county. Ballydaheen, in the Mallow area, was the scene of several gatherings by the local IRA, who waited in vain for the enemy.

JOHN MOLONEY BMH WS 1036, 17

James 'Spud' Murphy and Jim Lane, two officers in Clonakilty Company, spent two days evading the Auxiliaries by hiding out in the loft and in the back garden of a house in Rosscarbery. They eventually found their way to Mill Cove, and thence by boat around the Galley Head to safety.

JAMES MURPHY BMH WS 1684, 23

The body of John J Walsh, described as being a former member of the British Army reserve, was discovered by accident near Midleton in 1927. He was believed to have gone missing in June 1921.[297]

A training camp for the Third Cork Brigade was set up at Droumfeagh, Dunmanway in late June of 1921. It was in the command of Denis Lordan, adjutant of the Brigade flying column.

SEÁN MURPHY BMH WS 1445, 16

---

[297] Keane, p272.

July 1921

2 July 1921

Jeremiah O'Carroll (OC F Company, Third Battalion) was the target of an arrest bid at his home in Farnanes on this date. O'Carroll managed to escape, his brother Denis being arrested in his stead. O'Carroll maintained that the trauma brought on by the raid led to the premature death of his mother.

JEREMIAH O'CARROLL BMH WS 706, 6

Fermoy Battalion flying column moved to Tallow in Co Waterford to ambush a patrol of Black and Tans. A policeman was shot dead and two others wounded. Constable Francis Creedon, from Macroom, had twenty years' service in the RIC.[298]

CON LEDDY BMH WS 756, 15; WILLIAM BUCKLEY BMH WS 1009, 22

3 July 1921

Maurice Cusack of Ballycotton, a civilian, was fired at and killed by a party of the Cameron Highlanders in his home village. He had no connection to the IRA.[299]

EDMOND O'BRIEN BMH WS 623, 3

A plan by members of Fermoy Battalion was made to attack a group of British officers on the outskirts of Fermoy. Urgent messages were sent to the IRA that the enemy had knowledge

---

[298] Abbott, p262.
[299] Keane, p273.

of their plan. The house was duly surrounded by Crown forces, but the column had escaped.

JAMES HACKETT BMH WS 1080, 9; WILLIAM BUCKLEY BMH WS 1009, 23

Eugene Dunne, IO Adrigole Company, Castletownbere Battalion, was arrested as he ran into an enemy round up. He was released after the signing of the Treaty.

EUGENE DUNNE BMH WS 1537, 8

Edward Swanton, a Skibbereen draper, was abducted by the IRA; he 'was suspected of co-operating with the enemy'. Swanton was released after the Truce.

DANIEL C KELLY BMH WS 1590, 8; STEPHEN O'BRIEN BMH WS 603, 3

4 July 1921

A plan was made to attack a British military encampment at Farnalough, Newcestown, but for some unspecified reason it was never pressed home.

DANIEL CANTY BMH WS 1619, 34

Seán Healy was identified at Victoria barracks as having been in possession of arms near Jail Cross by Stevens, a student of UCC. Healy appeared at a British military court that day but Stevens failed to show. The trial was adjourned, and the Truce intervened a week later.

SEÁN HEALY BMH WS 1479, 72

5 July 1921

An extensive roundup was conducted in the Castlelyons area of north Cork by the British military. Fermoy Battalion flying column had a shelter in Barrafohenagh measuring 22 by 18 by 16 feet constructed half way up a hillside.

JAMES HACKETT BMH WS 1080, 10; WILLIAM BUCKLEY BMH WS 1009, 20 & 23

6 July 1921

Brady, a resident magistrate from Ballylickey, was arrested by Coomhola Company. 'It later transpired that this man was friendly to our side and he was released within a couple of days.'

JOHN J O'GORMAN BMH WS 1578, 21

7 July 1921

Foxe's Hole, a swimming-place near Dunmanway, was the scene of an ambush where members of Dunmanway Battalion fired on a party of Black and Tans. Seán Murphy, OC Aultagh Company, wrote in his witness statement that one policeman subsequently died, but there appears to be no evidence of this.

SEÁN MURPHY BMH WS 1445, 16

Coolcower House, situated about a mile east of Macroom, was burned by members of Toames and Macroom Companies. Richard Williams, the owner, also had a hotel in the town. Charles Browne, an officer in the Seventh Battalion, gave the date as 3 July 1921.

JEREMIAH MURPHY BMH WS 772, 9; CHARLES BROWNE BMH WS 873, 51; DANIEL MCSWEENEY BMH WS 1651, 12

Newmarket and Millstreet flying columns, under Second Cork Brigade vice OC Paddy O'Brien, moved into the west Limerick area, where they lay in wait in Templeglantine for an enemy patrol. It was while they were here that news of the impending Truce came through.

JAMES CASHMAN BMH WS 1270, 17; JAMES J RIORDAN BMH WS 1172, 20

An attack was made on Ballinhassig RIC barracks, during which a policeman was killed some distance from the building. Machine gun and rifle fire was returned by the garrison. Constable James Connor, aged twenty-four, was a member of the Black and Tans. He was a Tipperary man.[300]

JOHN BARRETT BMH WS 1538, 3

William McPherson, an ex-British Army sergeant major, was suspected by the IRA of being a spy. He was arrested by members of Dromahane Company and held for some days before his trial. He was executed one mile from Mallow.[301]

JOSEPH P MORGAN BMH WS 1097, 18; CORNELIUS O'REGAN BMH WS 1200, 14; LEO CALLAGHAN BMH WS 978, 25

---

[300] Keane, p273; Abbott, p263.
[301] Keane, p274.

8 July 1921

Ardcahan, on the Macroom road near Dunmanway, was the location chosen by ten members of Dunmanway Battalion to ambush a patrol of Crown forces. Very few British patrols ventured out in the days approaching the Truce, and the IRA party disbanded.

SEÁN MURPHY BMH WS 1445, 16

The home in Strawberry Hill, on Cork's northside, of Volunteer Denis Spriggs of C Company, First Battalion, was raided by a patrol of the South Staffordshire Regiment in command of Second Lieutenant d'Ydewalle. Spriggs was killed soon afterwards, the British military being told he had been shot while attempting to escape. Bearing in mind that Lieutenant d'Ydewalle had been involved in other incidents where IRA prisoners and civilians had been killed in the same circumstances, it is probable that the killing of Volunteer Spriggs was planned.[302]

P J MURPHY BMH WS 869, 30

9 July 1921

Daniel Healy and Liam O'Callaghan, two members of Cork city active service unit, were given the job of travelling to London to shoot Patrick Connors. Connors was believed to be the informer who gave information to Crown forces which led to the deaths of six IRA men at Ballycannon, in the Kerry Pike area (see 21 March 1921).

---

[302] Keane, p274; Ó Ruairc, P, *Truce: Murder, Myth and the Last Days of the Irish War of Independence*, Mercier (Cork), 2016, pp233, 240.

DANIEL HEALY BMH WS 1656, 15

Innishannon barracks was fired on for the last time on this date.

FRANK NEVILLE BMH WS 443, 16

10 July 1921

Second Cork Brigade area was considered too unwieldy to be effective, and it was decided at a brigade meeting at Dromahane, near Mallow, to form a Fourth Cork Brigade, comprising Mallow, Kanturk, Millstreet, Newmarket and Charleville Battalions. Paddy O'Brien of Liscarrol was its first OC.

JEREMIAH DALY BMH WS 1015, 13; TADHG MCCARTHY BMH WS 965, 18; JAMES O'CONNELL BMH WS 949, 10; MICHAEL O'CONNELL BMH WS 1428, 23; JOHN WINTERS BMH WS 948, 10; WILLIAM C REGAN BMH WS 1069, 13

One of the last actions of the War of Independence in the north Cork area was at Staples Cross, Castlelyons, when Fermoy Battalion took up positions at 11 pm in the expectation of a cycle patrol of over fifty British military passing by. The column stayed until 6 am. This being within a day of the Truce, most, if not all British units would have been under orders to stay in barracks.

JJ BRENNOCK BMH WS 1113, 19

A British soldier based at Ballyvonaire camp was captured, while out walking, by Doneraile Company; he was executed.

Private William Edward Larter of the First Battalion Machine Gun Corps was a native of Norwich, England.[303]

WILLIAM C REGAN BMH WS 1069, 13; THOMAS BARRY BMH WS 430, 28

A well-armed party of British soldiers tasked with getting supplies of water at Mitchelstown was fired on by members of Mitchelstown and Ballygiblin Companies, Second Cork Brigade. During a furious exchange of gunfire, several soldiers from both armies sustained injuries, although there were no fatalities.

LEO SKINNER BMH WS 940, 6; PATRICK J LUDDY BMH WS 1151, 22; WILLIAM ROCHE BMH WS 1362, 7; SÉAMUS O'MAHONY BMH WS 730, 17; GEORGE POWER BMH WS 451, 20

Four soldiers – two Royal Engineers and two from the South Staffordshire Regiment – left their post at Cork jail on the Western Road; they were unarmed and travelling on foot. They were captured by a patrol of seven IRA men. Dan Hallinan, OC H Company, in his report to IRA headquarters, wrote that they were searched by their captors before being taken to Ellis Quarry, where they were executed before 9 pm. Connie Neenan, one of the senior IRA men in the city, viewed these killings with disgust, suggesting that they were futile and wrong. Pádraig Óg Ó Ruairc, in his book *Truce: Murder, Myth and the Last Days of the Irish War of Independence*, says that Captain Hallinan was a close friend of Volunteer Denis Spriggs, a member of C Company, First Battalion, and that he was 'shot dead while attempting to

---

[303] Keane, p276.

escape' by Second Lieutenant d'Ydewalle of the South Staffordshires, thus suggesting that the Ellis Quarry killings were an act of revenge. There is no reference in the BMH to these killings. Those killed were:

Lance Corporal Harold Dakar

Private Henry Morris

Royal Engineer Alfred Camm

Royal Engineer Albert Powell[304]

John Foley, a civilian, was in his house in Leemount, Coachford, when it was raided by the West Yorkshire Regiment. Locals maintained that he died from being shot deliberately in the back.[305]

Major George B O'Connor, a justice of the peace from Rochestown, was a unionist whom the IRA accused of passing on information about them to the British military in Victoria barracks. He was found shot dead near his home.[306]

MICHAEL MURPHY BMH WS 1547, 36

11 July 1921

Seán Hennessy, lieutenant of Ballynoe Company, Fermoy Battalion, was one of about sixty prisoners removed from Spike Island in Cork harbour to Bere Island. They were released following the signing of the Treaty in December 1921.

---

[304] Keane, p276; Ó Ruairc, p162-174.
[305] Keane, 275; Ó Ruairc, 249-251.
[306] Keane, p277; Ó Ruairc, p88.

SEÁN HENNESSY BMH WS 1090, 11

John Begley was arrested in Patrick Street in Cork by the IRA on the day of the Truce. He was shot as a spy some time later.[307]

SEÁN O'CONNELL BMH WS 1706, 9; WILLIAM BARRY BMH WS 1708, 11

Cornelius Connolly, OC Skibbereen Battalion, and Tadhg O'Sullivan, QM Third Cork Brigade, were involved in the fatal shooting of a policeman in the town on the day the Truce came into effect. 'He was chief intelligence man to the British and was very much wanted by us.' Constable Alexander Clarke was aged fifty-two; he was from Co Tipperary.[308]

CORNELIUS CONNOLLY BMH WS 602, 2

William J Nolan, a youth from Friars' Walk in Cork, was abducted by the IRA, accused of spying and joining the RIC. His body was never found.[309]

Lieutenant Daniel Browne of Meelin Company, a member of the flying column of the newly-formed Fourth Cork Brigade, was part of a group of a hundred men, together with Limerick volunteers, lying in wait for a British military convoy between Newcastlewest and Abbeyfeale. At mid-day, the start of the Truce, the IRA commenced to take up land mines on the road. The expected convoy arrived, and tense moments passed before both sides exchanged souvenirs.

---

[307] Keane, p279.
[308] Kingston, p117; Keane, p278; Abbott, p266.
[309] Keane, p278.

DANIEL BROWNE BMH WS 785, 12; PADDY O'BRIEN BMH WS 764, 60; JAMES J RIORDAN BMH WS 1172, 21; SEÁN HEALY BMH WS 1339, 17

Volunteer Leo Skinner, of Mitchelstown Company, lay recovering at O'Donoghue's house in Gurteenaboul. The previous day he had been shot through the thigh in a gun battle with British soldiers at Mitchelstown.

LEO SKINNER BMH WS 940, 7

A second Cork Brigade Council meeting at Lombardstown, near Mallow, sent Commandant 'Dorney' O'Regan to disseminate news of the impending Truce. 'Tired and weary, he returned in the early hours of Monday morning, July 11th, bearing definite news of the "Cease Fire". Straightaway the necessary dispatches were got ready and despatch riders set out to reach the various Company OCs by mid-day. It was in Mitchelstown, as we have seen, that the last shots were fired in the Battalion area, and it was here that the despatch rider, Tom Lee, narrowly escaped death at the hands of enraged enemy forces as he arrived on his hunter for the "Cease Fire" Order for the local Company OC. Fortunately, through the good offices of the late Monsignor David O'Connell, P.P, V.G., he was spared and subsequently released, with apologies.'

SÉAMUS O'MAHONY BMH WS 730, 18

British troops were observed to have gone through Clonakilty Junction at Gaggin every Monday morning. A party of volunteers from Newcestown Company took up positions there on the morning of the Truce. They disbanded just before mid-day and took refreshments in local houses. 'We remained in the area until about 2 p.m., when we decided to return to our home areas. Just as we were about to move away, a party of British troops moved along the railway line from the west. Their strength was one officer and about twenty men. They were marching with arms reversed. We moved away and they just laughed, so that finished the fighting to the Truce to July 11th 1921.'

DANIEL CANTY 1619, 35

Captain Seán Healy, OC A Company, First Battalion, First Cork Brigade, gives an account of events at Victoria barracks on the day of his release: 'From the date of the signing [of the Truce, Saturday 9 July 1921] there was a noticeable change in the attitude of the camp officials towards the prisoners. Sergeant Grant, of the Hampshire Regiment, who was in charge of the camp, became very friendly, in the knowledge that it would only be a short time before before all the prisoners would be released and the camp closed down...After saying farewell to my companions who were left behind, I shook hands with Sergeant Grant to show there was no ill-feeling between us as soldiers, and walked out of Victoria Barracks (now Collins Barracks) into a free world. It was a glorious sunny evening. The feeling of emotion which came over me when I left the cage behind was one that I shall never forget. I felt as if I was walking into a new world and fervently thanked God for bringing me through the perils and trials which I had endured. I was a free man once more.'

SEÁN HEALY BMH WS 1479, 73

July 1921 (no date available)

Daniel M J O'Connell, grandson of Daniel O'Connell the Liberator, 'was another loyalist and no friend of ours'. Members of Skibbereen Company kidnapped him shortly before the Truce, but he was released on the orders of Michael Collins.

STEPHEN O'BRIEN BMH WS 603, 3

Major Percival's Essex Regiment surrounded a large portion of the barony of Carbery and made a sweep in the direction of the sea. Flying column section leader James 'Spud' Murphy and two comrades were forced to hide in a cave at Dunnycove, near Ardfield. They eventually travelled through seven townlands, breaking out at Sam's Cross and on to Bealad and Carrhuvouler.

JAMES MURPHY BMH WS 1684, 25

In the month of July, up to the signing of the Truce, Kilbrittain RIC barracks was sniped on three occasions.

JAMES O'MAHONY/ DENIS CROWLEY/ JOHN FITZGERALD BMH WS 560, 21

In the days leading up to the Truce, members of Dunmanway Battalion flying column drove through Dunmanway by car, engaging in an exchange of gunfire with some Auxiliaries. An IRA man was wounded.

EDWARD YOUNG BMH WS 1402, 22

The city active service unit attacked Tuckey Street and Shandon Street RIC barracks, and Douglas RIC barracks was fired on, in the days coming up to the Truce.

PATRICK MURRAY BMH WS 1584, 26

Probably the last great British sweep of the War of Independence took place in west Cork, when the flying column of the Third Cork Brigade, under Commandant Tom Barry, marched from Drinagh to Glengarriff, knowing that Major Percival's Essex Regiment was on their trail. They then marched to Coomhola, where they climbed, with the aid of a guide and in the command of Barry, the mountain ridge that borders Guagán Barra. At dawn they descended, entering the barony of Muskerry, and were fed at Cronin's Hotel. It was rumoured that Percival, on hearing that Barry's men had given him the slip, took a train back to Bandon, leaving his men to make their way back on foot.

WILLIAM MCCARTHY BMH WS 1255, 14

Appendix 1

The Cork Brigades: Bureau of Military History – Witness Statements pertaining to lists of personnel within the First, Second and Third Cork Brigades

First Cork Brigade

Officers of First Cork Brigade, 1919

O.C, Tomás MacCurtain

Vice O.C, Terence MacSwiney

Adjutant, Pat Higgins

Battalions of First Cork Brigade:

Cork City A

Cork City B

Macroom

Ovens

Whitechurch

Donoughmore

Passage West

Cobh

Ballyvourney

CORNELIUS KELLEHER BMH WS 1654

ARMY LISTS – FIRST CORK BRIGADE

Irish Volunteers/Irish Republican Army: First Cork Brigade

Witness statements where names of officers and men in each brigade are listed:

EDWARD HORGAN BMH WS 1644
Officers H Company, First Battalion, 1918.

THOMAS DALY BMH WS 719
Officers E Company First Battalion, 1920
Officers E Company First Battalion (at truce)

JOHN J. LUCY (and others) BMH WS 558
Officers B Company, First Battalion, 1917
Officers B Company, First Battallion (at Truce)

MATTHEW O'CALLAGHAN BMH WS 561
Officers G Company First Battalion, 1917-1921
I.R.B. Members G Company, First Battalion

CHARLES O'CONNELL BMH WS 566
Officers D Company, First Battalion

EDWARD SISK BMH WS 1505
Officers Carrigaline Company, Ninth Battalion.
Companies in Ninth Battalion

DICK COTTER AND OTHERS BMH WS 810

Officers Third (Ovens) Battalion – with succeeding officers.

Officers A Company (Srelane)

Officers B Company (Killumney)

Officers C Company Ballinora

Officers D Company Aherla

Officers E Company Farran

Officers F Company Farnanes

Officers Third Battalion (at Truce)

Officers C Company (at Truce)

JEROME COUGHLAN BMH WS 1568

Officers D Company Second Battalion

MORTIMER CURTIN BMH WS 1679

Officers Donoughmore Battalion

FRANCIS HEALY BMH WS 1694

Active Service Unit Midleton Battalion

Officers Carrigtwohill Company, Midleton Battalion.

JOHN MANNING BMH WS 1720

Officers, Donoughmore Company, Donoughmore Battalion 1915-1921

DANIEL J MCSWINEY BMH WS 1651

Officers and Companies, Macroom Battalion 1917

Officers and Volunteers, Macroom A and B Companies, Macroom Battalion 1920

MICHEAL MULLANE BMH WS 1689
Officers, Inniscarra Company, Donoughmore Battalion, 1917-Truce

JAMES MURPHY BMH WS 1633
Officers, Macroom Battalion 1918 – Truce

EDWARD NEVILLE BMH WS 1665
Officers, Rusheen Company, Macroom Battalion

EDMUND O'BRIEN BMH WS 623
Officers, Shanagarry Company Fourth Battalion 1917
Officers and Volunteers, Shanagarry Company at Truce

JOHN O'MAHONEY BMH WS 1662
List of companies, Macroom Battalion
Officers, Macroom Battalion
Officers, Kilmurry Company 1917
Officers, Kilmurry Company March 1920
Officers, Kilmurry and Crookstown Companies October 1920

HENRY O'MAHONY BMH WS 1506
Companies, Ninth Battalion
Officers, Ninth Battalion

PATRICK J. WHELAN BMH WS 1449
Officers and Volunteers, Fourth Battalion – Flying Column

CHARLES BROWNE BMH WS 873
Officers, Macroom Battalion, including addresses

Officers, A Company Macroom
Officers, B Company Macroom
Officers, C Company Clondrohid
Officers, D Company Ballinagree
Officers, E Company Rusheen
Officers, F Company Canovee
Officers, G Company Crookstown
Officers, H Company Kilmurry
Officers, J Company Toames
Officers, K Company Kilmicheal
Officers, Coachford Company

TIM BUCKLEY BMH WS 1641

Officers, Clondrohid Company, Macroom Battalion 1916

MICHAEL FOLEY BMH WS 1534

Companies in Third Battalion, First Cork Brigade.

DANIEL HARRINGTON BMH WS 1532

Officers Ballyvourney Battalion 1917
Companies Ballyvourney Battalion

CORNELIUS HORGAN BMH WS 1461

Pioneer officers, Rylane Company, Donoughmore Battalion 1917
Rylane Company Volunteers 1917

CORNELIUS KELLEHER BMH WS 1654

Officers Kilmichael Company 1918
Companies Macroom Battalion 1918

Officers Macroom Battalion 1918

Volunteers engaged full time on dispatch work, Kilmichael Company.

MICHEAL LEAHY BMS WS 1421

Companies in Fourth Battalion, January 1918

MAURICE FITZGERALD AND OTHERS BMH WS 558

Officers B Company, First Battalion, May 1920

Officers B Company, First Battalion, July 1921

ARMY LISTS – SECOND CORK BRIGADE

Irish Volunteers/Irish Republican Army – Second Cork Brigade

Witness statements where names of officers and men in each brigade are listed:

(Prior to the Truce, the Second Cork Brigade was divided in two. New section named the Fourth Cork Brigade)

MICHAEL GEARY/RICHARD SMITH BMH WS 754

Officers and Volunteers, Charleville Company 1917 – with addresses
Companies, Charleville Battalion 1917
Charleville Flying Column

JOHN FANNING BMH WS 990

Officers, Fermoy Company 1919
Officers, Fermoy Company, Fermoy Battalion, July 1921
Officers, Fermoy Battalion 1918
Officers, Fermoy Battalion, 6 January 1919
Officers, Second Cork Brigade, January 1919

PATRICK J. LUDDY BMH WS 1151

Officers, Castletownroche Battalion
Companies, Castletownroche Battalion
Castletownroche Battalion, Flying Column
Castletownroche Brigade, May 1921
Officers, New Second Cork Brigade

DANIEL MCCARTHY BMH WS 1239

Officers and Volunteers, Lombardstown, Mallow Battalion 1917

Officers and Companies, Mallow Battalion

PATRICK MCCARTHY BMH WS 1163

Officers and Companies, Mallow Battalion

Battalions in Second Cork Brigade

Second Cork Brigade, Flying Column

CON MEANY BMH WS 787

Volunteers, First Battalion 1917

Officers, Millstreet Battalion, Companies at Truce

JOSEPH P. MORGAN BMH WS 1097

Pioneer members, Second Cork Brigade Flying Column

Pioneer members, Mallow Battalion Flying Column

DENNY MULLANE BMH WS 789

Pioneer members, Freemount Company

Companies Second Battalion Cork Fourth Brigade, First Southern Division

MAURICE NOONAN BMH WS 1098

Officers and Companies, Charleville Battalion

PATRICK O'BRIEN BMH WS 764

Officers Liscarroll Company 1918

Second Cork Brigade Flying Column

DAVID O'CALLAGHAN BMH WS 950
Companies Castletownroche Battalion

JAMES O'CONNELL BMH WS 949
Kanturk Battalion Flying Column

JOHN O'CONNELL BMH WS 1211
Officers Lombardstown Company 1917
Officers and Companies Mallow Battalion
Officers Lombardstown Company, January 1921
Mallow Battalion Flying Column

MICHAEL O'CONNELL BMH WS 1428
Officers Second Cork Brigade 1919-1921

MICHEAL O'DONNELL BMH WS 1145
Liscarroll Company, Charleville Battalion, 1918 and 1919

HUMPHREY O'DONOGHUE BMH WS 1351
Officers Cullen Company, Millstreet Battalion

JOHN O'KEEFFE BMH WS 1291
Officers, Rathcoole Company, Millstreet Battalion 1919

SEAMUS O'MAHONY BMH WS 730
Third Battalion, Glanworth Flying Column

CON O'REGAN BMH WS 1200
Sinn Féin personnel 1918
Cumann na mBan personnel 1918

Officers Mallow Battalion 1918
Officers Mallow Battalion at Truce

JOHN O'SULLIVAN BMH WS 1376
Second Cork Brigade flying column (some names)

WILLIAM REARDON BMH WS 1185
Pioneer members Millstreet Company 1917
Companies Millstreet Battalion
Battalions Second Cork Brigade
Volunteers Millstreet Battalion February 1921

WILLIAM C. REGAN BMH WS 1069
Volunteers Doneraile Company 1919
Officers Castletownroche Battalion
Castletownroche Battalion flying column

JOHN ROYNANE BMH WS 1269
Pioneers Burnfort Company 1914

MICHEAL SHEEHY BMH WS 989
Officers Charleville Battalion 1917

RICHARD WILLIS/JOHN BOLSTER BMH WS 808
Volunteers, Companies of Mallow Battalion

JOHN WINTERS BMH WS 948
Bawnmore Company, Kanturk Battalion, 1918
Companies Kanturk Battalion
Officers Kanturk Battalion

CORNELIUS BARRETT BMH WS 1405
Kilcorney Company 1917 and 1920

JAMES BREANNOCK BMH WS 1113
Araglin Volunteers 1916

THOMAS BARRY BMH WS 430
Companies Fermoy Battalion 1918 and 1919
Officers Castletownroche Battalion April-July 1921
Officers Glanworth Battalion April-July 1921
Officers and Companies Glanworth Battalion
Officers and Companies Castletownroche Battalion
Third Battalion flying column

MATTHEW MURPHY BMH WS 1375
Officers Cullen Company 1917 and 1918
Sinn Féin Personnel Newmarket 1917
Officers and Companies Millstreet Battalion 1919
Volunteers Cullen Company at Truce

THOMAS ROCHE BMH WS 1222
Officers and Companies Newmarket Battalion
Companies Newmarket Battalion

DANIEL FLYNN BMH WS 1240
Officers Kiskeam Company Newmarket Battalion

CORNELIUS HEALY BMH WS 1416
Officers Millstreet Company Millstreet Battalion
Volunteers Millstreet Company 1917

Companies, Millstreet Battalion 1917
Officers, Millstreet Battalion 1917

SEAN HEALY BMH WS 1339
Battalions Second Cork Brigade

MATTHEW KELLEHER BMS WS 1319
Officers Ballynoe Company, Fermoy Battalion 1917
Companies Fermoy Battalion
Company OCs Fermoy Battalion
Officers Kilcorney Company, Millstreet Battalion 1917
Officers Fourth Cork Brigade

JACK LOONEY BMH WS 1169
Officers Analeentha Company, Mallow Battalion 1915
Officers Analeentha Company, Mallow Battalion 1919
Officers Mallow Battalion

TIMOTHY LOONEY BMH WS 1196
Companies Mallow Battalion
Officers Mallow Battalion

ARMY LISTS – THIRD CORK BRIGADE

Irish Volunteers/Irish Republican Army – Third Cork Brigade

Witness statements where names of officers and men in each brigade are listed:

CON FLYNN BMH WS 1621
Officers Bandon Battalion 1918

TED HAYES BMH WS 1575
Companies Clonakilty Battalion
Pioneer Officers Clonakilty Battalion
Battalions Third Cork Brigade
Officers Third Cork Brigade

JOHN J. O'SULLIVAN BMH WS 1578
Officers Bantry Company 1918-Truce

RICHARD COLLINS BMH WS 1542
Volunteers Schull Battalion flying column

JAMES MCCARTHY BMH WS 1567
Officers Eyeries Company July 1917
Companies and Officers Castletownbere Battalion

JAMES 'SPUD' MURPHY BMH WS 1684
Volunteers at Kilmicheal Ambush, 28 November 1920

SEAN MURPHY BMH WS 1445
Officers Dunmanway Battalion 1918 to Truce

FRANK NEVILLE BMH WS 443
Officers Knockavilla Company, Bandon Battalion

DENIS O'BRIEN BMH WS 1353
Na Fianna Ballinagree 1914

PATRICK O'BRIEN BMH WS 812
Officers Cork Third Brigade January 1919

STEPHEN O'BRIEN BMH WS 603
Officers and Companies Skibbereen Battalion May 1921

CHARLES O'DONOGHUE BMH WS 1607
Officers Farnivane Company August 1919
Officers and Companies Bandon Battalion

DANIEL DONOVAN BMH WS 1608
Officers Clogagh Company 1917-1921

DANIEL O'DRISCOLL BMH WS 1352
Officers Drimoleague Company, Bantry Battalion
Officers Bantry Battalion

LIAM O'DWYER BMH WS 1527
Officer Castletownbere Battalion, 1917-1921

WILLIAM O'NEILL BMH WS 1536
Officers Castletownbere Company, 1917
Officers and Companies Castletownbere Battalion

CORNELIUS O'SULLIVAN BMH WS 1740
Officers Inishannon Company 1917
Officers Inishannon Company October 1920
Battalions Third Cork Brigade

EDWARD O'SULLIVAN BMH WS 1501
Volunteers Schull Battalion flying column
Officers New Fifth Cork Brigade

JAMES O'SULLIVAN BMH WS 1455
Officers Bantry Company 1917-1921

PATRICK O'SULLIVAN BMH WS 1481
Officers Third Cork Brigade July 1920

MICHEAL O'RIORDAN BMH WS 1638
Officers and Volunteers Kilpatrick Company, Bandon Battalion 1916-Truce

RICHARD RUSSELL BMH WS 1591
Officers Third Cork Brigade April 1921
Officers Bandon Battalion

LAURENCE SEXTON BMH WS 1290
Officers Barryroe Company, Bandon Battalion 1918-Truce

JAMES SULLIVAN BMH WS 1528
Officers Bere Island Company
Officers and Companies Castletownbere Battalion

EDWARD YOUNG BMH WS 1402
Officers Dunmanway Battalion 1918-1921

TED HAYES BMH WS 1575
Companies Clonakilty Battalion
Pioneer Officers Clonakilty Battalion
Third Cork Brigade Battalions
Pioneer Officers Third Cork Brigade

DANIEL HOLLAND BMH WS 1341
Officers Barryroe Company, Bandon Battalion 1918
Officers Third Cork Brigade post death of Charlie Hurley (Brigade O.C.)
Officers Bandon Battalion March 1921

JAMES HURLEY BMH WS 1354
Volunteers Kilkerrin Section, Lyre Company, Clonakilty Battalion 1915
Officers Lyre Company, Clonakilty Battalion 1915
Officers Kilkerrin More Company, Clonakilty Battalion
Pioneer Officers Clonakilty Battalion
Pioneer Officers Third Cork Brigade, 1919
Officers Third Cork Brigade July 1920

DANIEL C. KELLY BMH WS 1590

Companies Skibbereen Battalion 1917
Officers Skibbereen Battalion 1918
Officers Skibbereen Battalion at Truce.

DENIS KEOHANE BMH WS 1469

Officers Caheragh Company, Bantry Battalion 1914
Companies Bantry Battalion 1918
Officers Bantry Battalion 1919, February 1921

WILLIAM LANNIN BMH WS 1520

Officers and Companies Schull Company early 1920
Officers Schull Company November 1920
Officers Schull Battalion at Truce.

Appendix 2
Members of Cumann na mBan – Co. Cork

Officers Cumann na mBan Cork City 1914

President: Mrs Sean Hegarty

Vice President: Miss Mary McSwiney

Secretary: Miss Nora O'Brien (Mrs Martin)

Treasurer: Miss Madge Barry

Cumann na mBan – Craobh Poblachtach na nÉireann Cork 1917

Drummond, M

Furlong (Mrs)

Harris, Mary

Harris, Nellie

Hegarty (Mrs)

Keating (Mrs)

Lucey, Eily

Lucey, Margaret

McSwiney, Mary

O'Brien, Nora

O'Mahony (Miss)

O'Sullivan (Mrs)

Phillips (Mrs)

Sheehan, Nellie

Cork Branch Cumann na mBan 1917

de Róiste (Mrs)

Duggan, Peg

Duggan, Sarah,

Fennell, Sheila

Good, Máire,

Moynihan, Molly

Murphy, Maria

Murphy, Maura

Ní Chuill, Máire

O'Leary, Madge

Craobh Poblachtach na Éireann

President: Mrs Sean Hegarty

Secretary: Miss E. Barry

Treasurer: Miss A. Murphy

Captain: Mrs Martin (Miss Nora O'Brien)

Number of members: 58

Cork Branch

President: Mrs M.E. Hegarty

Secretary: Miss Bastible

Treasurer: Mrs Murphy

Captain: Miss M. Aherne

Number of members: 40

Cumann Tomás Ceannt

President: (No Record)

Secretary: Mrs O'Mahony

Treasurer: Mrs O'Sullivan

Captain: Miss Peg Duggan

Number of members: 22

St Finbarr's Branch:

President: Miss M. Murphy

Secretary: Miss M Scanlon

Treasurer: Mrs Dineen

Captain: Mrs McMahon

Number of Members: 14

Tomás MacCurtain (Clogheen Branch)

President: Mrs E. O'Donovan – Kyrls Quay, Cork

Secretary: Mrs O'Mahoney – 4 Sheares St, Cork

Treasurer: Mrs J. Collins

Captain: Miss Nora Crowley

Number of members: 20

Douglas Branch

Captain and Secretary: Mrs O'Donovan, Douglas West

Treasurer: Mrs O'Sullivan, Douglas West

Number of members: 8

Blarney Branch

President: Miss E. O'Doherty

Secretaries: Mrs J. Cremin and Mrs C. Collins

Treasurers: Miss A. Harrington and Miss C. Callinan

Number of members: 13

Lehenagh Branch

President: Mrs Cunningham

Secretary: Miss B. Richardson

Treasurer: Mrs Ahern

Captain: Mrs Fennell

Number of members: 10

Shandon Branch

President: Miss B. Conway

Secreatry: Miss M. Conlan

Treasurer: Mrs L. Linehan

Caotain: Mrs N. Linehan

Number of members: 15

The Lough Branch

Captain: Mrs P. Sutton

Other branches: Bishopstown (Wilton), Blackrock, St Patrick's, University College Cork, Dublin Pike.

MARGARET LUCEY BMH WS 1561

Macroom Branch 1916

President: Mrs Dan Corkery

Vice president: Annie Murphy

Honorary Treasurer: Molly Lynch

Secretary: Molly Cunningham

Captain: Molly O'Shea

Third Cork Brigade Cumann na mBan

Bandon South District Council

President: Mary O'Neill (Mrs Walsh)

Secretary: Nora Crowley

Treasurer: Hannah O'Brien (Mrs O'Mahony)

Kilbrittan Branch

Captain: Mary O'Neill (Mrs Walsh)

Secretary: Nora Crowley

Treasurer: Hannah O'Brien (Mrs O'Mahony)

Timoleague Branch

Captain: Margaret Foley (Mrs Harte)

Secretary: Mary Kelly

Tresurer: Maureen O'Driscoll

Gaggin Branch

Captain: Catherine Walsh (Mrs Lombard)

Secretary: Josephine Flynn

Treasurer: Kate McCarthy

Barryroe Branch

Captain: Nellie Colman (Mrs Santry)

Secretary: Mrs O'Donovan

Treasurer: Nora Whelton

Clogagh Branch

Captain: Margaret O'Donovan (Mrs Burke)

Secretary: Janie O'Donovan

Treasurer: Kathleen Murphy (Mrs O'Donovan)

Ballinspittle Branch

Captain: Hannah Hannon (Mrs Curran)

Secretary: Mary Ryan (Mrs O'Sullivan)

Treasurer: Kate McCarthy

MARY WALSH BMH WS 556

Appendix 3

Dáil Courts

List of Safe Houses

Casualties

Personnel who participated in specific engagements

Houses burned in reprisal by IRA and Crown forces

IRA Training Camps

Miscellaneous

Dáil Courts:
Donoughmore - June 1920
MAURICE BREW BMH WS 1695

Schull -
WILLIAM LANNIN BMH WS1520

Clogagh -
DANIEL DONOVAN BMH WS 1606

Safe Houses:
Fourth Battalion Area
PATRICK J. WHELAN BMH WS 1449

Ballyvourney Battalion Area
MICHEAL O'SULLIVAN BMH WS 793

Newmarket Battalion Area
JAMES C. RIORDAN BMH WS 1172

Castletownroche Battalion Area
THOMAS BARRY BMH WS 430

Castlelyons Company Area
WILLIAM BUCKLEY BMH WS 1009

Lombardstown Company Area
Mallow Battalion Headquarter Houses
MICHEAL MCCARTHY BMH WS 1238

Lombardstown Company – Brigade Headquarters
MICHAEL O'CONNELL BMH WS 1428

Mallow Battalion Area
TADHG LOONEY BMH WS 1196

Mallow Battalion Area
JOHN MALONEY BMH WS 1036

Kanturk Battalion Area
JAMES O'CONNELL BMH WS 949

Kilavullen Company Area
SEAMUS O'MAHONY BMH WS 730

Burnfort Company Area
JOHN O'SULLIVAN BMH WS 1376

Kisceam Company Area
JAMES J. RIORDAN BMH WS 1172

Cork City Area
PEG DUGGAN BMH WS 1576

Knockavilla Company Area
FRANK NEVILLE BMH WS 443

Kilbrittan Company Area
DENIS CROWLEY AND OTHERS BMH WS 560

Dunmanway Battalion Area
PADDY O'BRIEN BMH WS 812

Casualties:

G Company, First Battalion
MATTHEW O'CALLAGHAN BMH WS 561

I.R.A. Killed at Clonmult
JOHN P. O'CONNELL BMH WS 1445

Third West Cork Brigade
CHARLES O'DONOGHUE BMH WS 1607

Timoleague Company
JOHN O'DRISCOLL BMH WS 1250

Lists of Personnel at Specific Engagements:

Dripsey Ambush
DENIS DWYER BMH WS 713

Lissarda Ambush
JOHN O'MAHONEY BMH WS 1662

Kilmurry Barracks Attack
Carrigadrohid Barracks Attack
Lissarda Ambush
Poulnabro (or Coolavokig) Ambush
Glen Gate (Macroom) Ambush
Macroom, Carrigadrohid Rd Ambush
CHARLES BROWNE BMH WS 873

Grenagh – attack on R.I.C.
MORTIMER CURTIN BMH WS 1679

Dooniskey Railway Station Raid
Inniscarra/Dripsey Rd, IRA Attack
JOHN MANNING BMH WS 1720

Mallow Barracks Capture by IRA 28 Sept. 1920
Mallow Railway Station Attack, 1 Feb. 1921
JOHN BOLSTER/RICHARD WILLIS BMH WS 808

Charleville Mail Train Raid 19 June 1920
MICHEAL SHEEHY BMH WS 989

Ballydrochane Ambush 11 Oct 1920
THOMAS ROCHE BMH WS 1222

Blackstone Bridge – Attempted Ambush 8 Dec 1920
JOHN FANNING BMH WS 990

Leary's Cross, Castlelyons Ambush, 10 Dec 1920
WILLIAM BUCKLEY BMH WS 1009

Schull Barracks Capture 4 Oct 1920
Fastnet Rock Attack, June 1921
CHARLIE COTTER BMH WS 1519

Rathclarin British Military Patrol – Disarmed
Kilbrittan RIC Barracks – Feb. 1920
Howes Strand Coastguard Attack
Timoleague – Arrest of British Soldiers 20 Dec 1920
DENIS CROWLEY AND OTHERS BMH WS 560

Barryroe Aeríocht
JAMES MALONEY BMH WS 1310

Bantry Raid Dec 1919
JAMES O'SULLIVAN BMH WS 1455

Farnivane RIC Barracks Attack
DANIEL CANTY BMH WS 1619

Innishannon Weapons Raids June 1920
RICHARD RUSSELL BMH WS 1591

Ballylickey Attack 14 June 1921
JOHN J. O'SULLIVAN BMH WS 1578

Timoleague Barracks Attack Feb. 1920
Courtmacsherry RIC Barracks Apr. 1920
Ahamonister Killing of RIC May 1920
Newcestown Ambush Oct 1920
Brinny Ambush Dec 1920
Kilbrittan RIC Barracks Attack
Kilbrittan RIC Barracks Attack Jan 1921
Burgatia House Attack March 1921
Bandon Attack 24 Jan 1921
Crossbarry Battle 19 March 1921
Rosscarbery RIC Barracks Attack 31 Mar 1921
JOHN O'DRISCOLL BMH WS 1250

Burnings in Reprisal by IRA and Crown forces

Timoleague Company, Bandon Battalion (by Crown forces)
JOHN O'DRISCOLL BMH WS 1250

Ryecourt House and Crookstown House, August 1920 (by IRA)
MATTHEW O'CALLAGHAN BMH WS 561

Kildorrery Area (by IRA)
DAVID O'CALLAGHAN BMH WS 950

Castletownroche and Fermoy Battalion (by IRA and Crown forces)
SEAMUS O'MAHONY BMH WS 730

Glanworth Company Area (by Crown forces)
THOMAS BARRY BMH WS 430

IRA Training Camps:

Glandore
JAMES MALONEY BMH WS 1310

Clonbuig
CORNELIUS O'SULLIVAN BMH WS 1740

Miscellaneous Lists:

Living Members of Fourth Battalion, First Cork Brigade Flying Column, 1956
PATRICK J. WHELAN BMH WS 1449

British Strongholds in North Cork
WILLIAM C. REGAN BMH WS 1069

Volunteers awaiting death sentence 21 May 1921
JOHN C. MURPHY BMH WS 1217

Alphabetical list of witnesses:

Ahern, Jim BMH WS 810

Ahern, Patrick BMH WS 1003

Ahern, Robert C BMH WS 1676

Aherne, Joseph BMH WS 1367

Barrett, Annie BMH WS 1133

Barrett, Cornelius BMH WS 1405

Barrett, John BMH WS 1538

Barry, Thomas BMH WS 1598

Barry, William BMH WS 1708

Begley, Florence BMH WS 1771

Bolster, John BMH WS 808

Brennock, James BMH WS 1113

Brew, Maurice BMH WS 1695

Browne, Charles BMH WS 873

Browne, Daniel BMH WS 785

Buckley, Jerome BMH WS 1063

Buckley, Leo BMH WS 1714

Buckley, Tim BMH WS 1641

Buckley, William BMH WS 1009

Burke, Michael J BMH WS 1424

Busby, Allan BMH WS 1628

Callaghan, Leo BMH WS 978

Calnan, Cornelius BMH WS 1317

Canty, Daniel BMH WS 1619

Carroll, Jeremiah BMH WS 810

Cashman, Daniel BMH WS 1523

Cashman, James BMH WS 1270

Cashman, Joseph BMH WS 1466

Chambers, Philip BMH WS 738

Clifford, Patrick BMH WS 946

Coakley, Daniel BMH WS 1406

Coleman, Michael BMH WS 1254

Collins, Denis BMH WS 827

Collins, Patrick BMH WS

Collins, Richard BMH WS 1542

Condon, Laurence BMH WS 859

Condon, Timothy BMH WS 1374

Connolly, Cornelius BMH WS 602

Coss, James BMH WS 1065

Cotter, Charlie BMH WS 1519

Cotter, Dick BMH WS 810

Cotter, Seán BMH WS 1493

Coughlan, Jerome BMH WS 1568

Courtney, Michael BMH WS 744

Crimmins, John D BMH WS 1039

Crimmins, Timothy D BMH WS 1051

Cronin, Cornelius BMH WS 1726

Cronin, Michael J BMH WS 1171

Cronin, Patrick BMH WS 810

Cronin, Timothy BMH WS 1134

Crowe, Patrick BMH WS 775

Crowley, Denis BMH WS 560

Crowley, Michael J BMH WS 1603

Crowley, William BMH WS 1502

Culhane, Seán BMH WS 746

Culhane, Thomas BMH WS 831

Cunningham, Mollie BMH WS 1681

Cunninghan, Nora BMH WS 1690

Curtin, Mortimer BMH WS 1679

Daly, Jeremiah BMH WS 1015

Daly, Daniel BMH WS 743

Daly, Thomas BMH WS 719

Deasy, Jeremiah BMH WS 1738

Deasy, Liam BMH WS 562

Deasy, Patrick J BMH WS 558

Delarue, Thomas BMH WS 1224

Desmond, William BMH 832

Dinneen, Michael BMH WS 1563

Dinneen, Timothy BMH WS 1585

Donegan, Maurice BMH WS 639

Donovan, Daniel BMH WS 1608

Donovan, Maurice BMH WS 1736

Doyle, James BMH WS 1640

Duggan, Peg BMH WS 1576

Duggan, Thomas BMH WS 551

Dunne, Eugene BMH WS 1537

Dwyer, Denis BMH WS 713

Fanning, John BMH WS 990

Feeley, Michael J BMH WS 68

Fehilly, Patrick BMH WS 604

Fitzgerald, John BMH WS 560

Fitzgerald, Maurice BMH WS 558

Fitzgerald, Séamus BMH WS 1737

Flynn, Con BMH WS 1621

Flynn, Daniel BMH WS 1240

Foley, Michael BMH WS 1534

Foley, Michael BMH WS 1534

Foley, Stephen BMH WS 1669

Foley, William BMH WS 1560

Forde, Daniel BMH WS 810

Forde, Maurice BMH WS 719

Geary, Michael BMH WS 754

Golden, Thomas J BMH WS 1680

Guiney, Daniel BMH WS 1347

Hackett, James BMH WS 1080

Hales, Dónal BMH WS 292

Hales, William BMH WS 666

Harold, Owen BMH WS 991

Harrington, Daniel BMH WS 1532

Hayes, Ted BMH WS 1575

Healy, Cornelius BMG WS 1416

Healy, Daniel MH WS 1656

Healy, Francis BMH WS 1694

Healy, Seán BMH WS 1479

Healy, Seán BMH WS 1339

Hennessy, Jack BMH WS 1234

Hennessy, Seán BMH WS 1090

Herlihy, Timothy BMH WS 810

Hickey, James BMH WS 1218

Higgins, Patrick J BMH WS 1467

Hogan, John J BMH WS 1030

Holland, Daniel BMH WS 1341

Holland, Stephen BMH WS 649

Horgan, Cornelius BMH WS 1461

Horgan, Edward BMH WS 1644

Hourihane, Thomas BMH WS 1366

Hurley, George BMH WS 1630

Hurley, James BMH WS 1354

Hynes, Frank BMH WS 446

Jones, John BMH WS 759

Keane, Dan BMH WS 810

Kearney, Joseph BMH WS 704

Kearney, Michael BMH WS 1418

Kearney, Peter BMH WS 444

Keating, Jeremiah BMH WS 1657

Kelleher, Cornelius BMH WS 1654

Kelleher, John BMH WS 1456

Kelleher, Matthew BMH WS 1319

Kelly, Daniel C BMH WS 1590

Kenny, Seán BMH WS 719

Keogh, Michael BMH WS 719

Keohane, Denis BMH WS 1426

Keohane, Timothy BMH WS 1295

Kingston, Samuel BMH WS 620

Lannin, William BMH WS 1520

Leahy, Denis BMH WS 473

Leahy, Michael BMH WS 555 & 1421

Leddy, Con BMH WS 756

Linehan, William BMH WS 1577

Looney, John BMH WS 1169

Looney, Timothy BMH WS 1196

Lordan, Denis BMH WS 470

Lucey, Margaret BMH WS 1561

Lucey, Seán BMH WS 1579

Lucy, John J BMH WS 558

Luddy, Patrick J BMH WS 1151

Lynch, Patrick J BMH WS 1543

Manning, John BMH WS 1720

McCann, Peadar BMH WS 719

McCarthy, Daniel BMH WS 1239

McCarthy, Daniel BMH WS 1457

McCarthy, Dan BMH WS 1697

McCarthy, James BMH WS 1567

McCarthy, Michael BMH WS 1238

McCarthy, Patrick BMH WS 1163

McCarthy, Tadhg BMH WS 965

McCarthy, William BMH WS 1255

McSweeney, Daniel J BMH WS 1651

Mac Swiney, Muriel BMH WS 637

Meany, Cornelius BMH WS 787

Moloney, James BMH WS 1310

Moloney, John BMH WS 1036

Morgan, Joseph P BMH WS 1097

Moylan, Seán BMH WS 505 & 838

Mulchinock, Denis BMH WS 744

Mullane, Denny BMH WS 789

Mullane, Michael BMH WS 1689

Murphy, Denis BMH WS 1318

Murphy, James BMH WS 1633

Murphy, James 'Spud' BMH WS 1684

Murphy, Jeremiah BMH WS 772

Murphy, Jeremiah BMH WS 744

Murphy, John C BMH WS 1217

Murphy, Kevin BMH WS 1629

Murphy, Matthew BMH WS 1375

Murphy, Michael BMH WS 1547

Murphy, Seán BMH WS 1445

Murphy, Patrick A ('Pa') BMH WS 1584

Neville, Edward BMH WS 1665

Neville, Frank BMH WS 443

Neville, Laurence Morrough BMG WS 1639

Noonan, Denis BMH WS 992

Noonan, Maurice BMH WS 1098

O'Brien, Denis BMH WS 1353

O'Brien, Denis BMH WS 1306

O'Brien, Edmond BMH WS 623

O'Brien, Patrick BMH WS 812

O'Brien, Patrick BMH WS 764

O'Brien, Stephen BMH WS 603

O'Callaghan, David BMH WS 950

O'Callaghan, Matthew BMH WS 561

O'Carroll, Jeremiah BMH WS 706

O'Connell, Charles BMH WS 566

O'Connell, Christopher BMH WS 1530

O'Connell, James BMH WS 949

O'Connell, John BMH WS 1211

O'Connell, John P BMH WS 1444

O'Connell, Michael BMH WS 1428

O'Connell, Seán BMH WS 1706

O'Doherty, Felix BMH WS 739

O'Donnell, Michael BMH WS 1145

O'Donoghue, Charles BMH WS 1607

O'Donoghue, Florence BMH WS 554

O'Donoghue, Humphrey BMH WS 1351

O'Donoghue, Michael V BMH WS 1741

Donovan, Daniel BMH WS 1480

O'Driscoll, Daniel BMH WS 1352

O'Driscoll, John BMH WS 1250

O'Driscoll, Michael BMH WS 1297

O'Driscoll, Patrick BMH WS 557

O'Driscoll, Seán BMH WS 1518

O'Dwyer, Liam BMH WS 1527

O'Dwyer, Seán BMH WS 54

O'Keeffe, Christopher J W BMH WS 1587

O'Keeffe, John BMH WS 1291

O'Keeffe, Tim BMH WS 810

O'Leary, Diarmuid BMH WS 1589

O'Mahony, John BMH WS 1662

O'Mahony, Eoin BMH WS 1401

O'Mahony, Henry BMH WS 1506

O'Mahony, James BMH WS 560

O'Mahony, Séamus BMH WS 730

O'Mahony, Séamus BMH WS 730

O'Neill, Edward BMH WS 203

O'Neill, William BMH WS 1536

O'Regan, Con BMH WS 1200

O'Regan, Michael BMH WS 1524

O'Shea, Joseph BMH WS 1675

O'Sullivan, Cornelius BMH WS 1740

O'Sullivan, Edward BMH WS 1501

O'Sullivan, James BMH WS 1455

O'Sullivan, John BMH WS 1376

O'Sullivan, John J BMH WS 1578

O'Sullivan, Michael BMH WS 793

O'Sullivan, Michael BMH WS 1186

O'Sullivan, Patrick BMH WS 878

O'Sullivan, Patrick BMH WS 1481

O'Sullivan, Patrick BMH WS 794

O'Sullivan, Tadhg BMH WS 792

O'Sullivan, Ted BMH WS 1478

O'Sullivan, Timothy BMH 719

Ormond, James BMH WS 1289

Powell, William BMH WS 1699

Power, George BMH WS 451

Reardon, William BMH WS 1185

Regan, William C BMH WS 1069

Reidy, Thomas BMH WS 1477

Riordan, James C BMH WS 1172

Riordan, Michael BMH WS 1638

Roche, Thomas BMH WS 1222

Roche, William BMH 1362

Roche (de Róiste), Liam BMH WS 1698

Ronayne, John BMH WS 1269

Russell, Richard BMH WS 1591

Sexton, Laurence BMH WS 1290

Sexton, Timothy BMH WS 1565

Sheehy, Michael BMH WS 989

Sisk, Edward BMH WS 1505

Skinner, Leo B BMH WS 940

Smith, Richard BMH WS 754

Sullivan, James BMH WS 1528

Walsh, J J BMH WS 91

Walsh, Mary BMH WS 556

Walsh, Michael BMH WS 1521

Warren, Timothy BMH WS 1275

Waters, Thomas P BMH WS 1597

Whelan, Patrick J BMH WS 1449

Wickham, Mark BMH WS 558

Wilcox, Patrick BMH WS 1529

Willis, Richard BMH WS 808

Winters, John BMH WS 948

Young, Edward BMH WS 1402

Bibliography

Abbott, Richard, *Police Casualties in Ireland 1919-1922.* Mercier Press, Cork 2000

Crowley, Seán, *From Newce to Truce*

Keane, Barry *Cork's Revolutionary Dead 1916-1923.* Mercier Press, Cork 2017

Kingston, Diarmuid. *Beleaguered: A History of the RIC in West Cork during the War of Independence.* Cork, 2013

O'Rourke, Pádraig Óg. *Truce: Murder, Myth and the last days of the Irish War of Independence.* Mercier Press, Cork 2016

Whyte, Louis. *The Wild Heather Glen: The Kilmichael Story of Grief and Glory.* Tower Books, Cork, 1995

www.bureauofmilitaryhistory.ie

www.cairogang.com

www.theirishrevolution.com

Printed in Great Britain
by Amazon